No New Day
Tomorrow

NO NEW DAY
TOMORROW

Franz Haeussler

Archway Publishing books may be ordered through booksellers or by contacting:

Archway Publishing
1663 Liberty Drive
Bloomington, IN 47403
www.archwaypublishing.com
1 (888) 242-5904

ISBN: 978-1-4808-7528-9 (sc)
ISBN: 978-1-4808-7527-2 (e)

Library of Congress Control Number: 2019907149

Print information available on the last page.

Archway Publishing rev. date: 7/3/2019

Grand Valley. May 31 2018

This book I wrote in honour of my late wife
Gertrud and to my late teacher Felix Sasse.

"Semper bene erit libara in libara patria vitare."

"Immer wid es schoen sein, als Freier
im freien Lande zu leben."

"It will always be nice to live as a
free man in a free country."

Franz Haeussler

PREFACE

The international atmosphere is charged with explosive tension caused by "incidents" which seem to be unavoidable. Legitimate governments elected by the people suddenly crumble and their respective heads are murdered or disappear. Such conditions are intolerable and must be corrected. But how? One way to accomplish this purpose is to do away with the rigid barriers which divide the East from the West.

Currently, however, there is not only an "iron" and a "bamboo" curtain of isolation, but also a line of demarcation drawn through the hearts and minds of the diverse peoples.

In all of the strategic world centers, Communism has taken the ideological offensive among the distressed masses to impose Marxism-Leninism over the ancient cultures and religions by making fantastic promises impossible of fulfillment.

To achieve their aim of world Communism, the Russians

employ three instruments: the military, the economic, and the ideological. Hence, it should be the objective of the Western world to counteract those weapons of expansion not only by comparable pressures, but by the use of ideological projectiles fashioned in the arsenal of Western democracy.

It is imperative, therefore, that the free peoples of the West should actually know the thoughts and feelings of individuals under Communist domination.

The writer, from personal, actual experience gained in Iron Curtain countries has attempted by means of living, realistic fiction to convey to readers in America and other democratic countries, a vivid image of Europeans enmeshed in the shackles of Communism. Many young people, with an awareness of what is facing their generation, have been torn asunder by this agonizing inward struggle to escape from a monstrous evil which threatens to engulf the Free World.

Which is the right path? The author, using a central character, depicts a sentient young man rebelling against the pressures of collectivism. He stoutly resists the blandishments of the Marxism pseudo-religion, and eventually finds his way back to truth and human dignity.

Just as in seventeenth-century Europe, when religious wars

threatened the extinction of western civilization, we of the twentieth century are confronted by a comparable struggle with the rising Bolshevik titans for the survival of the democratic way of life.

The free democratic nations remain forever on the ideological defensive. With a constant awareness of our great spiritual strength, we must gird our loins determinably to face the Russians in the grim struggle to possess the minds and hearts of the human race.

May this book, on which I have spent countless hours of toil and thought, help bring about a rapprochement and understanding between the two mighty world contenders in the interests of the continued existence and progress of mankind.

August, 1958

--The Author

Principal Characters

Peter Andreyevich

Serge Andreyevich

Horst Altbauer

Inge Altbauer, Horst's sister

Mr. and Mrs. Altbauer, had a grain and feed business

Anton, Horst's uncle

Axel

Fritz Bode, a Latin teacher

General Bor-Komorowski

Frans, or Franchishek, Kabel, main character

Sergeant Grushenko

Gunther, a friend of Franz

Gustav, a worker with great physical strength

Major Ivanov

Mr. and Mrs. Kabel, parents of Franz

Kolya, Vanya, Seryoesha, young Cossack soldiers

Captain Michael Konstantinovich

Comrade Otto Lehmann

Comrade Link

Peter Maximovich, Serge Andreyevich's friend

District Magistrate Meier

Comrade Lieutenant Michael Petrovich Mikhailov

Misha

LIST OF CHARACTERS AND MISCELLANEOUS NAMES

Peter Andreyevich

Colonel Serge Andreyevich

Horst Altbauer

Inge Altbauer, Horst's sister

Mr. and Mrs. Altbauer, had a grain and feed business

Anton, Horst's uncle

Apparatchik

Axel

Baranow

Fritz Bode, a Latin teacher

General Bor-Komorowski (liberation)

Comintern (before), Cominform (later)

Dzhigitovka

Hermann Rosenfeld, state propaganda director

Rudi

Dr. Schmidt, history teacher

Simeon, a Russian who speaks German

Captain Smirnov

Joseph Vissarionovich Stalin

Anton Wolf, young party functionary

CHAPTER I

In the April days of 1945, combat missions and occasionally the thunder of distant guns were ever more insistently announcing the approach of the Russian army. A rising torrent of refugees poured westward through the German provinces, fleeing before the Soviet steamroller.

A mood of panic had spread among the German population. As everyone knew, the Russians felt the time had come to seize and smash Berlin, the last lair of the fascist beast. And everyone in Germany knew that the hour of retribution, for every atrocity committed by Germans under Hitler's generals in Russia and the rest of Europe, had struck.

During that storm-wracked and dreary springtime, Franz was still living with his father and mother on their stud farm near the village of Neubeck on the Berlin-Hamburg highway, about twenty-five miles east of the Elbe.

The road, about 65 feet across, carried an unremitting stream of beaten, broken and exhausted German divisions. No fighting units these, but shattered, scrambled, tired officers and men. They were fleeing an engine of irresistible force, and sought only escape, if escape there was. For four years they had unconditionally carried out the maniacal orders of their Fuehrer and his top war lords without protest. These were the son who through enormous exertions and privation had pushed forward from the Memel to the Volga and on to Mount Elbrus.

This was what remained of the chosen instrument of the doomed ideologists of the Third Reich, for their plans of world conquest and their invasion of the east. This is what a reckless gang of criminals had done to a nation of poets and philosophers.

The Fuehrer, as yet, was holed up in Berlin. As yet, from time to time, the propaganda artist Goebbels spurred the German people to werewolf prowess and party meal.

"Soldiers!" ran one such appeal. "Give your lives to free your beloved Leader." Fuehrer irresistible in the center of Berlin, leading the resistance to the Red flood.

But the kindling propaganda phrases of a Goebbels could not dispel the apathy of this jaded populace. The nerves of this people had been too often overstrained in the confusions of war. By and large, speeches brought no response.

Meanwhile Marshal Zhukov's army had tightened the ring about Berlin. Wedge-fashion, the Soviet tanks and assault guns pierced the city. His artillery took the range, and laid a dense barrage over whole sections of town. There was hard fighting for the approaches to the Chancellery. A few SS units and Hitler Youth met the Russians with anti-tank weapons; fought to the last man, and the armored machine rolled over them.

Among the defenders of Berlin, the rumor had spread that the Russians must soon withdraw. It was hoped that the German Army of Defense would dismay the Russians, and that then the whole nation could pass to the offensive. But all such hopes were self-deception and delusion. The phantom army was powerless. The Russians swept it across the lake country of North Germany to the west, while Zhukov was capturing and smashing the Berlin pocket.

On the morning of May 2, 1945, Franz Kabel was suddenly wrenched from sleep by the sound of lively machine-gun fire. No sooner had he hurried downstairs than a dusty motorcycle courier entered.

"How far off are the Russians?"

"About seven miles from here, and advancing on the village along both sides of the road."

This reply left Franz wide awake. In no time he was down in the courtyard, where an SS unit was camping, making preparations for defense. Franz mounted quickly to the castle tower. From here he had a view of the country for miles around. He could see distinctly the approaching Russian tanks and cavalry. Interspersed among them came assault guns, loaded down with infantry.

God, thought Franz, what's become of the German front.

For neither tanks nor artillery were in sight. Here and there, a few infantrymen, running like rabbits from the Cossacks, were pursued and cut down. Franz felt dismay at this grim picture. So, these were the Soviet Russians. What sort of people could they be? He had read a lot at one time about political and economic history in Russia and the Soviet state.

How will these people act towards us? What are these neighbors of ours like?

An intense curiosity possessed him. Something enormous, irresistible, an army, an avalanche, was descending upon him.

How did the minds of these men work? What did they think and feel? Surely, they must be motivated by revenge. Surely, they will exact a grim vengeance for all the terrible things that have happened.

A pale dread possessed him, and he came down again, shaken, from the castle tower, and found his way to the cellars of the building.

In that shelter there were a few detached soldiers, hastily changing their uniforms for civilian clothes. A few dozen women and children had collected there. All were silently awaiting developments. Each sensed that something enormous was impending. None had fear of the combat. What harm could that bring now? The Russian steamroller would pass over the countryside like surf, sweeping the few German troops before it like dry leaves in the storm.

And so, it was, before long. Heavy rifle fire was heard. Increasing from moment to moment, breaking out all along the front. Mixed with the roar of heavy tanks and the clatter of hoofbeats. The first wave of the Red tide had passed over. Franz looked eagerly at the cellar door. Out there lay the future; out there was Tomorrow, and the yet unknown.

Resolutely, he strode through the door into the yard. Now

it was occupied by Mongolian infantry. Along the main street outside, squads of swift Cossacks trotted in chase of fleeing German soldiers. Horsemen and foot-soldiers crowded their way into the houses. At first, they could only stare. "You must be a damned capitalist, to live in a house like this," said a young Russian to one of Franz's friends, a workingman's son. There were a lot of these young fellows in the house. A large number of Red infantrymen came into the room. They took everything that wasn't nailed down. They seemed to have a use for anything. Whatever they couldn't carry, they wrecked.

Herd by the castle stood a distillery. Liquor -- vodka -- was the sap of life to the Russian soldier. With vodka to drink he was happy. But dangerous, too, and capable of any villainy.

Franz went over to the cow barns. Some dairy maids were busy with the milking. The Cossacks and Red Army men were not long in coming. They asked no questions. Brutally they dragged the women and girls away from the cows, jumped upon them and raped them. No sooner had one Cossack quenched his lust than the next fell upon the groaning, fainting victim.

In the meantime, the first supply units reached the area. Not to be outdone by their comrades, they robbed and plundered what was left of Neubeck. An Order of the Day by Marshal Stalin was their warrant. This was the terrible revenge of the Red soldiery for the German attack on the citadel of Communism. Whatever the Red Army had taken was, as it were, its prize and booty, and at its unlimited disposal.

From the mansions and cottages of Germany, movables were being piled on trucks and hauled off eastward. Silver and china were broken, trampled, and the remnant packed up and shipped off. Special crews were tearing up the rails, to be taken to the Soviet Union by the quickest way.

Systematically, all German territory held by the Russians was plundered to the uttermost. All dead and livestock in every branch of industry was carried off to the Soviet Union.

Franz talked about it to a Soviet officer, who intimated that all those things would still fall short of paying for the damage the Germans had done in Russia. More explicitly, he went on: "For you Germans there is going to be nothing but work and more work. We are going to take everything you have away from you, and then you will have to make a fresh start from nothing. But even on your peacetime production, we are going to keep on levying our tribute until you have made up for every wrong you have done, until your war guilt has been expiated."

Franz was dejected. He saw clearly that the Russians were indeed working towards the utter denudation of German soil. Eastern Germany in those two weeks was set back a hundred years economically. This was the grim truth, the fruit of the violent policy of a dictatorial regime.

So, the two weeks went by under the Red terror. Soldiers quartered themselves in droves on the houses of the citizens and made themselves comfortable after their fashion, or as comfortable as one can be at the front. Almost all timepieces, cars, radios, had been requisitioned by this time. Russians were everywhere to be seen publicly trading in bicycles. All the Russians Franz saw in 1945 had a wild desire for any products of civilization. Many were astonished to find light and water coming out of the wall. These men of Asiatic Russia stared open-mouthed at all civilized arrangements. They were simply unable to conceive that such dwellings, with such valuables, could be the abode of workingmen and petty clerks. These men from the broad steppes and forests of the east had had a one-sided Bolshevist teaching hammered into them for decades, and now Franz saw the result.

Everything, these men from the Soviet Union had been told, that comes from the west or has anything to do with the west is obnoxious and intolerable to the new society. For, the simple Soviet citizen was taught, were not the gentlemen of the west those same wicked monopoly capitalists whose only purpose was the exploitation and annihilation of the working class. Add to this, that in the Stalin era, a ruthless power policy had been pursued, thrusting all human values into the background. Besides, the Soviet Union is covered with a network of secret agents, responsible for the reliable and smooth operation of this enormous engine of terror. Throughout the Red Stalinist empire, from the highest party functionaries down to the poorest kolkhoz workers, there reigned an iron discipline, a discipline ever maintained, if not intensified, by Draconian measures of the Soviet government. If this fact is kept in mind, the behavior of the Russians in European countries under western influence becomes plain. These men simply felt the urge towards a better life. They slowly were becoming critical. Some realized that there must be a good deal wrong with the teaching of their commissars. The Red Army men talked with German workers about their previous living conditions, began to do some comparing and figuring.

This, of course, the Stalinist leadership was expected under all circumstances to prevent. Soviet man was to remain

Soviet man. Moreover, he was to remain a unilaterally organized man. The soldier was to remain a blind and willing tool
of his masters in the Kremlin. And he was also to bear the
banners of the world revolution, to the greater honor of the
Kremlin's Red czar. Men of politically independent thought
and judgment were an impossibility to Stalin; they were her-
etics, cosmopolitans, provocateurs or Trotskyites. Such men
disappeared into the forced labor battalions of the giant empire, swelling the army of cheap slave labor. The slave battalions of our present century were used to carry out Communist
construction projects. They planted timber. They built canals
or erected any sort of "palace" of the new society.

Most of the Russians Franz met in Germany in 1945
were, after decades of suppression, exceedingly mistrustful
and cautious in all their utterances. All the same, they were
curious and eager to learn something of life in Germany.
Many questioned the natives about amenities of life that the
westerner takes for granted.

On the 8ᵗʰ of May, 1945, the Hitler regime surrendered unconditionally to the Allies. In the farthest corner of its lair it had
been eliminated. Europe and the rest of the world drew a long
breath, for the scourge of the democracies and of world peace had

been wiped out. The Allied Armies met in the heart of Nazi territory, as victors and as guarantors of a new order of world peace. During the same year the United Nations Organization was founded at San Francisco. From now on, everything was going to be different. This inclusive organization of the peace-loving nations of the earth was to see that henceforth the comings and goings of men should be ruled only by the forces of pure reason, by the forces of peace and progress. Never again should the world be encompassed by a militaristic clique. All the peoples of the world were in agreement about this in 1945.

One morning in June, the local Soviet command set up headquarters in a large farmhouse. At the entrance was posted an order by the commanding officer, directing the population to go back to work, and to elect a mayor. In the village square of Neubeck there soon assembled a crowd which, after much debate, reelected the former mayor of the place.

The Soviet commandant addressed the people through an interpreter.

"The Red Army has destroyed Fascism. The Soviet Union means to assist Germany in building a peace-loving and democratic nation. In that spirit, then, let us get on with the job of reconstruction."

The people dispersed, to stare at the ruined and war-ravaged landscape. Along the highway from Berlin to Hamburg, the Russians had put up triumphal arches at every crossroads. On either side of the road, in places of any importance, one might see more than life-size portraits of Soviet marshals and heroes of the Soviet Union. Side roads branching off to staff quarters were strewn with gravel, and these thoroughfares the Russians had flanked with newly felled pine trees. Here and there between them showed a half-length portrait of some Soviet hero, his chest studded with decorations. The castle had at first been commandeered by the staff of a Cossack regiment. When they moved on, the castle was thoroughly looted again, and became a scene of awful desolation. In the halls, the cupboards had been wrenched open; linen, crystal and silver had been cast aside and trampled underfoot. The picture gallery was a sorry sight. Paintings were crisscrossed with scars of small-arms marksmanship. The choicest pieces of furniture were loaded on little peasant carts, a Persian rug over all to preserve the precious freight against the weather, and the little vehicles trundled off.

The stud of the manor was the first prey to the advancing mounted contingents. Weeping, the proprietress stood aside and looked on while the Cossacks dragged the mares and stallions out of their stalls and distributed them as booty among themselves. The mounted regiments, anyway, were particularly given to looting. Some Cossack officers would appropriate pack horses and load them with their spoils. At the last minute, old trusted retainers managed to conceal the best of the brood mares and young stallions in a corner of an outbuilding. So, a few of the valuable animals escaped the greedy marauder. All the harness and saddlery on the farm was carried off. What they did not immediately need, the Russians packed on the carts of the supply units.

Among the passing troops of Cossacks, Franz clearly discerned a parade, a farewell show, of all the German breeds of horses. From East Prussia to the Elbe, those men had had no occupation but robbery and rape. Excessively, they were interested in watches, adornments of all kinds, and alcoholic beverages. The Russians badgered the population incredibly for liquor. They loved vodka above anything. They would give the farmers watches, horses, if only they could pay for them with liquor; that made everything all right. Franz was amazed to see a Cossack take raw gulps of straight spirit without killing himself. The estate, as ill luck would have it, had a distillery.

The full casks had been hauled off by the first arrivals. What was left the Cossacks divided among them. Then the still was deliberately dismantled. All the leather belts were cut up and made into shoe soles by resourceful Red Army soldiers.

But the latecomers were unwilling to be left out. Every one of them wanted all the liquor he could get. Everyone had an irresistible craving for hooch. Potatoes and barley were to be had in plenty. The manager was ordered by the commandant to get the still back into production. The best and quickest way to do it was up to him. But vodka must be forthcoming without fail. Some men were hastily mounted on bicycles and commissioned by the commandant to scare up the necessary belting. The commandant gave them a document certifying that they were on Russian official business. Otherwise the first Red soldier to come along would have taken the bicycles, and the vodka project would have evaporated. You couldn't start a distillery without drive belts. So, with their Russian documents, the men were able to pass all sentry posts and gained the headquarters of the nearest town.

When the town commandant, Major Ivanov, learned that a still was going to be rehabilitated, he dropped everything; ordered his special commandos to scour the town, and got the belts. This matter interested him personally. He could do with a drink himself. The Russians just then lacked for nothing -- except this one thing. With liquor, even Germans, vanquished and humbled as they were -- with liquor even the conquered could wind the conqueror around his finger, and wring concessions from him. As soon as the man with the belts arrived, raw materials were quickly hauled to the spot with hastily requisitioned teams and wagons. The farmers had to deliver barley, potatoes and fuel. The Russians could hardly wait. The commandant threatened to lock the foreman up when <u>vodka</u> did not flow immediately. The Russian roared at the man, again threatened him with imprisonment, and accused him of sabotage. The honest man replied composedly that these things took time, the barley would have to start working, the still and the machinery would have to be in perfect shape, before production could begin. Recovering himself, the Major ordered the German workers to look alive. He exhorted them to take example from the Stakhanovites and step up their rate of production.

Three days later, after much going and coming, the first of the proof spirit began to flow. The gauge glass was taken off, with a tank holding a few hundred liters set under the cock.

Right out of the gauge and into the tank flowed the noble liquor so eagerly awaited by all the Russians round about.

The men and officers of the place crowded around the tank like cattle at the watering trough and drank deep of the potent brew. In two hours Neubeck was brimful of drunken Russians. They lay snoring in every corner. Some celebrated by molesting women and fighting among themselves.

The news that the liquor factory was back in business spread through the cantonments like wildfire. Quite a few Cossack troops were stationed in the vicinity. Details came riding in from all directions and galloped straight to the distillery. Disputes arose between the local troops and the Cossacks. There were plenty of brawls and shootings.

Franz did not omit to provide himself with some miscellaneous containers full of the stuff, and soon was driving a lively trade with the Cossacks. One brought a horse, others brought watches and articles of clothing and victuals of all kinds. Franz improved the occasion to add to the depleted family larder. He guessed that hard times were coming, and was doing his best to provide.

The sheepfolds and cow barns of the estate stood empty. In the great meadows below the stables, the Russians had rounded up no less than 5000 cattle from other villages. The Neubeck cows had been taken away from the farms long ago. The mayor was required to recruit a force which was kept busy milking the cows. More herds were arriving daily. Groups of women were assigned to processing butter and cream. Major Ivanov ordered the mayor to have the council tell off one hundred boys immediately for driving cattle. One of the hundred was Franz Kabel. The boys had to fall in at the crack of dawn, to be counted off, divided up and put under guard. Franz tearfully said good-by to his father and mother and was off to the meadow with the rest. The stock was split up into bunches of a hundred. Five boys had to circle each bunch and keep it moving east. Russians drove among the bunches in carts to supervise the operation. Often some of the cows would get off the road. The boys would then have to chase them and drive them back. Now and then the drove was overtaken by trucks or returning armored columns. Then the herds had to be taken off the road and kept somewhere to one side until the road was clear again, and the weary march was resumed.

In June 1945, the days were burning hot. Franz soon felt terribly hungry and thirsty, but he trotted on behind the herd, urging the reluctant animals forward. All the time, he was looking for a chance to escape, for he noticed that the column was going over eastward. These cows were going to be driven all the way to the Soviet Union as reparations. Franz knew that was a long road to travel. It was the road to slavery. It meant farewell to his beloved home and all that was near and dear to him.

Every day's march was about thirty miles. At times the herds were driven off the road to give man and beast a short rest. In the evening, after sundown, Franz would stretch out anywhere near one of the fires and fall into a deep, leaden and dreamless sleep. Sometimes he kept awake half the night, peering around to weigh the chances of flight. He knew that all the boys were being closely watched by the Russians, who distrusted all Germans and saw a trap in any sign of friendliness. Franz got into conversation with the Russians once in a while, but he soon saw that all these conversations were viewed with suspicion by the other Russians. His interlocutors would soon fall silent. When he asked where or how far the cattle were being taken, he was usually answered with a shrug of the shoulders.

"I don't know any more about it than you do," one young

man said, indifferently. "Just keep going. You'll see when we get there. Just keep heading east, straight ahead, where <u>we</u> came from. You wrecked our country and burned our towns and villages, now you'll have to make it good. You're the ones who lost the war."

It was as simple as that, in 1945, to the ordinary Russian. But Franz couldn't see it that way; after all, he was only fourteen, certainly not a war criminal, and he couldn't see why the children of a nation should pay for the sins of their elders. So, he was resolved to run away the first chance he had, before they entered Poland.

The weather got so hot that they took to traveling at night. The road led past a lonesome farmhouse. Three steers broke away and disappeared behind the house in a moment. A Russian sent Franz after them, to catch them and drive them back to the bunch.

The idea came to him in a flash. This was his chance to get away.

He was still in his own country. His mother tongue would still help him make his way back home. Franz broke into a dogtrot after the runaway steers. When he got behind the barn he started running, and ran as fast as his legs and lungs would take him. He may have zig-zagged about three miles across fields and meadows before he sank exhausted at the edge of a wood. He crept into the underbrush and fell asleep.

He awoke towards noon of the next day. His head was ringing and his stomach grumbled. He sat up dazed.

Where am I, anyway? he wondered. Sure enough; over there he could see the highway he had run away from the night before.

All day, the road was choked with traffic. Red Army troops were marching homeward to the east. Streams of refugees struggled along the sides of the road in both directions. Franz watched all this activity carefully. That's the way back, he thought, just keeping to the road, but you could travel a little to one side, where there's more room. That would be better. You'd make faster progress. His brain was busy with those thoughts. Groaning, he arose and edged towards the highway.

At the end of the field stood a farm wagon. It was one of those refugee wagons that were clogging the roads. An old grandfather was sitting on the wagon tongue and gazing into the distance. Franz approached the wagon slowly, studying the old man. He decided to try for a handout, and opened the conversation at once:

"Hello! Could you please spare me something to eat? I'm terribly hungry."

The old fellow seemed pleased at the interruption. Franz saw that there were two women in the wagon.

"That's my wife and daughter-in law," explained the man. "They were both attacked by the Cossacks. Our horses have been taken. So here we are, a long way from home, with no way to get anywhere."

Saying this, he handed Franz a big chunk of black bread with a piece of bacon. Franz was overjoyed and lost no time in falling to. The old woman leaned out of the wagon and handed the boy a can of black coffee. Franz thanked her with enthusiasm. For twenty-four hours, in the scorching heat, he had had nothing to drink, and he sucked up coffee greedily.

"I suppose you're from the east," Franz said between swallows.

"East Prussia," replied the old man. "A long way. How am I ever going to get back with no horses? The Russians came. We had to leave everything. Is there any use going on living? I lost two sons in Russia. I've worked hard all my life, and for what? We've been tricked by political swindlers and cutthroats. How that they see the fruits of their crimes, the cowards commit suicide so they won't get what's coming to them. Remember, young man, all those violent solutions of political and economic problems never came to any good. What good was it to have the best army, the best guns, the best industry? A bunch of scoundrels misused them. The whole country's been sacrificed to their crazy ideas. Compared to the way things are now in Germany, the time after the first World War was a vacation. Troops of all the victorious powers are jumping on a drained and worn-out people. They blame all of us. All of us are war criminals. They don't care whether we were Nazis or not. Their day of revenge has come. They are just getting a taste of power, and are still dizzy with victory. Well, that's life, for great nations and little households. There's a time to sow and a time to reap. History goes on. Nobody can stop it."

The old man stopped, and swept his troubled glance over the war-torn landscape.

"Well," said Franz, "I'm going to wait and see. Things will change. The winners can't keep a whole nation down forever. They can't use Nazi methods on us when they claim to fight for democracy. We'll live through it. Our ruined towns will come back to life. After all, we're a great country in the middle of Europe. We're ground down and beaten now, but there are sure to be enough brave men for leadership. They'll show us the way to a better future, along with the other free peoples. There'll be trade and commerce, and industry and hard work will clear away all our troubles."

The old man heard him out. "It's too bad Germany couldn't summon enough strength and unity to stand up to Fascism. That's where we missed out. We couldn't kick out the Nazis ourselves; foreigners had to do it. How we have to pay for our failures." For a moment he was brooding again, but then he added, "Boys are optimists. They've got more spirit. They're not all worn out and weary of life like us old people. I wish you all the best of luck. God keep you from the mistakes we made."

Thinking about the old man's confession, Franz thanked his benefactors, bade them farewell and cheerfully resumed his journey.

In his wanderings homeward, he always kept a respectful distance from the main roads, which were so full of Russian army detachments that he never felt quite safe. When he came to a village, he always avoided the buildings and cut across fields. Russian military units were stationed in almost every village. They watched the movements of the population very carefully. Every stranger had to report to headquarters. Franz shrank from the questioning and the suspicion. He wanted as little trouble as possible. Only when he felt he was starving, he would cautiously approach a house and beg a little bread and coffee. He would hurry on as soon as hunger and thirst were appeased. He passed many a Russian picket with pounding heart. Always, there was the anxious question, Shall I be stopped, arrested, interrogated, beaten? Whenever he found himself past the end of a settlement, he breathed a sigh of relief. Bravely he made his way in wide area through wood and field towards the west.

CHAPTER II

Franz came to a patch of birchwood. Somewhere inside, he could hear a great noise of hoofbeats. Shouting men and neighing horses sounded frighteningly close. It was very confusing. What was he to do now? Panic seized him. There must be a lot of Cossacks coming. Franz had seen enough Cossack brutality, and he looked about desperately for some way of escape. He was about five hundred yards from the wood when he first heard the noise. Now he ran quickly about three hundred yards towards the right, to get away from the road, and raced for the edge of the wood. There he would be able to hide, and the cavalry would ride past, leaving him to continue on his way.

When he got to the wood, Franz saw that he had miscalculated. Horsemen were spread out all through the area. They were not sticking close to the line of march as Franz had assumed. The objects of plunder that the Cossacks wanted might be found anywhere. Two of the riders must have been watching Franz running towards them for some time. Now they were about a hundred yards away. Feverishly he tried to plan his next move, but it was too late for that. One of them was yelling at him.

"Hey, Hitler Youth! Where do you think you're going?"

In terror, Franz ran faster than ever. But the two Cossacks on their trained mounts headed him off in no time; before he could turn, he was seized from behind by the collar and his ears soundly boxed. Twisting slowly around, he tried to get a look at his captors. They were ordinary-looking Cossacks, of medium size, stocky, with the appearance of a bird of prey. The older of the two wore huge handlebar mustaches. His age was about fifty. He was looking at Franz coolly, sitting his horse a little way off, while the younger Cossack was cuffing and searching Franz for weapons. He seemed to be a practiced highwayman. When he found Franz was not carrying any concealed weapons, he started hunting for valuables. This search was as fruitless as the other. To Franz's astonishment, the fellow who seemed about eighteen, proceeded to question him in German.

"You're one of those Hitler boys, aren't you? What are you spying around here for? You cure ought to be shot on sight. Then you wouldn't bother us anymore!"

The Cossack raised his pistol and held it to the boy's chest. Franz's mind went blank. He turned white as a sheet. He could feel his heart beating, and cold sweat running down his back. Franz was convinced his last hour had come.

The older Cossack now interrupted, speaking to his companion:

"Misha, leave him alone. You can't shoot the kid in cold blood like that. He doesn't look like a spy to me. You know how strict the regiment is about things like this."

When that didn't work, and the older man saw Misha's eyes gleam murderously and his finger tighten slowly on the trigger, he jumped from his horse, jerked the gun in the air, and bawled at the young Cossack:

"You should be ashamed of yourself, killing a child: We of the Gardo-Kuban Regiment won't stand for that kind of stuff. We're an outfit with honor and tradition, not a mob. Leave the boy alone. He's unarmed and couldn't hurt you if he tried. What do you want to kill him for?"

"Oh, all right, Peter Andreyevich, have it your way. We'll

take him in to headquarters, if you think so. They'll take care of him."

Somewhat reassured, Franz marched off to headquarters between the two Cossacks.

Very soon they came upon the main body of horse. Franz stared eagerly at the troop, riding by at a fast trot. Two officers headed each company, followed by enlisted men in threes. The horses of each unit were matched. The band were all mounted on dapple-grays. Then came the other units on blacks, bays and chestnuts. Franz could tell that about half the mounts must have been taken from German estates; unmistakably, several were Trakehner stock, the famous show breed. The baggage train brought up the rear. The carts were piled high with loot, looking very much out of place among the campaign gear. There were cartloads of radios, household china and plate, topped off with some gorgeous rug or tapestry.

The Cossacks knew well enough that all this plunder was a terrible handicap to a regiment on the move. But the war was over; there was plenty of time now, and to the victor belong the spoils. The whole countryside - people, land, livestock, things animate and inanimate - was forfeit. Stalin, the Little Father, had said so. Now that victory is ours, we will take it.

Franz was delivered to headquarters. He was taken in charge by a tall, gangling captain, who after looking him up and down from head to foot began talking deliberately in German.

"So, are you a fascist, or aren't you? Were you trying to spy on us, or weren't you?"

Franz answered quickly, "I'm not a fascist and I'm not trying to spy on anybody. I'm only trying to get home."

"Where is that?"

"That way, west, fifty kilometers or so."

"Then how did you get way out here?"

"I had to help the Russians drive cattle. Now I'm through with that, so I'm going home."

"I see. You got tired of helping to drive cattle and so you ran away. Now listen here. I suppose you can ride?"

"Yes, I've ridden some," Franz answered.

"All right, you can stay with us and drive horses to Russia instead of cows," said the captain. "We've got hundreds of captured horses, and we're short-handed." Franz tried to protest.

"But I'm only fourteen! You can't just kidnap me and make me go to Russia!"

"Don't tell us what we can do, my boy. We're in charge

here, remember. You can be glad we don't shoot you like a dog. You Hitler youths are dangerous." Turning to a young man behind him, "All right, Simeon, turn him over to Supply. The sergeant will know what to do with him."

"Idi poshol," said Simeon to Franz, and led him out through the camp.

Simeon was a sly-looking boy of eighteen. He spoke very good German. He took a look at Franz's dejected face and asked him in a kindly tone, "What's your name?"

"Franz," was the reply.

"That's 'Franchishek' in Russian, and I'll tell the sergeant your name's Franchishek. Tell me, tovarishch, what have you been doing up to now?"

"I go to high school," Franz answered.

"Oh, then your folks must be rich. Only rich people can send their children to your high schools - the others don't have the money. It's different in the Soviet Union. Anybody can get an education there if he has the ability. It doesn't matter how well off his father is."

"Now wait a minute," said Franz. "It wasn't like that at all. I know there were children from all classes of people in our school. Even laborers. Some boys and girls had government scholarships so that they could stay in school."

"But could a worker's son follow a professional career later on, like the son of a manufacturer or other capitalist?" Simeon asked quickly.

"Of course, he could," replied Franz.

"Well, anyway," Simeon retorted, "things are entirely different in your country. In the Soviet Union there's no such thing as 'children from all classes.' We have only one class, the working class. The most gifted sons and daughters of workers get higher education. If they work hard and meet the requirements, they can continue in school, and the government pays for it."

"I know a lot of interesting things have happened in Russia since the revolution," said Franz. "I hope we'll have a chance to talk about it some more."

"I'll have to see what I can do for you. Now be a good boy and do what the sergeant tells you. The commanding officer is a good friend of mine. He knows my father. There are several of us Stalin scholars in this outfit who will be glad to talk politics and economics with you."

Franz found himself passed on to an old sergeant with a deep bass voice.

"Well, now, young fellow," grinning all over his face, "ever been on a horse in your life before?"

"I've been riding since I was five. My father used to train race horses."

"That's just fine. We can use you all right. Take that nag over there. There's a saddle that might do. Just stay close by me and I'll show you your work. You can rub down my horse to begin with, and first fetch my grub from the field kitchen."

The horse that old Sergeant Grushenko had picked for Franz was a spirited runner, and trotted impatiently along with a group of riders in the rear of the column. Franz's future prospects looked gloomy enough. The regiment was pushing east about sixty miles every day. Franz realized he was even worse off than before. True, he was no longer a cattle drover, but he was the only German among more than two thousand Russians, and he was getting farther away from home every minute.

During the long rides, one thought was uppermost in his mind. That thought was escape. He racked his brains for a plan. "How can I get away?" Perhaps at night? But that wasn't easy. When you'd been in the saddle all day, you were dog-tired. You were glad enough to lie down at night, and you fell fast asleep instantly. Franz was caught, and he had to make the best of it. Some time he would find a way out.

Most of the Russians viewed Franz with suspicion, and they kept a very close watch on him. As time went on, he thought a little less often about flight and tried to get what he could out of the situation. At least he was getting plain wholesome food from the regiment's field kitchen, so he was better off than many captive Germans. On thin cabbage soup, lashes and forced marching, he wouldn't have survived. Many of these prisoners had suffered cruelly under this Russian treatment, but he was not footsore and he was not starving. There he was in a Cossack uniform, one German riding east in a Kuban regiment. No one would have known he was German, except for his ignorance of Russian, and he tried hard to learn. He took advantage of every opportunity to get people to talk with him in Russian. They liked this, and took pleasure in correcting him whenever necessary. It was not long before everybody knew him. Smiles of recognition and amusement would follow him when he rode about self-importantly on some errand.

He often used to meet Simeon at meals, and one day his friend presented him to the commanding officer.

"Well, my boy, how do you like the regiment?" said Serge Andreyevich. Franz lied cheerfully.

"Very much. I'm happy to be able to see all this, and pit note historic events. I've always been very much interested in Russia, and especially the Cossacks."

"Is that so," said the Colonel. "What do you know about our country, and why is it so interesting?"

"I admire the energy with which the Russian people solve their problems. For example, the way you have managed in a few years to develop from an agricultural to an industrial economy. What I like about the Cossacks is their enthusiasm for military glory, through centuries of history. I also like your devotion to a free and independent life. You always had a special place in Russia under the Czars, and you still have an autonomous republic under the Soviet state today."

"You're not so far wrong at that," replied Serge Andreyevich.

"Suppose you stay around headquarters from now on, and look after the horses. You can take care of my baggage, too."

Franz came to attention, said "Yes, sir!" - about-faced, and took himself off.

Outside, he found Simeon waiting.

"Come along with me, Franchishek, we've got hold of something very special. We're going to have a regular feast."

Franz followed willingly; he was always ready to eat. Four more Stalin scholars made up the party. Simeon introduced Franz to the others.

"Here's our new friend Franchishek." Turning to Franz, he went on: "Franchishek, let me present my friends from military school - Kolya, Misha, Vanya, Seryoesha."

"Very glad to make your acquaintance," said Franz drily. "I certainly hope we'll get along."

"Why, of course we will," replied Kolya. "Misha, pour the vodka. We'll have a drink on it."

No sooner said than done. Misha brought an armload of bottles and announced, "Let the orgy begin."

Seryoesha was already engaged in carving a great ham. A pile of eggs rested beside it. Misha swiftly built a fire. He set some stones around it and put the frying pan on top. The whole job took about fifteen minutes. Before long the boys were feeling in a very good mood. The ham and eggs, washed down with vodka, tasted fine. The group of merrymakers, around the fire, had grown to some ten in number.

Other campfires glowed along the edge of the wood. The Cossacks were getting ready for the night. The munching and snorting of horses were plainly to be heard. The sunset reddened in the west. Then quietly the regimental chorus began to sing. It was a nostalgic hymn to Mother Russia. The young people sat and listened to the Cossack voices. The leading basses would resound, followed close by the chorus in unison. They sang old Cossack battle songs. Nearly all the songs were heavy with nostalgia and melancholy. One song was about the fate of a young Cossack who had to part from his beloved to go to the Turkish wars. There he fell into the hands of the Circassians and was slain. But his faithful comrades stole the body and bore it home to the beloved. So, she gave him a hero's burial and planted roses on his grave.

All these songs made Franz feel very sad, and he was seized with a violent homesickness. At this point he found himself simply overwhelmed by human emotion. A boogie beat might have cheered him up, but the Russians would have had their own views on that. At any rate, these Cossack veterans were anything but jazz fans.

"What do you say, Franz, how do you like our songs?" asked one.

"Very beautiful, but very strange too. There is so much mystery and tragedy in them. They are just like you," Franz responded.

"Yes, that's the way we are," the other answered thoughtfully. "People always say that we aren't human. They think all we know is raiding and tearing around. We can be very happy, and very sad. We are gentle, and if necessary cruel. After all, for centuries we were the chosen imperial guard. After the revolution, they wanted to root us out. But history records that we were too tough. Our people suffered years of misery and despair, but our Little Father Stalin remembered us at last. He rescued the land of the Cossacks from oblivion and created new combat regiments. And as it turned out, in spite of all the modern weapons, it was no mistake to bring the Cossacks back to life. In the great Patriotic War, we proved our worth all through the wide-open spaces of our land. When the enemy's infantry had marched its feet off, then we were the swift troop following up our armor and cutting off the enemy's communications. We were splendid in the big encirclements and pincer movements. Of course, it would have been suicidal to pit our Cossack squads against the German artillery and machinegun emplacements; but in those tremendous spaces, the enemy couldn't field enough men and material to build up a strong front. So, with our tommy guns and light field pieces, we were able, by the help of our mobility and knowledge of the country, to wipe out many enemy divisions, and do our share towards victory."

"But," Franz put in doubtfully, "in line with military progress, I suppose, even if the Cossacks were very successful in this war, cavalry won't be able to hold its own indefinitely."

"No," Simeon answered, "I guess you're right there. Our leaders have thought of that. All the Cossack outfits are going to be modernized eventually. Instead of horses, we'll have trucks or maybe light tanks and motorized artillery. But such changes won't affect the permanence of the Cossack nation. What I mean is, we'll keep our customs and traditions, like our favorite sport, the djigitovka."

"Djigitovka?" Franz interrupted. "What's that?"

"Our friend doesn't know about that yet," said another voice, "but he will soon enough, down on the Kuban. It takes plenty of guts, let me tell you. Wait till we get home. If you feel like trying it, we'll be glad to let you practice."

All the Cossacks laughed heartily. "When he's seen it, he'll have had enough."

Secretly, Franz wished the whole Cossack nation at the devil, and would have been happy to escape his captivity at any opportunity. But the regiment had now passed far beyond the Oder, and was heading briskly for the Polish city of Poznań. He had lost his chance. His Russian was not nearly good enough, and he realized that flight through foreign territory would be hopeless.

Only a few days later, the regiment stopped in a Polish village. The staff set up headquarters in the schoolhouse. The Cossacks unsaddled their mounts and tied them to the trees in the square to let them rest in the shade. A billeting detail was sent a day's ride ahead to find the next suitable stopover for the outfit. A few squads rode out to forage in the neighborhood for the horses. In the center of the square there was a well. Cossacks were taking turns drawing water. It was a hot and dry Polish summer. Horses crowded around the troughs. The animals were suffering from thirst, but each man held his horse and waited his turn. The horses sucked up the cool well water greedily. Then they lay down wearily in the shade.

The horses were of many breeds. The original Russian stock had been largely replaced by German remounts. Among the best of the Russian horses were the Turkmens, long, sinewy thoroughbreds of great endurance, even tougher and hardier than those of the Kuban and Don Cossacks. The Turkmen horses somewhat resembled Irish hunters in conformation, but were leaner and wirier.

The fabulous horses of East Prussia were of course foremost among the animals taken in Germany. For speed and endurance, they compared well with the horses from Turkmenistan. The Cossacks had had ample opportunity to supply their shortage of mounts from the great stud farms of Trakehnen. They had continued to requisition horses all along their march through the German provinces as far as the Elbe. They never wearied of re-living the glorious days of that advance from Koenigsberg to Berlin. German resistance had slackened noticeably by that time. The German armies of the east were breaking up. Desertions were increasing daily. The Cossacks had been overjoyed by this triumphal progress into Germany. Had not their commander-in-chief Generalissimo

Joseph Vissarionovich Stalin promised them complete freedom to plunder? They exercised it in one village after another.
Then about every twenty-five miles there would be a small
or medium-sized town. Every day there were better and more
valuable prizes to be liberated, theirs for the taking. The
countryside had never before been touched by the storm of
the Red armies. Germany seemed a land of abundance compared to the provinces of Russia and Poland. No wonder
the Cossacks had such happy memories of their vacation in
Germany. Only one thing annoyed them; they clearly felt it
was not right that the other half of Germany should be occupied by their allies. The Russians should have been allowed
to march in triumph all the way to the Rhine. But there was
nothing to be done about that now. Little Father Stalin was
withdrawing his Cossacks from Germany, and they were sure
he knew what he was doing. They were resigned to the fact
that their holiday was over. Eagerly they pushed forward towards their waiting homeland.

In Polish territory, nevertheless, they followed their time-
honored practices. But the problem was not quite so simple as
it had been in conquered Germany. The Polish country people
watched the passing cavalry suspiciously. The strong Polish

militia was ready to protect the population from being victimized. Despite all these precautions, the headquarters officer, Captain Smirnov, got plenty of complaints from citizens. Cats had been stolen from one, chickens from another. Every time, the Poles with their police would come to the regimental staff to complain. The peasants indignantly demanded payment of damages and punishment of the offenders. But Smirnov was imperturbable. He was as thick-skinned as an elephant.

"What are the names of the guilty parties? Can you identify them?" he would ask. "Of course, this is a matter for the military police and courts martial. It's outside my jurisdiction," he would always conclude. Sometimes he varied his tactics and his tone of voice.

"I shall proceed immediately to see that those responsible are punished." The peasants would be satisfied for the moment and depart. Next morning the regiment would have moved on. The Poles had to put up with these depredations as best they could.

During this long ride to the east, Franz had ample opportunity to converse with the Russians about their and his own political and economic attitudes. Quite a few young officers of the regiment, Stalin scholars like Simeon, spoke German quite well. Franz had some impression of the problem that reconstruction would present in conquered Germany. The Nazis had left German youth with a bitter inheritance. There were no German newspapers to be had. Franz tried to glean some information from the Russian army newspaper, but the Cyrillic print defeated him. So, he asked Simeon to help him learn to spell it out. Simeon read some of the articles to him, and helped Franz learn the Russian alphabet.

"Look here, Simeon," Franz said once. "Do you think there's any way out for the German people?"

"Of course, there's a way out. Even during the great Patriotic War, Comrade Stalin kept saying that neither the Russian nor the German people could be exterminated. You must have heard of his famous remark, 'Hitlers come and Hitlers go, but the German people remain.'"

"All right," said Franz. "Suppose the German people do remain. But how? Germany has been through a long period of war. Everybody is worn out and apathetic. People have nothing left. Hunger and disease threaten. Without outside help, the country will never recover."

Simeon replied magnanimously:

"What you say is true. But we will be helping you to

rebuild your country. And please don't forget that we have a lot of reconstruction of our own to do. The Germans penetrated more than two thousand kilometers into our territory, destroyed the best of our factories, burned our towns and villages, and did all the damage they possibly could."

"Well, Simeon, if that's the way things are in your country, you'll need outside help yourselves to rebuild your shattered economy. In that situation, how could you extend any material aid to the German economy?"

"You simply don't understand the Soviet attitude in such matters, or you wouldn't be so pessimistic. In the Soviet Union, problems are solved much faster than is possible in countries with a capitalistic set-up. Look, Franz," he went on, "our land and factories are not the property of a few; all means of production belong to the people, and all products are distributed equitably among the population. Now since each individual produces more than he consumes, by the end of the first post-war five-year plan all the destruction due to the Hitler war will have been repaired. Remember that the Soviet Union is the biggest country on earth. Not all parts of our country were ravaged by Hitler's troops. From those other regions of the U.S.S.R., a stream of reconstruction materials will flow into the devastated areas."

Franz put in, "I guess that's not the only stream of re-construction materials flowing into your country. There's another one from the west - all the reparations you are getting from Germany."

"Yes," retorted Simeon. "That's the way it has to be. After all, you started the war, and you lost the war. I hate to think what you would have done to the Russians if you had won."

"That's true enough. But what do you mean when you say that you nevertheless want to help the German people rebuild their economy? I don't understand that. You say you liberated us from Fascism. All right. But you can never make friends with the Germans when you rape the women and de-port the men and systematically plunder the whole country. The Germans will say Bolshevism is much worse even than Nazism. You will only be raising up a new enemy against yourselves. You can't expect to solve such problems in the twentieth century by brute force."

Simeon answered excitedly, "We don't expect to and we won't try to. You will see how Soviet experience will be put to use in Germany. As soon as our armies have left Germany, a determined attack will be made on your most pressing po-litical problems."

"What do you mean by our most pressing problems,"
Franz wanted to know.

"You've got to realize one thing; the German master-race
theory is done with for good. The German people will have
to accept a lower standard of living. To begin with, our government will go to work and mercilessly liquidate all fascist
and militaristic institutions. Banks and factories will be nationalized. That is the first decisive step the Soviet government will take. Those war-mongering, aggressive militarist
and monopoly capitalist elements will be fought to a finish.
They are the ones we hold responsible for the first and the
second world war. We will turn over the holdings of the great
landowners to the peasants. The workers will take over the
factories from the capitalists. Then the German people will
be able to prove that they have dissociated themselves from
their former rulers and are ready to be accepted into the community of free nations of the earth.

"The masses of the German workers and peasants will
have to erect a democratic Germany out of nothing. But they
will be able to learn from the Soviet Union. We had much
the same situation at the end of World War I. We were
still an agrarian country, and what are we today, thirty years

later? Next to the United States, the greatest power on earth. This was possible only under the leadership of our glorious Communist Party. We needed no loans from the capitalist states, either. We refused such offers for the hypocritical pretenses that they were." Simeon continued:

"When the imperialists saw that wars of intervention and counterrevolution were of no avail, they tried to stop the advance of communism by binding us with export capital. Everybody knows how the Soviet government refused to be tripped and took its own road to socialism regardless of such temptations."

"Yes," Franz said, "and how did you do it? How did you manage to develop your great heavy industry in thirty years? What did you do to people? You destroyed their souls. You forced them into the mold of your communistic standards. You banished millions to the silent camps of Siberia, to a miserable existence. You came to power through heaps of corpses and a sea of blood. And when Stalin came to power, the biggest purges in history were carried out in the ranks of your own Communist Party. People in your country breath a never-ending terror. I read about the big Moscow purge trials. Your country is ruled by an oriental despot, nothing but a Red Czar, who really has nothing to do with socialism. Under the pretext of socialism, he pursues his ambitions aims of power politics. A lot he cares about the welfare of his people. He is wearing out two hundred million human beings in his economic experiment. Isn't that depriving the proletarian revolution of its historic and human significance?"

Simeon answered him sharply. "Just for that I ought to report you to the political officer as a counterrevolutionary. But I realize you were brought up in fascist Germany, so this time I won't. I hope you will learn better while you are in our country, and change your opinion. It would be too bad if your stubbornness brought you to a bad end. We need each individual to build up the land of socialism. I assure you we don't liquidate a comrade the minute he makes a mistake and deviates a bit from the party line. If he sees the error of his ways, and is willing to learn from his mistakes, we are always ready to take the repentant offender back into our ranks. Of course, he will be on probation for a while. Somebody has to keep an eye on him."

"Oh well," muttered Franz, "all this is very new to me. After all, I have never seen any of those things. All the new ideas you've presented to me will give me a lot to think about.

Anyway, I'm tired. I think I'll catch a couple of hours sleep. Maybe I'll dream about some unimaginable paradise on earth."

Exhausted as he was, Franz stretched out on the mossy ground, huddled himself in a couple of heavy uniform cloaks, and soon fell into a deep dreamless sleep.

The blare of bugles waked him in the morning. Sleepily he arose, rubbed his eyes and set himself in motion towards staff headquarters. He went to work tending the horses of the Colonel and his adjutant Captain Smirnov. Then he took his own beautiful Caucasian gray in hand.

This was an uncommonly intelligent animal, and full of tricks. When Franz came to groom him in the morning, he would bite and kick until he got a lump of sugar. Then and only then would he stand still. During the day, on the long ride, Franz's four-legged companion would indulge in whimsical notions. If he spied anything suspicious on the scene, he would point his ears like a cat, flare his nostrils, utter a snort of terror, rear on his hind legs and execute an instantaneous about-face, galloping off in the opposite direction. Franz needed all his horsemanship to get Nabor back into line. These exhibitions, which Nabor puts on every chance he got, never failed to rouse the merriment of the whole party. Franz got used to it, and was glad to have such a temperamental and inventive mount; sometimes he felt more like an acrobat than a rider. It passed the time, and Franz was diverted somewhat from the monotony of the long ride.

Another part of Franz's job was to take care of the saddlery for the three animals. After doing those chores, he would wash up and pick up the day's rations for the two officers and himself from the headquarters kitchen.

Scrubbed clean and cheerful, he would report to the Colonel, who would be quartered in some village homestead. Serge Andreyevich would ask him at breakfast how he liked life among the Cossacks. Franz would express enthusiasm, and hope he could remain with the regiment. He quite understood that as a German prisoner, he was in a privileged position. If the Cossacks had handed him over to some prison camp, he would have been much worse off. He might have died of starvation and mistreatment, as so many prisoners in Russia had done. But in this Cossack regiment he was to all intents and purposes a Russian, and his status as the Colonel's orderly would protect him from actual want. So, he was safe from going hungry as matters stood.

Epidemics had assumed devastating proportions in the stricken areas of Central and Eastern Europe. Filled with pity, Franz rode past slave caravans of captured Germans being driven eastward. In the suffocating summer heat, too many of his countrymen were dying on the march. Hunger was not the worst of it. In the flat, dry countryside, there was an acute shortage of water. The Russian units were supplied first, and then the prisoners. They sucked up the refreshing wetness greedily into their parched bodies. The water, not boiled, was often contaminated. Masses of prisoners succumbed to cholera and typhoid. Emaciated wretches fell fainting to the ground, unable to rise. Somewhere in the shoreless spaces of the east, the victim was mercifully shot where he lay. Many welcomed this end; they submitted to being driven until they fell flat from the heat. When a man could go no further, he was left lying by the roadside. He might be the father of a family, an only son, or a bridegroom; at least whenever Franz saw one of these unfortunates, beyond all chance of help, he couldn't help thinking of the man's loved ones. They would never know what had happened. No International Red Cross would ever discover his resting place. The Bolshevist engine of terror had struck him down. Countless prisoners and deportees vanished in the early years after the war, on the roads, in the camps of silence, and in Stalin's dungeons.

The Cossacks would ride past the convoys of prisoners without comment. Even their robber souls were touched with compassion. Franz asked Simeon: "What's the point of all this now? The war's over, isn't it? Why take revenge on defenseless human beings? The war wasn't their doing. They too, most of them, were caught in a ruthless organizational machine. No one asked them whether they approved or not."

"My friend, you can't cut wood without dropping chips. These prisoners are the chips, that's all. During the war, eighty million Russians lived under German occupation. Millions of my people perished in German camps. There were those among the Nazis who favored exterminating all the Russians, and the Nazis would not have stopped at carrying theory into practice. But the indomitable will and self-sacrifice of our nation prevented them in time. Your own Himmler said that whether ten thousand Russian women lived or died made no difference at all. As a German, all that mattered to him was getting these slaves to build fortifications in order to stem the red tide from the east. What happened to the ten thousand Russian women didn't interest him. The line had to hold. Nothing else counted. What's the use of talking? How could you expect the Russian soldier not to feel hatred when he got to Germany? All this is merely just retribution. The aggressors must pay their debt. I don't care just how much guilt or punishment falls on each individual. Hitler couldn't have done it all by himself. He had to have the help of large sections of the population. Now let the whole German people expiate their crimes."

"Well, I think you should consider that by this procedure you are practically descending to the Nazis' own level. People will soon find that they've fallen out of the frying pan into the fire. If you pursue such a policy, you will have no friends left in the civilized world. And the preparation and success of the world revolution you hope for depends on the cooperation of working people in the advanced industrialized countries of the west. Without them there can be no revolution. If you indulge in these medieval methods in Germany, the spark will spread from that country to start a new anti-Soviet. Germany is the heart of Europe. You can never get Germany or Europe on your side in this way, no matter how strong a system of propaganda and terror you build up.

"Slavery is no match for the free human will. You can't

treat enlightened Europeans with the same primitive methods as your Asiatics. If you can't give your proletarian revolution and your Russian bolshevism a human character, all your plans are foredoomed to failure. Your only weapon will be the language of force, and that has always been a very temporary and uncertain tool."

Simeon replied hesitantly, "You may be partly right. But you can't deny that the Soviet government, under the leadership of the Communist Party, has created an industrial state in only three decades. You object that this advance was achieved at a cost to men and freedom. That may be. But somehow, the lead that the rest of the world had over us had to be made up. I assure you that in a nation like ours this was possible only by ruthless measures. Under a less resolute leadership, our country would have fallen an easy prey to our enemies, who always did everything they could to strangle bolshevism in its cradle. The fact that they did not succeed is due primarily to the resolution and iron discipline of our leadership."

"That's exactly the same story they used to tell in national-socialist Germany," Franz retorted. "The same thing exactly. Don't talk to me about iron strength and ruthless determination of leadership. I don't agree with you at all,

Simeon, because what I think is that in this twentieth century, we don't want any more stern and all-powerful Fuehrer types, willing to let whole nations bleed for nothing but their private ambition. In our time, it should be the other way around. Leaders should devote themselves to the welfare of their people. What is more, the leaders should be chosen and recalled by the people, and should be responsible to the people at all times, and exposed to continual public criticism. All their statecraft and ability should be subordinated to the public good. That's what strong and conscious leadership would mean to me. It seems to me that we disagree pretty basically. You accept the totalitarian and dictatorial system, and I am advocating the parliamentary and democratic system." Simeon replied to Franz:

"It's true we don't have as much democracy as some of the western states, but on the other hand our democracy is real. All the Soviet deputies were elected to hold office, too. All representatives are fully responsible to the people."

"I'm looking forward to seeing it all for myself," said Franz. On second thought, he decided he would be more careful about these discussions. An informer might be listening, and it would be just too bad for him.

By now, Franz had become accustomed to the long, hard rides, and he had become inured to the day and night marches. He knew mostly all the Cossacks by sight. Sometimes he would ask them when and where the long trek would end.

"You'll see when we get to Rostov-on-Don. That's where we're heading. The old man will get us there, don't worry." That was all Franz could get out of his captors.

Beyond Warsaw, the country gradually assumed the typical form of a flat, broad plain. They passed ruined villages and fortifications, and through fields of grain and flowering gardens. The regiment lodged in a chateau near Lwów. The Cossacks found a piano in the hall. No one knew how to play it, so a schoolteacher was fetched in from the neighborhood. The poor man had to play polkas and mazurkas the whole night long. The regimental chorus took up a position by the piano and sang lustily, their Cossack melodies. Some young soldiers demonstrated traditional dances. Franz had an opportunity to admire the Russian temperament and the agility of the Cossacks. The dances called for great acrobatic prowess. Some of the men had found some vodka, making the gay mood complete. Polish girls, curious to see what was going on, came in and looked at the Cossacks with suspicion.

But the singers and dancers earned appreciative applause for their performance. "Come on," shouted the burly old Sergeant Grushenko, slamming the schoolmaster heartily on the shoulder, "You old devil, play the Rosamund song again!"

The tired pianist started playing again, accompanying the many-voiced Cossack choir. The girls timidly approached and sat down among the Cossacks. Franz was soon surrounded by a laughing, carousing company.

"My friends," Captain Smirnov addressed them, "we'll never be any younger than we are now. So, let us merrily dance and sing. We Cossacks have always been a gay people, and we must be true to our traditions."

He bowed to one of the girls and led a graceful mazurka onto the floor. The others followed his example, and the hall of the chateau was filled with dancing couples. Towards midnight, the party reached its climax. Pigs and fowl were brought in to the field kitchen from round about and a feast was prepared without delay. Serge Andreyevich stood, straddle-legged, on top of the table, beating his glass with a spoon for order. Everyone quieted down.

"My friends," began the Colonel. "I am happy to announce that I have just completed the fiftieth year of my life. I want the whole regiment to celebrate my birthday in company with our Polish friends. Long live Polish-Russian friendship! Comrades, let us enjoy ourselves."

"Long life to our Colonel," yelled the Cossacks with one voice. They raised Serge Andreyevich on their shoulders and carried him around the table in triumph, drinking his health again and again. One toast followed another. After all, Serge Andreyevich's birthday came only once a year. That was one chance for everybody to break loose and have a real celebration. What matter if wives were waiting impatiently at home? The Cossacks consoled themselves with the Polish beauties, and enjoyed the cool of the summer night while they were about it. Vodka flowed all night in torrents. The dancing got wilder and wilder, the Polish girls keeping up as best they could.

"Davai!" the men cried again and again, "Play the Rosamund song again."

Everybody started clapping, and the weary schoolmaster began to play again.

"Devai!" the men cried repeatedly. "Play the Rosamund song again."

Everybody started clapping, and the weary schoolmaster again began to play.

Chapter III

Next morning the roaring feast was all but forgotten, and the regiment, a little heavy-headed, was pushing on across the Polish landscape. They had left the region of Warsaw behind, and were marching southeast, approaching Lwów. The roads leading southeast through Poland were not as overcrowded at that time as the east-west highways. That was a tremendous journey, in the summer of 1945. Each day's march was a hundred kilometers. Often the road was broken by ruined bridges and overpasses, and the regiment had to wait until other units ahead of them had got past the spot. This sorely tried their patience. Standing about for hours in the heat jangled everybody's nerves. The horses became very restless and had to be quieted. Franz, being fond of horses, enjoyed working with the Arabs and other thoroughbreds that had helped him through so many hard times in this

endless waste. The Cossacks began to feel that he was trust-
worthy. They saw that he was interested in all their ways, and
helped him all they could. Franz wanted to understand the
philosophy of these Soviet soldiers. Their propaganda kept
insisting that the Bolshevik system had completely reeducated
the Russian people. The workers and peasants of the Russian
empire had brought forth a new type of individual. This
type had been the product of decades of concentrated ideological training. What were this individual's real thoughts?
What was his attitude towards the other human beings of
the earth? What distinguished so-called Soviet Man from the
citizens of the rest of the world? For what ideals and aims was
this type of individual working? All these questions occurred
to Franz, and he tried to gain a clear picture of the being
and consciousness of the Soviet personality. In all Russian
military units, there were political officers who had been
through a long course of training for their task. Their task,
essentially, was intellectual surveillance of the other officers
and men. The commissars held special authority from the
commander-in-chief, and had the power to institute summary
punitive measures at need, if the ideological or moral fidelity
of troops was jeopardized. Individual political officers were

closely supervised by higher commissars, in the performance of their duty. Thus, the government had assurance that everything was functioning smoothly and the machinery of power kept well lubricated.

Particularly in the course of 1945, Russian political officers and ideologists had their work cut out for them. For years the Russians had been told repeatedly that the toiling masses in the western countries led a miserable existence and were mercilessly exploited by the bosses and big landowners. Those countries, the Russians were given to understand, were permeated with the degeneracy and parasitism of a dying stratum of society, whose historic tasks were long-since performed. The proletarian masses, the ideologists said, suffered bitterly under the rule of these feudal masters and capitalists, and were eagerly awaiting the day of their liberation by the Red Army.

Now of course Russian human beings have exactly the same faculty of thought as any other human beings on earth. When the Soviet troops came to Germany in 1945, they could see that much of the teaching of their party leaders was not factual. Soldiers and officers saw how the German worker lived in reality. They were invariably astonished when they saw workingmen's dwellings in Germany. They could not get over their surprise that a worker should have more than one suit of clothes, and several rooms, with modern conveniences. At first the Russians thought these must be capitalists. But it was the same everywhere, and the Germans couldn't all be capitalists. It was very embarrassing. It was embarrassing especially to the political commissars, responsible as they were for the ideological orthodoxy of all the Russians.

Stalin had developed Marxism into a very special doctrine. This doctrine, in the Red empire, constituted unimpeachable dogma, and no one dared venture to criticize or question it. So, the commissars and other functionaries were more junior Stalin's, charged with the execution and consummation of his plans.

From Vladivostok to the Elbe, all life was regimented. The tune was called by one man in the Kremlin, who with unparalleled demagogy and despotism hitched the nations of the east to the chariot of his ambition. But in 1945 the Russians were beginning to suspect that they had been sorely misled and deceived. It was the facts of conditions in Germany that enabled Franz to make his discovery of ideas unfavorable to the Soviets in the Russian soldier's mind. The Russians were shocked to find how German workers had actually been living before the Nazi era. They inquired minutely into wages and prices in Germany at that time, and made comparisons with the purchasing power of what the Russian worker received for his labor. They compared the working hours, intensity of labor and private pursuits of individuals in Germany with those of people in Russia. They came to the conclusion that the Soviet Union, too, had been proceeding on the principle of guns, not butter. The difference between Soviet Russia and the rest of the free world was simply that Russia for decades had been striving only to develop heavy industry and armament production. Stalin had been violently forcing the rate of economic and industrial development in the Soviet Union. Whether such experiments cost hundreds of thousands of Russian lives had been of secondary importance.

Stalin understood that Russia had been an agrarian country before the revolution. He planned by drastic measures to catch up with the nations of America and Western Europe. But this economic and industrial construction of the Soviet land was to be accomplished without foreign aid or capitalist imports. Stalin solved his problems by simple disregard of elementary human rights. He unscrupulously appropriated the machinery of power. All his political opponents vanished into imprisonment or slavery.

The workers of Russia had evolved the Stakhanovite system. Stakhanov was a man who had over-fulfilled his quota of production by a hundred and thirty percent, a shining example to all Russian workers. Every sector of the economy came to have its own Stakhanov. The system functioned by utmost intensity of labor on the part of the toiling masses of Russia, and a very low standard of living. The idea was for the Soviet Union to catch up with the other leading industrial countries within a very short time. Next, the western powers were to be surpassed in the sphere of international industry.

The whole Russian people was exposed to training courses from morning to night. Training was largely political, but technology was not neglected. For Stalin was quite aware that his world revolutionary plans of conquest could be carried out only with the aid of intellectually trained personnel. All the same, in spite of all training programs and special courses, the best-trained Bolshevists were not to be compared with Western European or American intellectuals. They were educated in a pragmatic, single-track sort of way. They did not go in for the liberal arts, nor were they in any position to inform themselves about the facts of social and political life in the Western World and thus arrive at independent opinions.

The Soviet propagandists were always talking about criticism and self-criticism in the budding Utopia. A citizen of a western country, reading their fine words, might have visualized a thoroughly reasonable and useful institution. But all this criticism and self-criticism tended to one purpose only, to contribute to the stability of the Red regime. If a worker had failed to meet his quota, for example, he would be stood up in front of his associates, and say:

"The fact is, I didn't meet my quota because I committed such-and-such mistakes. Now I have learned from these mistakes, and I know how I can improve my performance in future. I shall do everything in my power to accomplish this."

That is more or less what self-criticism came to in the socialist state of the workers and peasants. Criticism was not much different. Thus, if the political director of some factory found that the work of Comrade X had not been what it should be of late, then Comrade X would get criticized before the entire assembly, and exhorted to mend his ways. If the accused confessed his fault repentantly, all was well. But if he had anything to say in his own defense, or spoke out against the exploitative policy of the regime, the political director would see a danger to the Soviet order, and it would be his duty to take steps towards eliminating this fascist provocateur. Before very long Comrade X would have vanished from his post and found a new home in some labor camp or prison. Such examples were both deterrent and incentive to the others. The regime had created a state within a state, a mammoth organization of police power. Fear and terror were the main attributes of Russian might. They were the twin engines that propelled the Soviet colossus.

These facts had to be borne in mind by Western men in any conversation with Soviet man. He would soon find that the latter was extremely cautious and mistrustful in all discussions of economic and political problems of our time.

Among the Cossacks on their homeward march, things were naturally rather different. Franz had plenty of chances to chat with individuals about their political and economic attitudes. On these marches through Russia's wide domains, the political commissars were unable to keep such close watch as among the workers in a factory. Anyway, the Cossacks were a much freer people than others in the Soviet Union. The Kremlin's political educators had a lot of trouble with them;

for centuries, the man-at-arms of the feudal Russian regime had been drawn from their ranks. After the revolution, their own Cossack republics grow up within the Russian federation. Stalin later created Cossack guard regiments, and they fought outstandingly in the war against the Germans. Franz had wondered why the Russians still set so much store by cavalry in the Second World War. When he saw the endless expanses of the east, he came to see that in the muddy seasons of the spring and fall, even the best mechanized troops might be reduced to utter uselessness. But the Russian cavalry units always got through. They were much more mobile than the infantry, and played a decisive part in encirclement maneuvers. Notwithstanding all advances in military technology, they remained a formidable weapon in Russia. Every man was equipped with a tommy gun firing seventy-three rounds without reloading, so these mobile troops had a respectable fire power. Franz would have thought the Cossack spirit could not survive under bolshevism, but he learned otherwise. True, they had to part with their property and allow themselves to be organized into collective farms, but even under the Red terror, this people were able to assert and maintain its national identity. Their traditional songs and ancient words of command were used as always.

In the flatlands behind Lwów, the landscape began to assume something of a Russian character. The hard, dry clay roads were dusty in summer, firm as cement in winter. The prospect was sad and interminable. Waving fields of grain were the exterior and dominant features of the Ukrainian countryside. Virtually every village had been burned by the Germans in their retreat. Most towns had been destroyed, and the main bridges blown up.

At noon one day, the regiment halted on a Tartar mound. Franz had tended his horses and taken a frugal meal. He was sitting around with some of the Russians, talking. Simeon acted as interpreter when necessary.

"What is the reason for these mounds in the middle of the steppe?" Franz wanted to know. "You can see them a long way off."

"They are burial mounds, from Tartar days. There are a lot of stories about them. Some are said to be resting places of the great Tartar chieftains, and they have also been used for watch fires and landmarks. It was through this country that the horde of Genghis Khan overflowed into Europe, sweeping over the Russian steppes like the wind. All in their path were overrun and destroyed."

"Yes, I heard something about that in school," said Franz. "But I never thought I would see anything like that."

"What do you mean?"

"What do I mean? The Russian conquest and occupation of Germany, of course. Wasn't that a horde? Could Genghis Khan have been any worse?"

"There you have the difference between East and West - the struggle between Pan-Slavism and Pan-Germanism," said Seryoesha. "But we must try to forget about that now. When we get home, we'll rebuild what has been destroyed. We have smashed the aggressor, and can go back to peaceful work."

"That's what you say," said another young man. "My three brothers got killed. My mother and I will be alone. My father's still in the army, and our house is destroyed, and you want enthusiasm for reconstruction. All you German's ought to be shot."

"Oh, come now," said Franz, "In the first place you can't shoot a whole nation, and in the second place there are a great many of us who hate fascism just as much as you do. When anybody says anything about Germany, all you think of is Hitler and fascism. I tell you there's another Germany. A nation that respects all human beings, and human rights, and intends to work together with the other free peoples for a better future and international understanding. The war wounds have not yet healed. But better nations will rise from the ruins. We who are young must believe this; what will become of us if we start reproaching each other again? We can't help it that you're a Russian and I'm a German. We just have to learn to respect each other, and learn from each other, or in twenty years we'll have another war which would probably finish mankind. We have to understand this and be reasonable, or else let feelings of hatred and revenge rage on. That would conjure up a new world catastrophe. We have no choice left but to live peaceably together."

"Ultimately, of course, you're right," the Russian agreed. "But the destruction brought about by the Germans in Russia must be paid for by the whole people. You can't get around that."

Franz had many conversations like this with the Russians, often lasting into the night. At length all would be overcome with drowsiness and stretch out wearily by the campfire. The monotonous champing of the horses was the music to which Franz nightly fall asleep. At dawn, reveille roused him. So, it went, day after day.

From Lwów their way led by Tarnopol, Vinnitsa, Usan, Kirowograd, Dnepropetrovsk, Zaporozhye and Taganrog to Rostov-on-Don.

The country around Rostov was the regiment's home ground. All were overjoyed when this objective was reached at last. They could hardly wait to be demobilized. Franz wondered what was going to happen to him next. Would the Russians turn his over as a prisoner of war? Or what? He knew that his prospects in a detention camp would be anything but rosy. Finally, he was able to dismiss these gloomy thoughts, and hope calmly for the best. For the time being, he was still taking care of the horses for the Colonel and Captain Smirnov. He tended them and exercised them. But he did not neglect his best friend, Nabor. Franz liked to ride through the beautiful environs of the town of Rostov. It gave him a wonderful feeling of freedom, and made him forget the woes of captivity, to gallop along the beach on the Sea of Asov just after sunrise. He gave the spirited Arab his head. The animal lunged out until he was flying along like an arrow. When Franz had exercised the other thoroughbreds, most of his day's work was done. Tired, he went to bed early.

One morning Serge Andreyevich came down to the stables

and said shortly, "My boy, I've left the service and am to become manager of a state farm in the Kuban. Would you like to come along? It's in the Krasnodar district, mostly horses and cattle. We raise Arabs and English-Arab crossbreds. I hope you like the idea. I would adopt you, as it were. Think it over and let me know tonight."

To Franz, his course was clear. There was no great need for reflection. He was going to have to find some sort of place for himself in the vastness of Russia. If I go with the Colonel, he thought, at least I'll be well off for board and lodging. This was no small matter in Russia at that time.

On the evening of the same day, Franz reported smartly to Serge Andreyevich and said:

"Sir, I'd like to go with you to the Kuban."

The Colonel replied, "Good boy. Get everything ready. We ride first thing in the morning."

Franz executed the angular about-face he had learned from the Cossacks and was dismissed.

Next morning, he was about very early, grooming his horse for the ride southward. Two noncoms and a veterinary surgeon from the regiment were to share the journey to the south. Serge Andreyevich said a few words of farewell to his regiment. "Comrades in arms, the time has come for us to part. I shall always keep a fond ??? of you. Our deeds together in this war have made a blood brotherhood among us, and the glory we won in battle from Stalingrad to Berlin shall be eternal. Never shall your heroism in the service of Russia be forgotten. Long live the Cossack nation! Long live our mighty Soviet Union! Long live our wise leader and great general, J. V. Stalin."

An honor guard presented an enormous bouquet, and said good-by to the Colonel on behalf of the regiment. The regimental standard was furled, a proud military march closed the brief ceremony, the Colonel mounted his horse, and the little group trotted leisurely southward.

"And that," said Serge Andreyevich, "is the last of military life for me. We're all civilians now. - We can't miss our road, all we have to do is follow the railway track from Rostov to Novorossisk. That will bring us straight to Krasnodar, and we can report to the district commandant there. Anyway, I remember this country pretty well from the civil war."

"Did you fight in the civil war?" asked Franz. "Were you a White or a Red?"

"Why, what do you know about the Russian civil war?"

"Well, a little bit, Serge Andreyevich, as you see by my question," Franz admitted. "Were you a White or a Red?" He had noticed that Serge Andreyevich preferred not to answer, but he was persistent.

"Let me tell you, my boy," the other replied slowly, "that was a very bad business. Russians were fighting against Russians. A civil war is the worst thing there can be. That war sapped the strength of our people terribly, and gave the forces of foreign intervention a chance to sink their teeth into us. I was a young Cossack lieutenant at the time, and for a while after the October Revolution I fought on the side of the Whites. When the Red Army was about to push us into the sea at Novorossisk, I went over to the Reds too, and served under Budjënny on the Polish front. We were victorious over the foreign armies of intervention, and made possible the first socialist state on earth."

"Didn't you say, sir, that we were going to a <u>sovkhoz</u>? What kind of a place is that?"

"A <u>sovkhoz</u> is a state farm. It belongs wholly to the community, that is to say to the socialist state, unlike a <u>kolkhoz</u>, or collective farm, where the individual peasant has a certain private interest. That may sound complicated, but it's simple enough. Each peasant on a collective farm works just like a worker in a factory. As a matter of fact, especially in the Ukraine, such enterprises are referred to as grain factories. Every man receives his hourly wage, and must meet his quota. He must hold to regular procedures and hours of work. Individual collective-farm peasants may have some land and stock of their own. They are able to eke out their family provisions from this little bit of private enterprise. The peasants can buy industrial products in the stores and on the open market. They get the money in the form of wages and incentive pay."

"What is incentive pay?"

"Simply this," replied Serge Andreyevich. "Suppose a worker produced more than one hundred percent of his quota; then he would get extra pay on a sliding scale. That is, for what he turned out over and above the assigned quota, he would get paid <u>pro rata</u>, plus about thirty percent."

"So, it would always depend on what the quota was?" Franz asked.

"Of course. And the higher the quota, the harder it is to overfulfill it, in order to earn any incentive, pay."

"Yes, I see that. What proportion of workers in Russia would you estimate actually get incentive pay?"

"Oh, possibly something like ten percent. The quotas are usually quite high, and only a minority of workers can meet them. It takes more than average skill and experience. Those who overfulfill the quotas are called activists and heroes of labor."

"But, sir, I don't understand how that would work out on a farm. It's all right in a modern factory, but among the country people, and especially the Cossacks, you wouldn't think such an arrangement could be popular. After all, they've always lived on the land. Why should they take an interest in socialist theories? Don't these sovkhoz's and kolkhoz's kill the peasants' initiative? There's no competition in your system. People must get listless and lose interest."

"It's not as bad as all that," said Serge Andreyevich with a smile. "We have socialist competition., something quite different from what is meant by competition in other countries. Every factory or collective farm is divided into teams. These groups vie with one another in fulfilling their quotas and planned goals ahead of time, and this spirit of emulation contributes to the construction of a new society."

"But what does the individual worker get out of it? Why do the proceeds of all this labor have to go into the state treasury, to be invested mostly in armaments? Why shouldn't the standard of living in the Soviet Union be higher, after nearly thirty years of socialist labor? Why don't people have more to eat? Why do you spend so little on consumer goods and so much on heavy industry?" Franz wanted to know.

Serge Andreyevich sat thoughtfully in the saddle without saying anything for a while. At last he swung slowly around and looked at Franz as if he were a visitor from another planet.

"You ask a lot of questions at once, my boy. Let me give you a piece of advice. It's not a good idea to show too much curiosity in Russia, or talk too much. You'll have to get over that. In all this time, we've learned to say amen and so be it to everything, and keep our mouths shut. Some of what you said was outright counterrevolution, and could be interpreted as rebellion against the state power here. We live under a dictatorship of the proletariat. Just a couple of ambiguous remarks in public, and you might be done for. You'd find yourself in some prison cell, or in a labor camp. Our state is governed by the all-powerful Communist Party. That party in turn maintains an enormous police apparatus to check up on the entire population. They are inexorable towards renegades and reactionaries. So, you will find it best to keep still and be careful in public, or your candor may cost you dear. Now as to your questions. Stalin spends more money for guns and tanks because he wants to carry out the program of world revolution. To do that, he needs force in the form of tanks and guns. The population can do nothing about it because it is held in check by terror. And that is why the standard of living is no higher. Our colossal administrative apparatus, too, is a spawn of the socialist regime, compelled by its quotas and five-year-plans and statistics to maintain the structure."

"You said all this was necessary to carry out the world revolution," said Franz, "but at the Moscow Conference, Stalin promised Roosevelt, in return for American aid in the war against Germany, that the Comintern would be dissolved after the victory."

"So, he did," Serge Andreyevich replied. "At the moment, he had no choice. But now he is strong and victorious. He will find a substitute for the Comintern. The old fox doesn't change. If he can't get through, he'll go around. But he'll never give up. Joseph Stalin is a fearless fighter, tempered in the fires of revolution, outlawry, civil war and invasion."

Franz remembered something. "Why do you call the

four-year war with Germany the great Patriotic War? I
thought the proletariat had no country. Isn't the Soviet citizen
an internationalist first, and a Russian second?"

"That may have been true until 1941," Serge Andreyevich
replied. "But it's different now. When Hitler attacked this
country in 1941, some Russians thought this was the time to
throw off the Bolshevik yoke. In the early battles in Western
Russia, the Germans took millions of prisoners. The morale
of our combat troops was low, and the civilian population
showed little enthusiasm as well. That was when the Nazis
made their big mistake. They treated the Russian prisoners of
war barbarously, and deported many civilians to Germany as
forced laborers. The Russians soon learned this. Ivan found
out it would do him no good to surrender to the Germans.
Stalin saw his chance. He promised a better life after the
war, and launched the big slogan of Patriotism. The Russian
soldier thought he was fighting and dying for a truly patriotic
cause. This new propaganda line began to get results. The
winter battle of Moscow was Stalin's first big victory. The
tide of the fascist armies froze solid in the bitter cold of the
Russian winter."

"Did Stalin really have as much to do with the military

victory at Moscow, and later in the siege of Stalingrad, as people say?" Franz wanted to know.

"That's a debatable question. Some maintain that Zhukov and Timoshenko and Voronov were the real commanders. But Stalin was generalissimo, and all the other generals acknowledged him as the foremost military genius of Russia. Anyway, he took care to claim all the credit. Just wait and see. Some of the famous marshals of the Red Army are going to drop out of sight. The monuments will be built and the odes composed in honor of Stalin. He will be worshipped as the best and wisest of all the Russians. He pushed his way ruthlessly into the tyrant's seat after Lenin's death, and now he rules as a Red Czar over an enormous empire."

"I see," said Franz. "You still have a Czar of all the Russia's. He has a different program and a different cloak, but he's a despot all the same."

"Yes," rejoined Serge Andreyevich, "it has often been like that in history. Former revolutionaries and fighters for freedom become dictators themselves when they have beaten their political rivals. It is very ironical."

✫

After many days they came to the end of their journey. They saw the whitewashed stables of the farm from far off. There were miles of paddock fences. Marvelous horses grazed on the green meadows. Franz noted a strong influence of the English thoroughbred. All the herds were separated by ages and distributed among the paddocks. Here in the south of Russia, Franz saw every breed of horse that the Cossacks had captured in Poland, Hungary, Romania and Germany. These noble beasts were the product of centuries of careful breeding. How their true owners must have raged at the robbery committed so casually by the Russians. The brood mares grazed tranquilly under the grateful Caucasian sun. Here they would undoubtedly remain for the rest of their lives, far from the ancestral pastures and stables of Europe.

Not all the horses were of captured Central European stock. The Russians had developed an Arab and an Anglo-Arab breed, and Franz saw some magnificent specimens of the Russian art of cross-breeding.

The travelers rode through the gates towards the administration building. The manager welcomed his guests cordially and showed them the best of Russian hospitality. Serge Andreyevich had the horses unsaddled and turned loose.

The incumbent manager was a Ukrainian, being transferred to some collective farm in his own country. When Serge Andreyevich had inspected the offices, the foremen were assembled, and he formally assumed the direction of the Sovkhoz.

Franz was given a room in the residential quarters attached to the administration building. Serge Andreyevich set him daily lessons to study. In due course, he had him enrolled in the high school. His former commanding officer took a lively interest in his progress. When Franz had finished his assignments, which were not always easy, he sometimes thought sadly of home, and the days of the long march from Germany to the Caucasus. He talked Russian as much as possible with anyone who would listen to him. He wanted to know how people really felt. He was quick to tell Serge Andreyevich that he liked Russia very much, and that he wanted to learn as much as possible about the Soviet Union and its political and social institutions. Continuous activity, and work with the horses on the farm, made him forget his homesickness and helped him bear the hard lot of the exile.

He saw how the ordinary Russians and the prisoners of war were starving and toiling their way through life. The fate of the prisoners, who were dying in the camps by hundreds of thousands, was appalling. They were worked hard all day, on a diet of thin soup and beatings. There were endless interrogations by NKVD officials. Occasionally the guards were able to find a stool pigeon among the captives, who would betray his fellows to the Russians for some trifling privilege. The Russians had automatically extended their own system to the administration of the prison camps, which were scenes of unspeakable misery. Starving forms slunk disconsolately along the walks. Every man was kept at work until he was a physical wreck. With luck, he might be sent to a special camp to be treated for dystrophy, but most simply died.

This typically Asiatic Russian treatment softened up the toughest individuals in time. Time was the secret weapon of the NKVD, exemplified by its motto <u>Samper cadendo gutta cavat lapidem</u>. ("By constantly falling, the drops hollow the stone.") If thirty days and nights of ceaseless interrogation, with a beating now and then, didn't break you, then a sufficiently long course of hunger and cruelty would make you confess yourself a spy and a traitor to the Communist cause. The tortured victim would utter, attest and sign his own indictment. The machine functioned with smooth perfection to perpetuate the red regime. At that time Stalin and his Politbureau laid down the general line, or direction, in which all Soviet people were to move for the five years to come. And woe to him who deviated from the line. The renegade would be hunted down by Stalin's bloodhounds.

Everything was calculated and regulated down to the smallest detail. The peasants had to raise so much produce per hectare. Of this fixed yield, they had to give up so much to the state. Every bit of land and every head of stock, every man, woman and child, had to be accounted for and be harnessed to Stalin's chariot. And so that people should know what all this was for, they were subjected to hours of indoctrination daily. Thus, in the days of Stalin's harsh reign, the whole Soviet people were continuously regimented and watched not only in their work but in their attitudes. Especially the youth of the Soviet Union was being groomed to become the vanguard of the world revolution and trained in national bolshevist patriotism. Schoolteachers told the children that it was Ivan Polsonov who invented the steam engine, and so it went in all fields of science and technology.

In the Soviet Union, after World War II, no time was lost in realizing that the setback to technology had to be made up at all costs. This applied above all to development of the Soviet air force and the production of atomic weapons. The Soviets did not shrink from brutal means to achieve these ends. They spent huge sums for the development of their own science. They promoted scholarship in every possible area. German specialists in critical fields were kidnapped and made to work in Russia's factories and laboratories to strengthen the Soviet state.

Nor did the Soviets hesitate to spend money for espionage in the Western democracies. It was perfectly understood in the Kremlin that the mastery of the world could be gained only by a decisive lead in the development of atomic weapons. The Russians worked as if possessed, but they worked silently. If any advance was made in atomic science, they did not generously announce it but gloated in secret and worked on.

Serge Andreyevich received his directives from the District Soviet, and was responsible within his sphere for keeping to the correct line of march: That is to say, for fulfilling the Plan. This called for a lot of playacting. The men pledged themselves unanimously to breed the best horses and raise the most productive cows. A competition was organized with a neighboring sovkhoz. Such competitions were going on all over the land of the Soviets. They were reported in the factory newspapers, and the daily press carried whole pages of results and statistics. By such measures the government hoped to step up the capacity of various branches of industry and to encourage higher and higher output. There was no end to planning and quota-fulfilling. When a plan was fulfilled, the Soviet workers proceeded to over-fulfill it, and when that was done the year and the plan came to an end, and the citizens were faced with another plan year. Then the whole cycle repeated itself. The economy was supposed to run with the precision of a machine, but sometimes things didn't go as the Kremlin strategists had calculated. Even in the Soviet Union, the mood of nature was not amenable to planning. And when the unremitting toil made people discontented, the secret police descended mercilessly to expose economic "saboteurs", spies and foreign agents. That was their answer to everything.

Human beings, fallible by nature, were held strictly responsible for any slip-ups in the state planning machinery, thus protecting Stalin's prestige and his aura of infallibility. The Party and the communist state were the invariable victors in this struggle. Confessions from the guilty were always forthcoming. A Soviet citizen might well wonder what life was worth on these terms. The average man was working for utopian aims but had to submit to an awful enslavement. Daily he was obliged to listen to the worn-out, mendacious phrases of Party ideologists, while himself unable to speak or act. Franz didn't see how people could have stood it for so many years.

But the Russian people were possessed of infinite patience. Stalin himself had said that he could never have carried out his plans if the Russian people were not so patient. Any other nation would scarcely have been able to steal itself for such economic experimentation. There had been the transformation of the Russian countryside from small peasant holdings to collective farms and "grain factories". How many human lives were lost in the famines of the thirties? Anyone who knew the Russian peasant and his fierce attachment to his land might imagine what this meant. All his property was simply taken from him, and he was obliged to work on the collective farm like a serf. The peasants were forced to deliver their grain and all their harvest to great storehouses, and received so little in return that they went hungry most of the year. If the more desperate dared to approach the storehouse and take a bit of corn for their hungry families, they risked deportation to the labor camps, where their lot would be more hopeless than ever.

Nevertheless, want and the acute shortage of consumer goods of all kinds in the Soviet Union meant that theft was very widespread in town and country, despite harsh measures taken by the government. The people toiled on year after year, and fulfilled one five-year-plan after another, but the individual never won more freedom or a higher standard of living. Undismayed, the functionaries continued to affirm that someday Soviet collectivism would produce so much wealth, fairly and equitably distributed, that everyone in the new communist society would live in abundance.

All this sounded fine in theory. But in Soviet practice it took on a different aspect. After all, the individual worker in the factories and on the collective farms of Russia need not have been condemned to such a miserable life; and in the long run, so great an empire could never have been brought to real prosperity by cruelty and violence. The leadership of the Soviet Union knew this perfectly well. If a country like Russia, an agrarian state only forty years before, was to aspire to equal the heavy industry of the west in so short a time, something had to give. The Russian people went through decades of poverty because the Kremlin so decided.

The Kremlin had no other intention than to use the Russian people to subjugate the rest of mankind, as they had so long enslaved the Russians. That was the basic reason why the peoples of the Soviet Union were subjected to these privations.

Correspondents from the free world visited the Soviet Union and wrote much about Soviet life. They were shown carefully selected projects and institutions of the regime. But the underlying thoughts and concerns of the people were often overlooked. In 1945 the Russians were beginning to form ideas about their future that did not jibe with the plans of their rulers. It must not be forgotten in the west that in Russia, too, the people long for real freedom and the fruits of civilization. Deep in his heart, the average Russian rejects the Stalinist policy of violence. People tried to tell themselves from year to year that things would be better someday, and that a dawn of freedom and self-determination might appear on some distant horizon.

Franz kept trying to get an idea of the attitudes the Russians had towards the western democracies. He realized that the ruling stratum in Russia was comparable to the Nazis in principle, but he soon saw that the Russian official elite used entirely different methods. The Soviets worked underground. They were less often aggressive and warlike than the Nazis. They preferred the war of nerves and the strategy of harassment. They busily organized underground movements all over the world and financed them, to soften up the cardinal fronts. They ventured as close as possible to the edge of war, but they always calculated skillfully how they might reopen the door to negotiations at the last minute.

Having taken three steps forward towards their world revolution, their cold war strategy could always afford to take one step back without losing political ground.

Even to harbor such thoughts as these was a crime in the Russia of Stalin's over lordship. If anything of the kind were overheard by a stool pigeon, the indiscreet speaker might expect summary arrest. But by this time Franz knew a number of the men well enough to talk with them in confidence. After school, he had continual opportunity to talk to people and become acquainted with their point of view. He noticed that after the war the chief aim of Soviet propaganda had become to attack its foremost adversary of tomorrow, the United States of America.

By the end of World War II, the Soviets knew that they had been able to win their victory over fascism only with American assistance. In their hour of need, they went so far as to promise the Americans that they would dissolve the Comintern, thus abandoning the project of world revolution. Accordingly, the communist fifth columns in all western countries suddenly suspended their agitation. The leaders of the western nations failed to realize that Stalin would go back on his promises. When the war was over, the Soviets did not hesitate to bolshevize all the countries they had conquered. The plans had been worked out in advance, before Soviet troops ever invaded the present satellite countries. In the Soviet state schools, English became the principal foreign language after World War II. All preparations were made in the direction of world revolution, and every branch of industry, every national institution, was built up and promoted for one purpose only, to consolidate and expand Communist influence throughout the world.

The idea that the Soviet system was the only decent system was drummed into the boys and girls incessantly. Every argument was used to explain to people again and again that the obvious duty of every communist was to fight for the abolition of free enterprise and the liberation of the working classes from the yoke of capitalism.

Franz had lots of conversations with Serge Andreyevich, and once he asked him:

"Tell me, Serge Andreyevich; there is so much talk about the evils and injustices of the capitalistic economic and social system. Now we know that workers in the western world have a higher standard of living than Soviet workers. So how can it be true that your system is better?"

Serge Andreyevich answered him, "That's only temporary. We are convinced that it will change in a few years. Since we don't wish to be dependent on foreign capitalists, we must develop our own industry."

"But why do you do it on the guns-not-butter principle? You could live much better if you gave up your ambitious plans and supported light industry rather than heavy industry."

"We don't want to do that. We can build a consumer-goods industry only on the basis of a strong heavy industry. We must remain strong against the forces of international reaction. That's why our first concern is to hasten the reconstruction of heavy industry."

"But what about the other side of your planning system?" asked Franz. "Your strictness and discipline require a big non-producing administrative apparatus which must be a heavy drag on the economy. Besides, it throttles any independent initiative and makes people into robots. Contrary to your doctrines, it puts you on the side of the inhuman, on the side of slavery and violence. I don't think such a system can be the way to a better and happier future, because it allows the individual no freedom or dignity."

"So, you think that the bourgeois form of the state is better than the proletariat."

"Well, it seems to me that the western attitude towards life has its good and bad points too, but perhaps it is the lesser evil."

"But of what use is personal freedom to the workers if they do not have possession of the means of production? All your people are really dependent on their employers."

"I know, but any worker can get an education in the capitalist countries too. He can go to night school and rise to be an engineer or factory superintendent. Besides, in the western country's workers' rights are protected by unions and other labor organizations. The worker can give some force to his demands through the strike weapon. But when a strike occurs in the Soviet Union, the leaders are immediately branded as foreign agents and liquidated. In the western countries, nobody has to be afraid of falling into the hands of the secret police, never to be heard of again. Isn't that the important difference?"

"Hitler had his concentration camps, and so did the British in South Africa for that matter," was the reply.

"Of course, but the British learned better. So much so that even in World War I, the Boers fought on their side against Germany. England's arch-enemy, Jan Christiaan Smuts, became her best friend. As for Hitler, he was a crazy politician. He was just as much of a menace to freedom as Bolshevism is still. Only he was a right-wing radical and his methods were reactionary. It's a good thing he and Stalin could never get together."

"Never?" said Serge Andreyevich. "Why couldn't Hitler and Stalin get together? We had a non-aggression pact from 1939 on. If Hitler hadn't attacked us, commerce between Russia and Germany would have continued. It might have worked out very well."

"That shows how much you know about Adolf Hitler.

I'm sure Stalin didn't trust the Nazis even when he signed the pact. I think he did it because Russia gained so much by it. There was no one then to prevent Stalin from doing what he wanted except Hitler. After all, the Russians got the lion's share of the booty - the Baltic states, eastern Poland and Bessarabia. The two dictators divided the eastern part of Central Europe between them. All Hitler wanted was to look his back door before attacking in the west. He had to avoid fighting a war on two fronts. England and France couldn't compete with what he had to offer. They couldn't have sold Poland to Stalin, but Hitler had no scruples. When Poland was divided between the Germans and the Russians, Hitler thought it was time to attack the others. He could be sure everything was taken care of on the eastern frontier."

"Then what do you think made Hitler attack the Soviet Union?" Serge Andreyevich objected.

"That must really have been his ultimate aim," Franz suggested. "He wanted to make Germany not only a great power, but a world power. What did all his previous conquests amount to compared to the great raw-material resources of the Soviet Union? In his insane imagination, Hitler saw a German colonial empire extending to the Volga. Germans

would pioneer all this territory and use it for their own purposes. The eastern nations were to be kept on a low cultural level and made dependent on Germany. The Americans
rightly recognized the danger and intervened. A Germany
backed up by the tremendous resources of the orient would
have become a serious danger to America."

Serge Andreyevich replied indifferently, "Hitler and his
power are smashed now, and the German people are paying
the price."

"Are you going to reorganize your zone along Soviet
lines?" asked Franz.

"I think so, yes. Long before our troops reached the
German border, German Communists were being trained for
the formation of a Soviet state in Germany. The same thing
happened with the Communist parties of other countries we
occupied."

"Well, I don't think the Polish and German peoples can be
handled by the same methods the Communists use here in the
Soviet Union. If the trend towards bolshevization should continue, the nations oppressed by the Russians are likely to rebel."

"They won't find that so easy," said Serge Andreyevich.
"They are building up the same kind of machine there as we

have here. But let us adjourn all this political discussion until later. We have work to do. Let history take its course. We have to round up some horses to be sent to the tracks for a try-out."

Franz was to take the horses to Krasnodar for shipment. The animals were duly delivered to the station. Franz had some extra time and visited the black market. This was officially prohibited, but illegal commerce flourished in the U.S.S.R. just after the war.

Everyone who could afford it patronized the black market to supplement his ration allowance. Franz had obtained a couple of bottles of vodka from Serge Andreyevich, and tried his luck with an Armenian merchant. But the man was too determined to get the better of him. Franz moved on. Finally, he came to terms with an old Jewish trader. They got to talking. It was just mid-day, and the Jew, Ivan Petrovich, kindly invited Franz to dine. Franz told him his story. The two soon came to an agreement. Franz's new friend paid for the vodka with some hundred-ruble notes and a new pair of Cossack boots. Vodka was at a premium.

"Tell me, my friend," said Franz's new acquaintance, "have you more of this vodka, or can you perhaps get me some of the stuff?"

"Why not," was the reply. "It all depends what you can offer me."

"Well, I can get you all the things that are in demand in Russia today. Gold, watches, jewelry, anything," said Ivan.

"That's fine," said Franz. "But I don't need any of those things."

"Oh, you don't, eh? Then what do you need?" asked the Jew in surprise.

"I'll get you all the vodka you want," Franz promised, "if you can get me some good connections. I need someone who is being transferred from here to Germany, I mean an officer or something. Then I'd need Russian papers. I could go along to Germany as his orderly, maybe, and when I got there I could disappear."

"Now, wait a minute," said the Jew. "You don't want much, do you? You're playing with fire. So many people to let in on a confidential matter. And whom can you trust nowadays?" Franz's friend, Ivan, wondered.

"I don't care about that," Franz urged him. "All I want is to get out of this lousy country. I could get hold of another thirty bottles or so. Please try and arrange it for me. I have to go back now. Next time I get a chance I'll come to see you again."

"All right, I'll see," was the reply. I know a member of the District Soviet who sees a lot of the officers. And I think I could find someone to take care of the documents. But look here, all this is going to take a long time. We must plan very carefully, and everybody will have to be paid off. You've picked an expensive hobby."

They said good-by. Franz went back to the Cossacks, saddled Nabor and cheerfully started for the farm. As the horse jogged along, Franz became anxious about his situation. He became indifferent to the possibility of betrayal. One thing he knew beyond a doubt. He had to try to get home again, and meant to lose no time about it.

Franz had already decided that there was no future for him in the Soviet Union. He did not hate the Russians. But he did hate the system that was grinding two hundred million people so harshly, depriving them of the most basic freedoms. In a way it seemed more inhuman and beastly than the Nazi regime, which had not been exactly benevolent. No, he was going to have to escape from the Soviet paradise if there was any way to do it. He hoped his parents in Germany would still be living where he was taken from them. Still, he was not so bad off materially, like so many other prisoners-of-war and convicts in the Fed empire; Serge Andreyevich simply adopted him, and that made him a Soviet citizen.

Such procedures were quick and easy in Russia, without very much formality. Meanwhile Franz kept on being pleasant to everybody, and openly praised the benefits of the Soviet system, in order to avoid suspicion. Nor did he omit to requisition as many bottles as he could from his foster-father's cellar. He did not stop at stealing vodka, there was champagne and cognac too; very precious fluids on that market. He never doubted he would find someone to take him to Germany.

One day at dinner, Serge Andreyevich said, "I think I must be missing a couple of dozen bottles down in the cellar. I wonder who can have broken in."

Franz looked as innocent as he could, and hastened to say, "I don't think the cellar's locked securely enough. This is a bad time to be careless about things like that. The carpenters and all the clerks go in and out as they please; they'd think nothing of stealing the stuff."

It didn't seem to occur to Serge Andreyevich that Franz might be the culprit.

"Anyway," Serge Andreyevich rejoined, "I've had the cellar

locked up properly. I'll find the thief, too. A fine thing, I should say."

Franz was glad he had cached a good supply while he could, and determined to guard his secret. But he went right on talking.

"The trouble is, this paradise doesn't provide enough consumer goods. The poor devils of Cossacks are parched, and here we are with a cellarful of vodka. What about equality in the Soviet Union? There you have the germ of a privileged social stratum. Can you call that a classless society?"

In putting these questions to Serge Andreyevich, Franz knew quite well he was talking counter-revolution, but he also knew Serge Andreyevich for a very reasonable man. When it came to ideological contention, Serge Andreyevich would always try, quietly and patiently, to convince Franz of the correctness of Communist doctrine.

"Well, I'll tell you," he began calmly. "Our idea is to live by the principle of equal pay for equal work. Now if a manager or an official earned no more than a laborer, there would be no incentive to effort. Our critics always say there's no competition in the Soviet Union. Of course, we have competition. Only the system is entirely different from what it is in capitalist countries. With us, the product goes in the first place to the collectivity, meaning society. In capitalist countries, all proceeds of competition go to individual top industrialists. That is the basic difference between the two economic systems in the world."

"But," Franz objected, "then why should there be so much want in your society? You have an enormous difference between theory and practice. The great bureaucracy of the police and all the other official institutions robe your consumers of the collective product. Besides, I begin to doubt whether you have really pushed the individualist very far into the background. You go to extremes in idolizing heroes of the Patriotic War and heroes of Socialist Labor. All those activists - not to mention Stalin himself. I know what you say, but it seems to me the Soviet Union doesn't have a classless society at all. Instead, we have a thin upper crust and a mass of discontented and oppressed people."

"Wait and see," Serge Andreyevich replied. "After the next Five-Year Plan, we'll have got over the war and life will be better."

"You told me that before," said Franz. "You've fulfilled a number of Five-Year Plans under Stalin by this time. How is the experiment coming out? You have heavy industry now, at the expense of the consumer. Lots of Russians are in labor camps. The government is severe, but can't put a stop to thieving. Give people a free and comfortable life, and the Russian will be content with his lot."

"Well, we're living through the aftermath of the Hitler war. The coming Five-Year Plan will dispose of that," said Serge Andreyevich, yawning. "Let's hope it all ends well. Good night."

Slowly, Franz went upstairs to bed.

One night, Serge Andreyevich was rudely awakened by loud knocking at the door. The secret police wanted to inspect the records. They asked questions about everything.

The Commissar asked Serge Andreyevich:

"How many cows has this Sovkhoz? What is the average production per head? How many clerks does this enterprise employ? How many of the workers are members of the Communist Party? What about socialist propaganda and education in this installation?"

The head of the board of inspection introduced himself curtly as Comrade Olshanov, and gave Serge Andreyevich a bawling-out.

"What do you mean by not having a political director on the job to handle agitation? This place is a pigsty. I shall report to the District Committee and see that this condition is rectified at once. And where are the 'date foaled' entries on all these horses?" Olshanov wanted to know.

Serge Andreyevich waited until he had finished, and replied in his usual quiet tone.

"Take it easy, Comrade, and I'll explain. First, suppose we take a glass together and clear the air. Hand me those glasses over there, Franz, will you? Now. 'Your health.' … There, that's better.

"Now, my dear Comrade Olshanov," Serge Andreyevich continued pleasantly. "The thing about the political director will be taken care of. I've been very busy so far getting the farm on its feet. I really didn't have a chance to do anything about it, what with the pressure of work. You must realize that most of our thoroughbreds are captured stock from Germany and countries of Eastern Europe. All we can do is try to get in touch with the studs there, to identify the horses; which isn't going to be so easy."

"Twaddle," said Olshanov. "You're an expert, aren't you? This is your job. Just estimate the ages yourself, and make out the papers. When you get done, send the whole file to Rostov with your report. Don't be so conscientious. What's the difference if you're a year or two off? The point is to get the nags certified and the records complete." Olshanov frowned. "By the way, you didn't meet your milk quota."

"We did what we could," Serge Andreyevich told him. "The cattle have been driven so far, you can't expect any record production just yet. It's impossible. You have to reduce the delivery quota. Those bureaucrats just dreamed it up anyway."

Olshanov made some notes and dictated a summary to an assistant.

"Very well," he concluded. "I shall report in full to Rostov." Turning to Serge Andreyevich, "You'll hear from them. Good-by, Comrade."

"Good-by!" Serge Andreyevich called after the departing Olshanov. "Next time I wish you'd come at a more reasonable hour!"

Inspections like this were frequent in every corner of the Soviet economy. Citizens lived in fear. Tomorrow a man might be sitting in jail if he fell short of the labor standards. He could expect stern discipline. On this point, little Father Stalin was mercilessly severe, and tolerated no deviation from the plans of his economy. All functionaries thought with a shudder of the great purges of the thirties. They knew that the Stalinist machine would ruthlessly sweep any obstacle from its path. Would the Soviets make the other Eastern European countries like Russia? Would they be able to erect the same economic system and the same apparatus for crushing public opinion? Franz wondered. If the Soviets tried to do that, he thought, they would have to fight another revolution. The face of society would be utterly changed. Franz was sure that Europeans opposed and abhorred Bolshevism. But had not the Russians great armies of occupation in all those countries, and had they not plundered all their conquered territories? How was there to be any reconstruction in East Germany? He could see the tendency of political developments plainly enough in the Soviet press.

The papers were already talking of liquidating landlords and capitalists, and care out for establishment of worker and peasant power in the conquered Eastern European countries. It did not occur to the Soviets to keep the promise they had given the Americans during the Second World War. They were not disposed to recognize democratic freedom and human dignity. If they had done so, they would have been betraying themselves. The police apparatus would have lost its meaning. The principles of the Stalinist dictatorship would have been shaken. The Russians knew all this even as they promised the Americans to become truly democratic. But at the hour of the German invasion they had no choice but to accept Roosevelt's terms. The old fox in the Kremlin meekly said Yes to the Western Powers, and after 1945 got busy digging the grave of free democracy. Stalin was very skillful. An appearance of rectitude was to be kept up abroad in the west.

The Soviets always said they were for democracy too. A straightforward lie to the free peoples of the world. Roosevelt meant to encourage the Communist world of the east to dwell in peace with the free world of the west. He brought Churchill and Stalin together, becoming the guarantor of concord and reasonableness in the Allied camp.

If only he had been able to accomplish his aim, to impel Stalin towards coexistence instead of cold war after Hitler's defeat. And what else could Roosevelt have done? many people asked. After all, it was better to help the Russians than the Nazis. However, it would have been better for the free world if both totalitarian states had dropped out of sight after 1945. The Soviet state is at least as great a danger to the free world

as the Nazi state was. What would have happened if the
Americans had not helped the Soviets? Probably the Germans
would have conquered Russia, and been utterly exhausted in
consequence. It would have been a Pyrrhic victory. Then if
the Americans had resolutely attacked the Nazis, they could
have killed the two birds with one stone, and been rid of both
disturbers of the peace.

Now what have been the disastrous consequences of the
Americans' policy? The free world is once more in peril.
All conceivable means have had to be mobilized to stop the
Communist advance. The Soviets knew they were far behind
the Western Powers in all technical branches of warfare. But
the Soviets have left nothing undone to catch up with America
in the development of aerial and nuclear weapons. No effort
has been too great. Now, after the end of World War Two,
the Russians by their ruthlessness have managed to establish
an equilibrium in the nuclear field. What is the free world
to do next if the Soviets work just as hard in the coming ten
years? The question must arise whether the west can afford to
stand by and see Soviet technology expanded and improved
until it towers over the rest of the world. If that should ever
happen, the free peoples need entertain no illusions. For this

is the overwhelming Soviet threat. They have set themselves the aim of conquering, regimenting and Sovietizing the entire free world. All that mankind has built up by centuries of labor would be in vain, and marked down for destruction. All tradition would be made subservient to the purposes of the regime, and anything that couldn't be used would simply be chucked overboard.

A great many people in the Eastern European countries have tried to work with the Soviets. They have had to confess their folly. Some have committed suicide, some have languished away in imprisonment. The Bolshevist giant has become dangerously big and strong of recent years. The west has had all it could do to contain Russian expansionism by a globe-encircling strategy. And what was it about the Russian Bolsheviks that proved so mortally dangerous to the west? It was the firm intention of the Communist Party leaders to conquer the entire world and organize it after the Soviet Russian model. What was being done in Eastern Europe today was to be repeated in the west tomorrow, unless the free nations summoned the needed energy to lessen the peril. But what could they do except concur in the Russian idea of coexistence? The west was obliged to rely on the Russian's practical common sense. Even they could not carry out their plans if terrible weapons of annihilation were used against them. They, too, were forced into the policy of coexistence, whether they liked it or not.

But the states of the eastern bloc were more powerful than the west in land forces. With more troops, they were able to wage a war of nerves. They could provoke local conflicts, and thus attack the Americans without risking a world war. The United States would thus be compelled through their treaty commitments to go to the assistance of the defenders. Thus, the Soviets would have achieved their aim. They planned to gradually paralyze the striking power of the west by tactics of attrition, and then to risk a decisive thrust at the proper moment. At best, the west could only adapt to the situation. Swift retaliation was necessary wherever the Soviets attacked. Now it is in the nature of the Soviet regime that it can exact great sacrifices from its people. The consumer goods industry was further restricted. This was not possible in the free western countries. Here the governments really represent the people, and the people's representatives cannot convert their constituency to a Spartan standard of living just because the current political situation demands it. That was the weakness of western policy. It would be unthinkable to trail behind Soviet Russia in armament and in development of modern weapons; but the national standard of living must not be inferior. A judicious balance had to be struck between production for the armament race and that for consumption. Otherwise the democratic peoples of the west would soon be discontented, and the democracies would be confronted with a crisis. The Russians had nothing of this nature to worry about, the will of the Politburo being the supreme law. Every free citizen of the western world should have seen his duty, and planned his political behavior accordingly. The Europeans should have risen above their traditions and frontiers, and thrown up a powerful continental rampart to stem the Red tide. Western Europe could not be asking help from America forever. It should have made a determined effort to unite and build fresh ideological defenses across national boundaries against the ideas of Communism. Particularly, the youth of the west should have realized that it would pay to enlist in the cause of freedom. That might surely have seemed the lesser evil, considering the consequences implicit for the west in letting things slide.

In those days of Communist triumph, Franz had little cause for optimism about the future of the western way of life, or liberty in any form. He was deeply shaken by the terrible violence of the Bolshevik machine. He was more determined than ever to break out of the Stalinist structure.

One day Serge Andreyevich sent him to town with the veterinarian to replenish the farm's store of medicines. Franz got into a jeep and rode with the doctor through the Caucasian countryside. In a big saddle-bag, he had stowed a number of bottles of vodka and plenty of paper money. He had decided to stake everything on one card, and risk the crucial move of flight. When they drove into town about noon, he took abrupt leave of the veterinarian and told him he would be back in a few hours. He grumbled a bit, but let the boy go. Franz went at once to see the man he had met in the market. He knocked at a shop door in the crooked, dirty street. Someone approached the door with a heavy tread and drew the latch. It was the owner himself.

"Ah, here you are again. Come on in. How's everything? What can I do for you?" asked the Jew.

"What can you do for me?" Franz replied. "You tell me. Here's some more vodka. What are the chances? When can I start back to Germany?"

"Patience, my friend, patience. Let's take it easy. I have

discovered an officer who is to be transferred in a few weeks, and is going your way. Come with me; let's try to see him now."

Franz's friend carefully packed a couple of bottles in his briefcase, and the two strolled leisurely through the town. They came to a private house, and asked the maid who opened the door whether the master was in.

"I'm sorry, the Captain's not back yet," was the reply. "Have the gentlemen some other business in the meantime? He'll come off duty at four."

The pair agreed to wait, and spent the interval walking in the Krasnodar park. When the time was up, Ivan said to Franz:

"Well, my boy, now let's see if the Captain is home. He should be off duty by now."

Again, they stood at the officer's door and rang the bell. Rapid steps were heard within. The handle turned, the door opened. Before them stood a tall, athletic Russian in captain's uniform.

"Well, if it isn't Ivan Petrovich," he greeted Franz's friend. "Good of you to come to see me again."

"Thank you, Michael Konstantinovich. I've come about this young man here."

"I see," replied Michael Konstantinovich noncommittedly, and courteously asked the two to come inside. They sat down in the plain sitting-room. Michael Konstantinovich looked Franz over with interest and said:

"Now, young fellow, Ivan Petrovich has told me all about your case. In about four weeks I am to travel straight to Germany from here; a special mission, do you understand?"

"I understand," Franz answered readily.

Ivan Petrovich had meanwhile opened his briefcase and handed the Captain some bottles of the liquor Franz had brought.

"Here you are, Michael Konstantinovich," said Ivan Petrovich cordially. "We've brought you some decent stuff, as usual. There'll be more later."

"Excellent. - Oho," examining the label, "this is my brand - Kontorovich! I shall chill a bottle at once." Michael Konstantinovich vanished from the room. The two heard him rummaging about in the kitchen. In a few minutes he returned with a big tray, loaded down with sandwiches and clean glasses.

"So," said Michael Konstantinovich. "First of all, we're going to take some refreshment. Then we'll be sure to get on.

Ah!" he groaned, dropping into his armchair, "It's been quite a day. I'll be pleased to get out of this place. It's really very nice in Potsdam, so I'm told."

"Yes," Franz agreed at once; "it really is. You're certain to like the resort of the old kings of Prussia. And the scenery, the lakes and woods all around - it's beautiful. You must get a camera when you're in Germany, that much I'd advise you to do. Take pictures and keep them for souvenirs. I know I could get one for you. My parents have connections."

Ivan Petrovich interrupted.

"In the meantime," he told Michael Konstantinovich, "I've obtained all the documents. The boy will have to travel with you as a Russian soldier. I'll give him a pass, and he'll ride in the truck with you as your orderly. Of course, you will have to rehearse him so he'll know how to act at the frontier and the inspection posts. Is that understood?"

"Yes. By Jove! What a lark. Why, this is a regular pirate dodge!" Michael Konstantinovich exclaimed. "Just like in the days of the slave traffic. Ha ha ha! That calls for a drink."

The Captain left the room and busied himself in the kitchen again. Beaming, he appeared in the doorway with a bottle of vodka. "Now, then," he said, "we know how we're going to do the job, and for the moment we can forget about our troubles."

Michael Konstantinovich poured Franz a tumbler of vodka, neat. Franz looked on doubtfully. He knew from experience that any protest against this sort of hospitality was useless. As an alien, one simply had to do as the Russians did and try to keep up the pace.

"You know, Ivan Petrovich," Michael Konstantinovich suggested, "we ought to have a little celebration. I'm going to have some of the boys and girls in to join us. That's not such a bad idea, is it?"

"Well, I wouldn't want any mention made of our plans. That could spoil everything," said Ivan Petrovich anxiously.

"Oh, don't be an old stick-in-the-mud, Comrade Ivan. We're none of us crazy." Turning to Franz, he continued, "Wasn't it your great post Goethe who said:

'Wer nicht liebt Weib, Wein und Gesang,
Der bleibt ein Narr sein Leben lang.'*

---

* Who does not love not woman, wine and song?
  Will be a fool his whole life long.

So, Ivan Petrovich, let us be merry, and no more of your grumbling. Goethe was absolutely right."

Michael Konstantinovich got on the phone, called up his friends, and invited one and all to a vodka party. Everybody came. They drank, sang and danced far into the night. Franz did his best to emulate the Cossack dancing, but he found it the most difficult sort of acrobatics. The veterinarian was going to get tired of waiting. It was such a good party, Franz forgot about him and let the doctor drive back to the <u>sovkhoz</u> as best he might. Franz would get home somehow. His new friend, the Captain, turned out to have a superlative baritone. In the middle of the night he started singing folk songs. Another officer accompanied him on the piano. The company was in a happy mood. Franz had his arm around a pretty girl and was rapidly forgetting any unpleasantness he might have known. Little Natasha was a raven-haired child of the Caucasus. She asked Franz questions about what things were like in his country; she could speak a little German herself. She was a high school student, and meant to be a doctor someday.

All good things must come to an end, and in the gray of morning the party broke up. Michael Konstantinovich told Franz and his patron, "You two may as well stay right here and sleep it off." Franz at least needed no second invitation. He staggered to the nearest couch and sank into a dead sleep.

Awaking towards evening he felt terribly hungry. Ivan Petrovich and Michael Konstantinovich were sitting comfortably chatting over a glass of tea.

"Well, young man," Ivan Petrovich said to him, "it's about time. We've got a horse for you. Now first get some breakfast inside you, and then let's see you gallop off home. Your friend Serge Andreyevich will be waiting anxiously."

"I suppose I'll get a lecture or a licking. That'll probably be the end of it," Franz replied, sitting down on a heavy oak chair and starting to eat everything in sight. After breakfast they discussed their plan again in complete detail. Then Franz took his leave and promised to bring another twenty bottles of vodka to the appointed spot in four weeks' time. The two saw him to the small back yard of the house, where a tall, red Anglo-Arab was saddled and waiting.

"Donnerwetter!" said Franz, "Michael Konstantinovich, this really is hospitality. You certainly take good care of your guests!"

"Now don't say another word," said the Captain. "Climb on your pony and get out of here."

Franz mounted, laughing, and was off, waving good-by. When he had got out of town, he rode slowly out across country, into the night. After a while he gave the horse his head. The beast struck out; his stride lengthening and quickening, and soon Franz was dashing like a ghost rider through the night towards his home sovkhoz.

It was dawn when Franz reached the outskirts of the farm. He slowed down to a walk. Some young stallions reared up, startled. The horses had spent the night in the pasture. They crowded to the fence and stared in the direction of the horse-and-rider, an unaccustomed sight at this hour. Franz ignored the neighing audience and rode on. He was busy thinking up excuses to pacify Serge Andreyevich. At last he decided to say he had met a girl in town, and that was why he hadn't got back sooner. Now he could see the outline of the main buildings. The windows of the manager's house were dark, so Serge Andreyevich must be asleep in bed. Franz unsaddled his mount and let him into a loose box in the stable. He heard Nabor whinny as he came in with the chestnut. Nabor was probably wondering where his master had been all this time, and why he was riding this other horse. Franz was in the habit of visiting Nabor first thing in the morning and giving him a couple of lumps of sugar. He had missed yesterday, and Nabor snorted impatiently.

The Cossack on watch got up sleepily and peered at Franz in surprise.

"Franz! Where are you coming home from at this time of night? The boss has been looking for you. He'll have something to say to you all right. - And where did you get the horse?"

"I borrowed him. Never mind, I can take care of myself," Franz replied, seeing the man's worried expression. When he had tended the chestnut, he paid another visit to Nabor, who had carried him from Germany to the Caucasus. Franz patted and spoke to his four-legged friend affectionately and gave him some lumps of sugar. Nabor nickered with pleasure, and Franz felt better. Then he left the stable and advanced upon the house.

When he had rapped at the door twice, he heard Serge Andreyevich's footsteps. The door creaked open. One look was enough. Infuriated by Franz's truancy, Serge Andreyevich beat him soundly and gave him a tongue lashing into the bargain. He wanted to know what the big idea was, anyway, and Franz told him the story he had prepared.

"I see," said Serge Andreyevich when he had finished. "I'm going to have to make some changes. This is a fine thing. A young boy like you, running around nights and in fast company at that. Just you wait," he went on. "I'll bring you to your senses. The wind has changed, you may count on that."

Franz had his own plans for the coming four weeks, but, he decided, Serge Andreyevich would calm down after a while. Anyway, he was very weary after his ride, and slept through the day and the night. Next morning Serge Andreyevich called him in the small hours and sent him out with the veterinarian and some of the men. Franz breakfasted and went out to saddle Nabor.

"Where are we going today?" he asked the men.

"We're riding out to one of the ranges where a couple of dozen young stallions have to be gelded and then they have to be broken," said one.

So that's why the doctor is going along, thought Franz. This is going to be quite a job. The doctor was looking at Franz sidelong in some amusement.

"Why," said the doctor, "here's our Franchishek. I thought we'd lost you in Krasnodar. So, the bad penny came back.

Do you suppose there could be some reason why Serge Andreyevich got you up so early to come with us on this job?"

"Sure, he had a reason," Franz answered the doctor. "I was gone a couple of days without leave, so of course Serge Andreyevich is angry with me. He means to teach me a lesson. Well, I'm going to have to make the best of it. Maybe I'll learn something."

"You might learn more than you've bargained for," said one of the riders. The summer sun was coming up, and the mist rising from the soft turf. The riders saw the yellows and greens of the steppe come to life before them. They turned into a lane and centered past some of the farm's horses grazing along the fences. The animals would bunch up at the fence and widen their nostrils curiously at the passers-by. They would trot along as far as the fence would let them. Then their leader would stop short. All the other horses would stop at the same moment as if rooted to the ground, whinnying after the party.

After a brisk five-hours' ride, they reached the outlying camp. The Cossack in charge was expecting them, and pointed out the colts, which were rolling and playing in a pasture meadow. One of the men, a Kalmuck, was an expert with the rope. He prepared his lasso with leisurely care. After a hearty meal, consisting of fried steak and potatoes, the man got to work. The doctor had his instruments laid ready on a field table. The Kalmuck horseman mounted and took up a position to one side of the bunch of stallions. A couple of Cossacks drove the colts past him. He picked up his rope and started whirling the noose overhead. Usually he picked out the last animal in a string, which was usually a little distance behind the rest. The roper would follow the straggler carefully, guiding his own mount with his knees. At the proper moment, he would throw the noose around the victim's hind legs. His aim was true, and the other men surrounded the fallen animal and tied it securely till it lay motionless and the veterinarian could do his work.

The job was difficult and sometimes dangerous. The colts kicked wildly in fear, and tried to bite their tormenters at every opportunity.

Shortly after noon, the doctor sent Franz back with one of the men to get some more creolin for disinfecting the wounds. The two had ridden a couple of miles when they saw one of the farm's older stallions galloping straight for them - a splendid gray, one of the most spirited of the thoroughbreds.

He pointed his ears and made as if to mount the mare Franz's companion was riding. The two horsemen separated until they were a couple of hundred yards apart. The stallion had to pursue one of them. He raced after Nabor and laid his ears back belligerently. Franz took his <u>nagaika</u> and out him as hard as he could, but the old rascal didn't give up so easily. When he saw he wasn't getting anywhere, he turned his attention again to the other pair. Once more he was rewarded with cuts of the whip. The stubborn brute alternated his attack several times in this way, until finally he abandoned the attempt and left them alone. Believed, the two continued on their errand.

Serge Andreyevich took care not to let time hang heavy on Franz's hands. When this job was over, the boy had to report every morning to the foreman, and was kept very busy. He had to exercise all horses from young to old on the sand track. He was always glad when he got through with his work at night, and he went to bed right after supper.

Serge Andreyevich ordered a celebration in honor of the twenty-sixth birthday of the Red Army. He had invited many of his former regimental comrades. Franz received permission to bring some of his friends from school. Most of them were sons of Kuban Cossacks. Franz meant to make the most of his opportunity to contribute to the success of the festivities.

"Serge Andreyevich," he told his foster-father, "I've asked a dozen of my friends, all of them very good horsemen. They'll bring their own horses, and we've planned a special entertainment. The guests will have nothing to complain of. We're going to put on a regular <u>dzhigitovka</u>."

Serge Andreyevich was very pleased. "What a fine idea. You have thought up something worthwhile this time," he applauded.

"We practiced all last year after school, and we're pretty good now."

"We'll see how good you are. I hope you realize you'll have a critical audience?" Serge Andreyevich added a word of warning.

"Don't worry," Franz reassured him. "We won't disappoint you."

The last of the boys had arrived by noon. Some of the senior officers started an argument about the institution of the <u>dzhigitovka</u>.

"What's the point of all this tearing around on horseback anyway?" said an elderly major to Serge Andreyevich. "Real horsemen would laugh at us and call us circus clowns if they could see our 'favorite sport'!"

"Every nation has its peculiarities, even in horsemanship," said Serge Andreyevich. "Among us Cossacks, it's the <u>dzhigitovka</u>. Besides, it trains horse and rider in agility, resolution and lightning quickness. What would the Cossacks be without it?"

"Ah, you're so right, my dear Serge Andreyevich. Let's keep up the old tradition. As long as we can do that, we shan't have to worry about the future of the Cossacks," conceded the major.

The guests had made themselves comfortable on the lawn. The great rectangle of the yard had been cleared for the performance. The eleven riders charged in like a whirlwind. The leader of the group was foremost. When he came level with Serge Andreyevich, he reined his horse to a full stop on its hind legs in mid-gallop.

"The <u>dzhigitovka</u> is ready," reported the young man to his host.

"Let it begin!" Serge Andreyevich shouted. "Show us what you can do."

At a word of command from the leader, the group scattered. A rider clambered under the belly of his galloping horse and reappeared on the other side. Some stood on their heads in the saddle, rushing at a breathless pace over the course. Girls among the spectators threw their handkerchiefs on the ground. Riders galloping by hung from the saddle to retrieve the bits of cloth and hand them to their owners without breaking step.

Two sturdy lads' rods side-by-side. Two more climbed on their backs, and a fifth stood straddle-legged on their shoulders. A murmur in the audience grew to a roar as the five riders and two horses went through all their paces like a well-oiled machine.

"That's pretty good all right," acknowledged the old major. "Perfect teamwork!"

The old gentleman was right. Not a moment could any of the performers afford to relax his attention. One false move, even the slightest miscalculation, and all would tumble down in a heap.

One young man had trained his Arab horse in some fancy maneuvers. He borrowed a chair from the host and jumped his horse over it - very difficult because of the precision required to produce an effect. Then the boy dismounted, took his whip in hand, and issued orders with it like a ringmaster. The horse lay down, get up, took a jump over an obstacle, rose on his hind legs and marched towards his master erect. Then he dropped on all fours again. The boy stroked him, gave him some sugar and remounted. This performance also was greeted with enthusiastic applause.

The eleven riders re-formed, and, as a finale, went into a formal quadrille. In close military order, the horses and riders left the field amid yells of approval from the assembled company of Cossacks and their guests.

Franz and his comrades took places beside the girls at one of the huge round tables in the dining hall, and gave themselves up to the pleasures of the feast until far into the night.

Franz thought anxiously of the twenty bottles of vodka he had promised Ivan Petrovich. They were hidden safe in the hay left over the stables.

When the appointed day comes, he thought, I'll pack them in a couple of saddle bags and take them to town. He was determined to carry out the plan.

As he had hoped, Serge Andreyevich proved a good deal more affable after the performance, and life returned to its former channels. There were a good many visitors of evenings, with whom Serge Andreyevich talked over the events of the day. The master of the house was expansive in his hospitality. He would send the housekeeper down to fetch a bottle of vodka or Crimean champagne to be chilled. On one such fine summer evening, a good friend of Serge Andreyevich's from the regiment was there. A table had been set up outdoors under a tree, and it was very pleasant. Contentedly they watched the long and ever-changing spectacle of sunset. Serge Andreyevich's friend, Peter Maximovich, was now posted at a machine station far off in the Ukraine, and he and his host talked over the problems of the first post-war five-year plan.

Peter Maximovich was a heavy-set man of medium height, and might have been in his early fifties. After the first words of greeting, when Franz had been introduced, Peter Maximovich sat down and said to Serge Andreyevich:

"How long has it been since we saw each other last, anyway?"

"I think it must be all of five years. Of course; it was in Rostov, shortly before the war," Serge Andreyevich replied.

"Yes, it must have been about that time," Peter Maximovich agreed with him. "What a dreadful time - the war, I mean. What unspeakable suffering it has caused. I see it every day, you know, in the Ukraine. Everything was destroyed. First, we scorched the earth in our retreat, and on the way back the Germans destroyed what little remained. So, there are the great extents of plain, the coal mines of the Donets Basin, and the industrial towns, razed to the ground. The fruits of decades of construction were wasted."

"Be thankful, my dear fellow," Serge Andreyevich answered, "that the Patriotic War ended as it did. If the winter, and the Americans, hadn't come to our assistance in expelling the invader, we would probably be in some concentration camp in Germany right now."

"You're right, Serge Andreyevich, it came out all right so far," Peter Maximovich admitted doubtfully. "But clouds are already gathering on the political horizon. I refer to our relations with the western world. As you know, the situation is anything but promising. I foresaw this, even during the war. Isn't it obvious that our society can never get along with bourgeois capitalist society? It's out of the question. After all, they're poles apart."

"Yes, that may be so. But don't forget," said Serge Andreyevich, "how we improved our strategic position by pressing on to the Elbe. That means that our order will be dominant wall into Central Europe."

"But do you really think that the Poles, Czechs and Germans will take up our system?" Peter Maximovich asked.

"It will take them up. They will have no choice," said Serge Andreyevich. "Not long ago I was in Moscow and attended a session of the Soviet of Nationalities. I can tell you one thing: The Comintern is not dead. The agitators are taking it out of mothballs, now that the war is over."

"Didn't we promise the Americans, during the war, that we would dissolve the Comintern, in return for their aid?" Peter Maximovich objected.

"Yes, of necessity," Serge Andreyevich replied. "So today we have the Cominform, with the same aims and activities as the Comintern - after all, we hold half of Europe."

Peter Maximovich was unconvinced. "The people of Eastern Europe are not willing to have our social and economic order extended to their own countries. They don't want to become carbon copies of our government and institutions."

"We have the power," Serge Andreyevich told him, "and we'll do as we think best."

"What will the western powers - especially America - have to say about that?" Peter Maximovich inquired.

"They will protest. Our relations with them will deteriorate. Do you imagine that the atom bombs dropped on Japan had no diplomatic significance?"

"Of course, I know the atom bomb was used to demonstrate America's scientific superiority," Peter Maximovich said. "But I know for a fact that our top leaders are aware of the danger. That is why we deported all the German experts we could find to our country, and are making them work under the most favorable conditions possible, for the Soviet state - to develop our aviation and rocket technology, and atomic weapons. We thoroughly realize our disadvantage, and have taken vigorous measures to close the gap."

"Do you think we'll succeed?" asked Serge Andreyevich.

"Well, of course, that's hard to say, but we have our Russian scientists too, working side by side with the Germans." Thoughtfully, Peter Maximovich went on: "I believe we might manage to catch up with the western powers in about ten or fifteen years."

"Do they have that much of an advantage in this field?" asked Serge Andreyevich in surprise. "What will happen if they make use of it? Is there not a great temptation for the capitalists to choose this moment to get rid of their archenemy? The Americans may never have another chance as good as this."

"I don't think the Americans will do that," said Peter Maximovich.

"Why not?" Serge Andreyevich wanted to know.

"The President of the United States is not a Hitler. Western democracy is an entirely different form of government from ours."

"What does the form of government have to do with it?" asked Serge Andreyevich.

"It has a great deal to do with it," was the reply. "Look here; the parliamentary democracies of the west are an apparatus essentially dependent on public opinion. A president or prime minister cannot possible start a preventive war all by himself. The opposition would immediately protest vigorously against any such action, and hold the government to account. Representative government is an expression of the national will, and the peoples of the west do not want a war of aggression. They want peace and prosperity. That is a great point in our favor. We must recognize and utilize this situation."

"That brings up another danger," said Serge Andreyevich; "we may be ready in a few years. Our government, by the same token, is dictatorial. If there should be men of less wisdom at the helm of our ship of state, it is conceivable to me that the temptation to aggression might be too great."

"Let us hope, my friend, that our state will continue in future to be guided by wise men mindful of the grave peril threatening mankind through the use of these weapons," Peter Maximovich answered.

"Then an equilibrium would have been established, geo-politically speaking. Perhaps the two giants will divide their spheres of influence, and the world be tranquil at last," said Serge Andreyevich.

"I don't suppose it will ever be tranquil," Peter Maximovich rejoined, "at least not in our time. If the two world powers should really come to an agreement, it could only be at the expense of other nations. Think of the par-tition of Germany, for example. I hope that mistake will not someday cost us dear. We have created an intense focus of unrest in Europe. Those countries are still crushed and bleeding, but in the coming decades we shall reap where we have sown. There will be a harvest of hate. No, I don't think we are going to have peace and tranquility. Such things don't come by planning and compulsion, as the scholars of the materialist camp keep trying to tell us. We have to do with an iron law of nature, the struggle for existence of nations and individuals. Still, I see some chance for a long interval of peace. I think it may be possible to enlighten mankind to a point where the devastating effectiveness of these weapons will compel a realization that their use would mean the death of the human race. Possibly fear will serve to prevent a third world war. But if the beast in man should triumph, the downfall of our world is certain, and the survivors, if any, will have to start over."

After a while they grew weary of conversation. The sun had set. In pale lantern light, the men sat under the tree in front of the main farmhouse. A broad, deep quiet spread over the South Russian steppe. This uncanny silence might well have been what formed the Russian character. Sitting there, alone under the night, one realizes the insignificance of the individual in relation to the universe. This aspect of physical nature might also account for the profound melancholy of Russian folk music, and of the Russian soul.

Franz finished his glass of vodka and quietly said good-night to the two friends.

A thunder of hoofs waked him next morning. The Cossacks were driving some young stallions to the main gate. Franz, as he dressed, cast a glance at the calendar. Well, he thought, it won't be long now. If nothing goes wrong, the day after tomorrow will be it. That's when I'll escape.

He had everything in readiness. His two friends in Krasnodar had done their part. He was to get back his home and his freedom, and in return the two Russians had received countless bottles of vodka and other hard liquor. It was a good bargain on both sides.

During his last two days, Franz conscientiously per-formed all further tasks his adoptive father assigned to him. On the eve of the appointed day he went to bed rather early, to be rested for the journey. A couple of hours after dark, he climbed cautiously from his bedroom window and dropped into the garden outside. With silent tread he crept to the hayloft and brought down the two saddlebags full of bottles. Once more he stole through the great stables and passed the box stalls. Nabor heard him coming. He looked at Franz searchingly as he approached the door of the box with the two saddlebags. His nostrils slightly dilated, his proud head bent somewhat forward, ears pointed, he seemed to say, what are you doing here in the middle of the night? Where can you be going now?

Franz hesitated. Should he take his favorite along after all? Should he expose him once more to the hardships of a perilous journey? "No, my friend, I can't do it. But who will take care of you now? Who will look after you and give you sugar lumps as I used to?"

Franz had privately said something to one of the young men about what would happen to Nabor if Franz should have to leave. Franz made him a present of a bottle of vodka, which was accepted with delight, and with a promise that Nabor should lack for nothing in his master's absence. That was all he could do for his beloved horse. Franz realized how badly he was going to miss his friend. He and Nabor had traveled thousands of kilometers together, night and day, in every season and at every pace. Nabor had never failed him. Slowly Franz stroked the horse's neck for the last time, and emptied a little sack of sugar cubes into the manger.

Franz glanced towards the clock on the wall. He felt a twinge of alarm. It was getting late. He had been in Nabor's box over half an hour without noticing the passage of time. He could not afford to loiter. At all events, he had reached a decision not to take Nabor with him. With heavy heart, he parted from his four-legged friend, closed the door of the box, and hurried down the aisle to the harness room.

There he picked a light but strong English saddle and buckled the saddlebags to it. He gathered the plain snaffle and reins across his shoulders, hoisted the saddle on his back, and emerged silently into the great yard, which was in complete darkness.

Slowly he groped his way towards the common stable where the men's horses were kept. Franz had picked his mount for this expedition in advance. With some difficulty, he opened the creaking stable door and found his way to the horse, a long, wiry English half-blood, like a hunter. He found his new friend lying down on a fresh bed of straw, with no idea of going for a ride. Franz clapped the good fellow lightly on the rump, and he got up. Soon Franz had him bridled and saddled. He tightened the girth as well as he could and led the

NO NEW DAY TOMORROW 139

horse out of the stable into the dark. The little door closed without a sound. Franz mounted.

It was about half an hour before the rider's eyes were completely adapted to the darkness. Meanwhile Franz rode at a fast walk, until the main group of buildings was well behind him. Then he reached the wide track paralleling the main road to Krasnodar. The horse, eager to run, fought the bridle, impatient for his rider to give him free rein. From a quick, short trot, the hunter broke into a fast gallop. Stretched out like an arrow, he flew with Franz through the night. Franz hoped his horse would hold out. He had shortened the stirrups, jockey-fashion, to give the horse more freedom of motion at a gallop. After six hours of hard riding, Franz reached the town. The horse was breathing hard and covered with sweat, and walked along slowly, chewing at the bit. From the main road, Franz turned into the side street, reaching his friend's house in good time.

From the street, Franz was unable to see any light. Probably the householder was somewhere in back. Relieved to have completed his night ride, Franz dismounted, stretched his legs, led his horse into the yard and tied him up in the little stable. Ivan Petrovich had heard him, and emerged sleepily from the back door.

"Better go in and get some rest," he said to Franz. "The Captain is already here, and sleeping. Everything is ready. You start in two hours. Did you bring the stuff? I see you did. Then that's all right. I'm going to have to give that fellow another couple of bottles."

"What fellow, Ivan Petrovich?" Franz asked him.

"Oh, you know," replied the other. "The one who helped me get your papers."

"I see," said Franz; "well, as long as I can leave, that's the main thing. It doesn't make much difference if the papers are blue or green, or if there's one signature more or less."

"It makes a difference to the authorities, my boy. But you'll be all right," and he led the way into the house.

Franz was astonished at the completeness of the preparations. His things were laid out on the table, a worn private's uniform and papers to match. The Captain was now up and about, and greeted Franz with the words:

"Well, and here's my orderly. Take a rest and change your clothes. Call me in an hour."

"Yes, sir!" said Franz smartly, coming to attention. The officer grinned and went back for another nap.

Franz greedily ate his breakfast. He was hungry after his ride. The master of the house came back into the room and gave him a reproachful look.

"But my dear boy, what have you done to that horse? The poor beast is half dead. I've put a couple of blankets on him so he won't catch cold. It's all right to be in a hurry, but you might ride sensibly."

Franz didn't seem to care just then. He went on punishing his breakfast, and remarked indifferently that this was an emergency. "Can you tell me exactly how I'm supposed to act the part of a Russian soldier. I'm going to change as soon as I've finished eating. Before the curtain goes up on the first act, we could have a dress rehearsal. While I finish your last sausage, you can give me my last instructions."

Ivan Petrovich was somewhat taken aback by the boy's coolness. "That's what you call gallows wit, I suppose. If you can muster all that nonchalance in an army inspection post, I can promise you won't have any trouble."

Then he started to go over the essential points again with

the boy; details of the daily life of a Soviet enlisted man, which Franz would have to know about.

"When the Captain gets up, he'll instruct you further," Ivan Petrovich went on -- "In case some unforeseen situation should arise. Otherwise you put on your uniform, stuff the papers in the breast pocket of the tunic, sit in the car and shut up. You'll be riding in a ZIS truck. Besides the officer and yourself, there'll be a driver. He is reliable and won't talk. You'll probably be stopped twice, at the east and west borders of Poland. Then quite possibly the Russians will stop you a couple of times without notice in East Germany. I think I've told you everything important. When you don't have to talk, don't say a word. Show your papers when you're told, and that's that. The Captain will do the talking. Everything clear?"

"It's perfectly clear the way you explain it. Nothing can go wrong," replied Franz.

CHAPTER IV

The officer, who was to be Franz's constant traveling companion in the coming days, had meanwhile been roused from dreams to reality and was busy washing and shaving himself. He kept pacing nervously up and down the room while he was about it, and asking Franz whether he was perfect in all the details of their plan.

"Yes," Franz answered Michael Konstantinovich. "My friend, Ivan Petrovich, has explained everything. But once we get to Germany, I'll need some civilian clothes. I can keep the shoes and socks, and the trousers, and I can get rid of the fur cap. Still, I'd need a plain coat or jacket."

"We'll see when we get there," replied Michael Konstantinovich. "I've got some friends in Potsdam who'll be sure to do me the favor of selling me a suit of clothes. A much more important things you must destroy your Russian

papers as soon as you're in Germany. I should even recom-
mend moving your home in Germany at least a hundred
kilometers farther away. It is entirely possible that our authorities are hand-in-glove with the East Germans. When
you've found your parents, you'd better make that clear at
once. The best thing for you would be not to be seen in your
home town at all. Go away with your parents right after the
happy reunion."

"That's something to look forward to," said Franz, astonished. "I never thought of that. I thought the whole thing
would be over with when I got back to Germany. I see that's
when I start moving around all over again, or the German
police authorities might investigate the whole matter."

"Well, you're not seventeen yet, are you?" said the Captain.
"That's a point in our favor. You won't need a pass in Germany
until you're eighteen. If you change domicile with your parents, you can just get new papers wherever you're living then.
When you fill out the forms, you just say you've always lived
with your parents. That won't arouse any suspicion. What
the government doesn't know won't hurt it. So long as all the
forms are filled out properly."

"That sounds good," Franz agreed, admiring his uniform

in the mirror. "It ought to be simple enough. So, I've got my marching orders. I'll follow your instructions to the letter."

Michael Konstantinovich stood up suddenly and looked out of the window. "Here's the driver with the ZIS. Time to go. Take care of yourself, Ivan Petrovich." The two men shook hands.

The travelers lost no time settling themselves into the ZIS truck. The officer and the driver sat in the cab. Franz made himself as comfortable as he could in the back. The ZIS started with a jerk, and they rode straight out of town towards Rostov.

From Rostov, they continued in a northwesterly direction towards Zaporozhe. The army inspection posts were passed without much difficulty. The officer would get out, report to the desk, show the clerk his orders, and perhaps ask for directions. Usually the officers on duty would wish the traveler pleasant journey and a good time in Germany, and that was all there was to it. The men would exchange laughing remarks, and the party would continue on its way after a good night's sleep.

The condition of the Russian highroads was still very bad in the year 1947. The truck had to crawl over pits and washouts, in constant danger of breaking a spring. The landscape stretched out dismally before them. Now and then they would pass a line of tractors from some collective farm, droning along with machinery in tow. The scoured parts of plowshares glared in the sunlight. In the fields, they sheared through the vegetation and buried it under the loose black soil of the Ukraine. The monotonous rear of the engines could be heard from far off.

The cities of this war-torn countryside still resembled great fields of rubble; the government had mobilized all its reserves for reconstruction, but the job could not be done in only two years. In the towns, the travelers saw many German prisoners, working at the arduous task of rebuilding what their war lords had destroyed.

The collective farms and the countless little villages presented a sorry appearance. Most of the cottages had been burned by the retreating Germans. Then the Russian workers and peasants had returned, and hastily erected make-shift mud huts. Clay and thatch were the commonest building materials to be seen. Gangs of workmen were laying railway tracks shipped in from Germany.

Before 1945, there were many double-track railroad lines

in Germany. The Russians felt the Germans could get along with single tracks, tore up the extra rails throughout Eastern Germany, and took them away to be credited to German reparations.

Told of this significant development, Franz began to feel that it was going to be very difficult in coming years to work out a normal political and diplomatic relationship between Germany as a whole and the Soviet Union. To judge from all this, the Russians were going to remain very suspicious of the German people, and very cautious. As it was, Bolshevik propaganda was doing all it could to make people in the Soviet Union fear the vindictiveness of West German militarism, as well as the western nations. The cold war was approaching its peak.

This was Stalin's device for continuing the "hot war." International Communism was now to gain its ends by other means. During the week-long drive through the south of Russia, Franz was reminded frequently of the miserable lot of the Russian worker. In the course of their labors to construct the Communist society, these people were completing one five-year plan after another, without change in their material conditions of life. Why should the Russian workers struggle so? Why were those in the satellite countries being exploited so mercilessly? The fruits of their labor went to strengthen the bastions of Communism. The millions of robots in the red empire were being kept in check by mutual fear and violence. These tactics proved quite effective for the time being. Franz had wondered now and then whether he was right to ignore the opportunities that offered themselves to a young man in Soviet Russia. But after all, it was a totalitarian state. Franz had always hated every sort of violence and inhumanity. In fact, that was the main reason he had decided to turn his back on this new order once he had seen its inhuman features. Little political experience was necessary to perceive some traits of resemblance to the Nazis. Such thoughts visited Franz on his long journey home to his conquered and divided country.

They arrived without incident in the border town of Brest Litovsk. Who was there in the broad expanse of Russia to trouble about a rattling military vehicle - a common enough sight everywhere? They got out briefly and showed their papers to the officer on duty, who satisfied himself that the marching orders were in proper form, and that the stamps and entries of previous inspection posts were all complete. The officer said shortly:

"All right, drive on."

When they had passed the frontier, they drove on unmolested as before, and as the roads were better now, they made
faster progress towards the west.

Things looked much the same in Poland as in Russia.
Even the flat terrain, as far as Warsaw, was very similar. The
houses, as well as the roads, looked a little neater. The war had
left terrible scars all over the country. Franz suddenly realized,
as they crossed the Vistula near Warsaw, how bravely the
Polish people had fought and suffered for the ideals of western democracy, despite five years of National Socialist terror.
Their will to freedom and resistance had never been broken.

It was here on the Vistula, in the winter of 1944-45, that
the most remarkable event in the history of Polish resistance
to oppression had occurred.

As the Russians were marching on Warsaw from the east in
1944, the members of the Polish Army of Liberation decided
the hour of rebellion had struck. General Bor Komorowski
gave the signal to strike against the Germans - certainly not
without consulting the Russians beforehand. But what did
the Russians do when the revolt broke out? They stopped at
the Vistula and kept the bridgehead of Baranow. They waited

for their reserves to come up, and halted their offensive for several months. The Germans had undisturbed leisure to smash the Polish insurrection before the eyes of the Russian armies. How was this possible? How could the Russians, as a kindred and allied people, permit this? All over the western world, people wondered.

But the shrewd impresario in the Kremlin knew exactly what he was doing. Why should the Soviets help the Polish nationalists? Stalin had already decided that all territories occupied by the Red Army were to become new states in his empire. And he knew that the stubborn Polish nationalists would not cooperate. Even before the war was won, the powers had promised the Poles full sovereignty after their liberation. The nationalists were not the people Stalin needed as submissive tools of Moscow. So, it was simply in the Russians' interest that the Germans should do their dirty work for them. In the first place, the German army was being sapped of its remaining strength; in the second place, it was doing what the Russians wanted done. Later, when the Polish Army of Resistance had been annihilated in the streets of Warsaw, the Red Army responded to the urgings of the western allies and mounted a big offensive, which was very successful indeed, and helped the Americans out of a tight spot in the Battle of the Bulge.

Meanwhile the Poles had been thoroughly Sovietized. Annual plans were projected, and had to be fulfilled and overfulfilled. The democratic opposition was put down. The Communist dictatorship was in the saddle. The estates of the landlords were turned over to collective farmers. The agrarian program of the Soviet government was imitated in every detail. The Polish workers and peasants were not asked whether they approved or not. In most instances, the Polish farmers were extremely hostile to the collective system, because it virtually enslaved them to Moscow. People felt uprooted, but submitted importantly to foreign tyranny. All the nations of Eastern Europe, like Poland, were compelled to revolutionize their social and political life. The Russians cared little whether the suppressed peoples liked it or not. Since the revolution in Russia, they had gained plenty of experience in dealing with such reactionary elements.

The truck rolled on, making good time, to Frankfurt on the Oder, on Germany's new frontier. The dusty ZIS clattered clumsily through former German territory. A few names of towns had been changed, but despite several years of uninterrupted Soviet rule and the expulsion of Germans from the Eastern Provinces, this country still plainly showed traces of the German heritage, however blurred. Franz watched eagerly for the frontier, which must be somewhere not far ahead. The Russian officer looked at him questioningly.

"Well, why are you looking so crestfallen? You ought to be happy."

Franz answered him, "Happy? What about? I'm taking a leap in the dark. You know, to tell the truth, I feel very uneasy. You can see that here in Poland, conditions have become exactly what they are in Russia. According to what I read in the papers, there have been tremendous economic and political changes at home, in the East Zone of Germany. I find it difficult to imagine a Soviet administration in my home town, and I wander what can have been happening. I have a vivid memory of capitalistic - and, as you say, reactionary and fascist - Germany. I wonder how my father and mother have come through this revolution," said Franz.

"Yes," the Captain replied calmly. "You're right, of course, there have been some great changes, which are sure to surprise you very much. But you've spent a year or two in the workers' fatherland, and had ample opportunity to study our way of

life. So, you shouldn't have too much trouble adapting yourself. What did your parents do for a living?"

Franz spoke slowly, looking the officer in the eye. "My
father was a retired army officer, and had a farm of his own
the last I knew. It must certainly have been taken from him
under the land reform. I have no idea where he may be now,
or whether my parents have survived at all. I must confess,
frankly, that even after all my ideological training in the
Soviet Union, I still cannot understand how in the twentieth
century, people can justify driving owners off their property,
summarily, without any compensation. Their reward for a
lifetime of effort is to become beggars in the streets. My old
man, for example, built up his business out of nothing, with
unfailing energy; his sons were to continue his work. What
is left to us now? We've become cattle in an enormous herd,
condemned to be driven without any real aim wherever your
doctrine may dictate. You cannot force your idea and your
way of life on the whole world. Mankind will rise against it
exactly as against Hitler tyranny."

"Well," Michael Konstantinovich replied, "nobody asked
you to invade our country? It was your idea. No one need be
surprised if we react as we do."

Franz went on more quietly. "Of course, Hitler's war was a typical imperialist war. But that doesn't entitle the Russians to adopt the same methods that the Nazis used in their European conquests. What I mean is that you Russians run the risk of showing the world by such conduct how closely your system resembles National Socialism. Such policies will not inspire the nations of Europe with confidence, that's certain."

"Get those fascist notions out of your head, my boy," said the officer to Franz. "In a quarter of a century, we've been through two wars of aggression. We plucked the evil out by the root, and started smashing feudalism and the bourgeoisie and all parasitic elements in our country. We knew that the majority of people in all countries were proletarians. When these toiling masses are mobilized against the capitalist stratum all over the world, the victory will belong to the Soviets. The dictatorship of the proletariat will rule the world from Moscow."

"My dear sir," Franz replied, "that's nonsense. It will never happen. Even if some of the countries of the world should come under bolshevist rule, they would never acknowledge the supremacy of Moscow for any length of time. They would seize the first opportunity that presented itself to get out of the clutches of Russian dictatorship. In fact, I don't think that Stalin with his methods of government could even get a majority of the workers behind him, because his form of government is anything but proletarian democracy. It is simply medieval despotism. Only think of the political tensions inside the Soviet Union. Think of the problem of nationalities. Your glorious Party has had its treason trials. Your leader Stalin won't live forever. Now he has the reins of dominion firmly in his hand, but when he departs from our terrestrial sphere someday there will be a bitter struggle for power among his followers. That will weaken your prestige decisively, all over the world. You have to be careful with these plans for world conquest. True, Stalin is not going about it the same way as Hitler did. He is trying to convince the masses of workers in all non-Communist countries of the truth of his doctrine and incite them to overthrow their governments. But the western powers are aware of that, and are mobilizing all their defenses against such intentions. There you have what we call the cold war."

"Well, there's no and to arguing about it. All that means nothing to me right now. I'm interested in the situation in Germany. Tell me about the women."

"Oh," said Franz, "I don't suppose you'll have any trouble. You speak German well, and will soon find your way about. Potsdam is a fine old royal city. You'll like it. I wish you'd think about getting me some civilian clothes when we get there."

"All in good time," Michael Konstantinovich assured him. "First we must get across the border. We can work out the details on the road from Frankfurt. But you must promise me one thing; don't say a word to anyone about our having come out together, because if there should be the slightest suspicion, we might both find ourselves in an eastbound cattle-car, direct to Siberia. Remember it will be your own funeral if you talk. You're old enough to understand what's at stake."

"Don't worry," Franz replied. "I'll keep still and not expose you to any danger. You Russians can be kind and helpful people when you want to, in spite of all the ideological trappings you have to put up with. On closer acquaintance, a person can get along with you all right."

Michael Konstantinovich accepted this tribute. He replied, "Yes, I too have come to the conclusion that there are people of good will in every nation, who are in favor of real understanding. But in European history these men of good will have often had a hard time of it. They were voices crying in the wilderness, and their words fell on deaf ears. The centrifugal forces always won out. When the slaughter was over, the people always paid the bill, victors and vanquished alike."

In due course they reached Frankfurt, now the German-Polish border city. Slowly they drove to the inspection station. A large number of Soviet army vehicles were lined up outside, all waiting to be cleared. On the other side of the road, similar American trucks, from occupied Germany, were going in the opposite direction. Franz climbed out and chatted with some of the waiting Russians. He shuddered to see the trucks traveling eastward. They were still loaded down with booty, Franz noted, especially household articles and furnishings of all kinds. On top of the heap sat members of the household of some Russian officer who had probably had a house allotted to him in Germany. He must have been recalled unexpectedly. Those who could afford it always tried to take the house furnishings back east with them. Franz had seen enough. Were the Russians still free to take away anything they chose out of Germany? If so, it was very unlikely that the people at home were still in possession. He wondered what Germany would look like after being Sovietized. What can have become of our place, he thought. Was it utterly destroyed, overrun? Perhaps his father was languishing in some concentration camp because he had been an officer. What about his mother? Had she died of grief at all the terrible things that had happened? Or was she still hoping - waiting - for her last and youngest son, who had vanished without a trace, to come back? She knew quite well that the three older boys had fallen in battle, a sacrifice to the madness of the Bohemian corporal. What would have become of all the boys at school? Did they stay in the East Zone, or did they flee to the westward?

Franz asked himself these anxious questions as he stood, chewing sunflower seeds like a Russian peasant, surrounded by other Russians waiting in line to be cleared by the inspecting officer. After a two-hour wait, he was next. His interviewer spoke briefly to the captain in charge of the section. One of the non-coms accompanying the captain demanded Franz's pass.

"You're pretty young yet, aren't you? Take care you don't get into trouble in Germany, or you'll be shipped back."

"I won't get into any trouble," said Franz. "I know how to act in an occupied country all right."

"Let's hope so," said the man, handing him his forged papers.

As soon as they were cleared, the three got in and drove over the bridge across the Oder. The paved streets and roads of Germany made for speed. Before long, they reached the outskirts of Berlin, where they turned off southward towards Potsdam.

The German scene had changed a great deal. Franz saw the same streamers painted with slogans, the same oversize portraits of leaders of the world proletariat, as in the Soviet Union and in Poland. East Germany looked like a small edition of the giant Soviet state, Russian-style. A revision, a display copy of the countries of the eastern blood for exhibition to the western world. To the unprejudiced observer, there actually seemed to be a sort of democracy. Some posters of other parties were to be seen on the public signboards. These parties had at first been tacitly tolerated by the Russians in the post-war years, and gradually manipulated into mere puppets. But they remained in existence, for use in propaganda for the benefit of the three western powers and the world public. Everywhere along the roads, Franz saw ruined buildings, though most of the towns and villages had been cleared of the worst of their debris.

"You're not saying anything, my young friend," said Michael Konstantinovich, "aren't you glad to be back?"

"Yes, of course I'm glad we made it. We got past all the inspection posts without difficulty. We gambled and we won. But everything around here looks strange to me. Actually, I think I really expected to find my home looking as if I had never left it. At least I thought nothing much would have changed. Of course, that was only wishful thinking. Realistically, I know from the Russian papers which way the wind was blowing. The same things are happening here as in the other Red provinces. All the same, I am very much obliged to you for getting me here, through a couple of thousand kilometers of dangerous territory. I really don't know how to thank you. You Russians aren't all Bolsheviks, anyway, any more than all Germans are fascists. Are you going to do me this one more favor about my clothes?"

"Of course, my boy," said the officer. "Before I go to where I'm billeted in Potsdam, I'm going to look up a good friend of mine. I went to school with him. He's a good fellow and likes his fun. We'll go straight to his place. Comrade Mikhailov is a lieutenant in a tank unit. We'll have no trouble doing business with him. I'll get some civvies from him for a spot of cash. The whole thing shouldn't take an hour, we'll just say hello. You can wait in the car with the driver."

"All right," said Franz, "but try not to be too long, or I'll start getting nervous. I don't feel quite right in this uniform anymore."

"You've waited this long," Michael Konstantinovich answered, "a couple of hours one way or the other won't hurt you. You realize I'm going to have to chat a little while before I start asking favors."

"Do as you think best, but please get me the clothes so I can go home."

The officer did not reply to Franz's plea, but pulled a notebook out of his coat pocket and gave the driver his friend Lieutenant Mikhailov's address in Potsdam. The driver, by dint of much inquiry, found his way to their destination. They halted in front of a bungalow on a side street, away from the main stream of traffic. A Russian sentry stood at the door. The Captain jumped out of the car and approached him, identified himself, and asked to see Lieutenant Michael Petrovich Mikhailov. The soldier disappeared into the house. After a little while he came back and said, throwing the door wide, that the Lieutenant would see the Captain now. Franz's friend entered, and the door was closed behind him.

Franz waited an hour. He waited two hours. Still his friend did not come out. Franz had half a mind to follow the inspiration of the moment and make good his escape. But he knew he would have to wait it out. He had no choice but to sit patiently in the car. He knew his friend couldn't resist vodka; those two are busy getting drunk, Franz thought, remembering how the Russians behaved on such occasions. Hospitality was in their nature. As long as there was plenty of liquor, Franz feared, he would be forgotten. Still, the officer understood what was at stake. He could not very well take Franz along to his billet; once there, the boy would not be able to get away unnoticed. The Captain had two sets of marching orders - genuine, for two persons, and false, for three. Before Michael Konstantinovich reported for duty in Potsdam, the forged papers would have to be destroyed. The genuine orders could be presented by the officer and his driver on arrival. So, it was high time Franz and the two Russians parted company.

At last the door of the house opened and his friend came walking quickly towards the truck, accompanied by another officer. He had a parcel under his right arm. At least he's got my clothes, though Franz. He seemed to be walking steadily enough. After an exchange of parting amenities, the Captain got in and curtly gave the order to drive on.

"Where to?" the driver wanted to know.

"Anywhere," was the answer. Turning to Franz, Michael Konstantinovich said, "Here you are. Change your clothes."

Franz obeyed with alacrity, and became a civilian in no time. He kept his Cossack boots. They were not noticeable under the trousers.

"There," said the Captain. "Now destroy your Russian papers before we separate. I want to see it done, for my own peace of mind. Be sure to do exactly as I told you. It's time for you to make yourself scarce. Here's some money," handing the boy a few bank notes. Franz tore up his papers into tiny scraps before the Captain's eyes, said farewell to the two Russians, and trudged off, whistling merrily, towards the railway station.

CHAPTER V

Franz didn't have much trouble buying a ticket to a small town just outside Berlin, where the game warden had used to be a good friend of his family's. That should be a good place to start inquiring for his father and mother. Mr. Reinhardt would probably know what had become of them.

When one returns from foreign travels, voluntary or otherwise, it often seems as though nothing at home had changed. Looking out of the window of his local train, Franz found it otherwise. The aspect of Eastern Germany had indeed changed very much during his stay in the Soviet Union. In the towns, the Communists had proceeded vigorously against private enterprises. Large and medium-sized plants had been taken away from their owners, and over the entrances of nationalized buildings there were large neon signs with anti-capitalist slogans. Elsewhere, posters urged the public to greater efforts in fulfilling the Plan. Others praised the glorious leader J.V. Stalin, honoring the heroic exploits of the Soviet liberators in grandiloquent phrases. Just the same as in the Soviet paradise, thought Franz. The Russians coming to Germany must feel quite at home. Their German partisans were doing everything they could think of to reconstruct Eastern Germany in the image of the Soviet Union as quickly as possible.

Great changes had taken place in the countryside, too. Russian ruthlessness, combined with the unscrupulousness of some of the German bolshevists, remodeled the economic system overnight. Owners of estates larger than 240 acres were expropriated without notice or compensation. Within the hour, they were obliged to clear out and settle not less than fifty miles distant from their former property. Many families had acquired their holdings by decades of hard work and thrift. Their mansions stood neglected, surrounded by their gardens, barns and stables. A coat-of-arms over the main gate might be the only remaining affirmation of the past. Properties were unconscionably mismanaged by thieving administrators. What the Russians lacked leisure to despoil, their German adherents cleaned up after them. With German thoroughness and industry, they carried out their orders to the letter. What was the tenor and intent of these orders? Moscow commanded German bolshevists to make a Red province of Eastern Germany, and coordinate all political and social institutions with the Soviets. The objective was the brutal violation of a people for colonial exploitation. Yet the Soviets did not hesitate to present themselves to the world public as democrats, and in fact had the effrontery to call themselves the true democrats. They pretended that the working class, a majority in any modern country, was behind them, and from this derived their claim to assume republican garb. But the plain facts were otherwise. The pro-Soviet leaders knew perfectly well that they did not have a majority of the people behind them. They relied on the bayonets of their Russian friends, and want to such extremes that they even alienated their ally, the Socialist Party.

Franz could see, now that he had returned to Germany, that a third of the population had fallen out of the frying pan into the fire. One might have thought that after the defeat of fascism, the whole world could breathe easier, but in the eastern half of Germany nothing had changed in this respect. The brown-shirted rule of force had been replaced by the far more stringent and intensive tyranny of the Reds.

The new dictators did not content themselves with utilizing all people living under their sway; from 1945 on, they proceeded systematically to deprive all their opponents of any tangible or intangible resources they might have. These were the first steps taken by the Soviets to transform the state of society in Germany. Franz's first look at the Soviet German newspapers confirmed his worst expectations. All of them, in Communist-controlled Eastern Germany, had taken over the same jargon as their Russian models, <u>Pravda</u> and <u>Izvestia</u>. They all saw things through the same pink spectacles. Franz tried in vain to find any sign of opposition thinking in Christian Democrat or Liberal papers. They, too, had degenerated completely into Communist puppets.

Franz, still occupied with his thoughts, get off the train and found his way to the game warden's residence. Twice he clattered the iron latch of the garden gate. Inside, a couple of dogs started barking clamorously.

"So," said Franz to himself. "He's still here." For if the hounds were at home, their master couldn't be far off. Franz heard, through the back door, a heavy tread, gradually becoming more distinct. The head of the house was heard ordering the dogs into a corner, and the big door swung open. The man stared at Franz, speechless. He recovered himself in a moment, however, and exclaimed:

"Why, it's Franz! Come in, my boy, come in. Make yourself at home. Where have you been? I thought at first I was dreaming."

"No," said Franz quietly, "you're not dreaming, Mr. Reinhardt. It's me all right."

"We all thought we'd never see you again. Have you been to your family's yet? They must have been overjoyed!"

Thank God, thought Franz, that means they're still alive. Still, he was most uneasy, and asked the old man fearfully, "What's happened to them? Where are they?" He seized hold of the other's coat sleeve. "Tell me. What's happened? I haven't seen them; I came here first to make sure. Tell me, won't you?"

The old man, astonished, began at last to speak.

"Calm yourself, my boy. They're both alive and well, though they've had troubles enough."

At these words, Franz relaxed. Mr. Reinhardt made him sit down in the living room. Quick, light footsteps approached. The mistress of the house entered and looked at Franz strangely.

"Don't you see?" said the warden to his wife. "It's our young friend come back again."

"Oh," cried Mrs. Reinhardt in astonishment, "then it's really he! Where have you been all this time? You look exhausted. I can get you something to eat, right away, can't I?"

"That would be fine," Franz admitted gratefully. The lady left the room.

"Well," said Mr. Reinhardt, "I suppose you've quite a story to tell. No one around here knew what had happened to you. You simply disappeared into the cast, and that was the last we heard of you. Your father and mother must have given you up for lost. And now you're back. I suppose you've had a bad time."

Briefly, Franz told the story of his adventures.

"But how have you been getting along, Mr. Reinhardt? I expect it hasn't been easy for you either."

"No," the old man replied, "it hasn't been easy. We've had our troubles, too. Only a week before the surrender, my boy in the air force was shot down. That hit us very hard. All of us are very poor now. Your father and mother were ordered off their property. Your father was arrested and beaten several times. I didn't escape beatings either. I keep some guns in the house, of course, and for that I was arrested and locked up by the GPU for a couple of weeks. Then they let me go, as there was nothing against me politically. I was not involved in the denazification. But plenty of innocent people did get departed to the east, or imprisoned in the confusion, without really finding out why or wherefore. That's the worst thing about the Russian system--the continual anxiety, uncertainty and unpredictability. Your folks had two hours to leave their place, though your father was never a Nazi. The fact that he had been an army officer and had property of his own was enough for the Soviet German authorities to brand him as a fascist and militarist. Somehow, they've managed to come through unharmed. They're living in a little place, not far from here, and getting along pretty well. I see your father every now and then."

The two of them in the living room fell silent, busy with their own thoughts. Mrs. Reinhardt brought in a tray. The hearty sandwiches and light wine tasted wonderful, and soon Franz felt better than he had for a long time. The old game warden gave him minute directions for finding the place where his parents were living. Franz thanked his friends warmly for their hospitality and guidance. He had not realized what a risk he was running by taking the train. Usually, passengers on all trains had to show their papers. Since Franz had no papers, and did not even know his parents' address, he was lucky not to have been arrested. He would be more cautious in future. The only prudent course was to travel the rest of the way on foot. He knew the country pretty well.

I'll be able to get food and lodging at farmhouses on the way, he thought, with the help of a little money.

So, he pressed on from village to village. It was the same everywhere. Eastern Germany had undergone a real russification. At the edge of every village, there would be one of the triumphal arches the Russians had put up for their victory celebration. Most of these structures were painted in gaudy colors. At the top of the arch, visible from afar, there would be the portrait of some Russian general. In a schoolyard, Franz saw a gigantic picture of Stalin, painted in luminous lettering with the words "Long Live the Wise Leader of All Peace-Loving Peoples - Our Best Friend, J.V. Stalin". Quite a sense of humor, thought Franz to himself. These people were being forced by a shameless administration to glorify the representatives of this hated system. What a sorry inheritance Hitler had bequeathed to the German people. Their brothers and sisters in the western part of the country at least had a chance to construct and organize a form of government that really suited them, and which they really wanted and valued. But here, Franz thought, there is no use even thinking about reconstruction. Willy-nilly, the people had slipped from one police state into another. As the vanquished, there was nothing they could do about it. The preponderance of force was too great. The chains of slavery were too heavy. A weary and exhausted people could not break them.

The farmers were going about their tasks in their accustomed manner. The great houses, chateaus and farm buildings in many villages had been torn down, and the land was supposed to belong to those who worked it, according to the Communist speechmakers. The big landed estates had been broken up into small parcels of twenty or thirty acres each. Most of the livestock had been driven off when the Russians first came. Thus, the homesteaders and the many refugees faced the task of raising new stock and at the same time undertaking intensive cultivation of the arable lands assigned to them. This was extremely difficult. The peasants were actually half enslaved, though the pro-Communist press referred to them as free peasants. The government told them how many and what kinds of animals they had to raise. Most important of all, everyone was told exactly what quantities of products he must turn over to the government annually. The entire land reform had been organized from the start in such a way that the formerly free peasants became workers under Soviet state capitalism and were exploited by the state more intensively than ever.

On the outskirts of the villages, Franz often saw little houses that had been put up in the Russian temporary fashion. Settlers got the raw materials from the great junk piles of the demolished mansions.

In a little country inn, Franz was able to order a simple meal and a bed for the night. In the bar, some farm workers were sitting, talking about local affairs. Franz represented himself as being from the city, and tried to strike up a conversation. It turned out that this was not so easy. People were naturally suspicious of strangers, and for good reason. Not a few in the vicinity had been arrested for criticizing the regime and its agrarian policy too freely, never to be seen again. Even in the villages, the Communists governed by the principle: Divide and rule. The class struggle was carried on in intensified form. A big farmer had to give up much more of his output to the government than a little one. Every year the thumbscrew was turned tighter. That meant that the quotas of the large and medium farms increased automatically year by year. Anyone unable to meet these exorbitant demands would be arrested and heavily fined. In this way, slowly but surely, the Communists hoped to gain their ultimate end of completely suppressing the independent element in agriculture and completely leveling all engaged in that branch of the economy. The predominantly individualistic peasantry was to be replaced by a mass of people producing agricultural products. The German Communists intended, and were required, to follow the Stalinist example of collectivization in every detail, though the experiment had cost the Russian people unspeakable misery, and the Soviet Union was drifting from one famine to another.

But the apostles of Marxist ideals did not care if a few people more or less were sacrificed to their economic and political experiments. All they cared about was that theory should be carried into practice. Nor did the planners pay any attention to special circumstances in a given country. They tolerated no excursions deviating from the party line. By and large, the Soviet Russian example was simply extended to the satellite countries. The administrations of these countries were directed by Moscow, and responded to the word of command. Their governments had degenerated into more outposts of Moscow. Opposition in town and country was ruthlessly crushed. To the old Nazi prisons, new ones had been added. In spite of the shameful facts, government propaganda never tired of talking about freedom, progress and democracy. Every thinking man in Eastern Germany know by this time that these were empty phrases.

Franz was curious to know what attitude the working people in the Soviet part of Germany took towards the Communist reforms. He walked right up to a table and asked permission to sit down. He was cordially invited to do so. Franz stood a round of drinks.

"And how's the farm program coming along?" he asked. "Going to make the quota?"

"What do you mean, going to make the quota?" one of the older men replied. "Nobody ever makes the quota. Nobody around here, anyway. This is light soil in this part of the country. Take me, for instance. I'm supposed to be growing rape, wheat and sugar beets; also, fertilizer. That's plain crazy. The allotments are much too small, and there's not enough stock to make manure. We haven't even got up to fifty per cent of the prewar herds; the reparations took almost all the horses and cattle. How are we supposed to make that up in a couple of years? It'll be a long time before we can raise enough even to supply the government and, besides, the stock is poor, because all the best sires and dams were taken away in 1945."

Franz wanted to know whether the government was doing something to help them.

"Of course," the man replied. "They do plenty. But the only thing they know how to do is demand more production. How can such methods alleviate poverty? We do the best we can, work ten hours a day and more to try to meet the government's requirements, but I don't think we'll ever meet the quotas. I have no confidence in the future any more. If the west can't help us, we're stuck. If the Communist economy wants to destroy us, it can. But it'll take a while. It'll be a gradual process. So far, the Reds with their agrarian policy are dependent on us large and medium farmers. After all, we turn out the greater part of the product the people have to live on. But I'm afraid that over the years the Soviets will build up the government side of German agriculture so much they'll be able to do without us. That's what they're working for. Already a lot of families find they can't put up with all the threats and extortions any more, and are pulling up stakes to escape to the overcrowded western part of the country, so they can at least get some peace."

Franz interposed, "What about tractors and machinery from industry?"

"Well, there are what they call the machine and tractor stations. They have all kinds of modern farm equipment. But the people in charge have a strong Communist bias, and are regarded as mainstays of the new system. They are strictly forbidden to do work on the farms of large and medium-size owners. The machinery is not supposed to do any good for the class enemy, but only for small peasants and homesteaders. So, all the machine and tractor stations are getting to be strong points of propaganda. They train the young fellows, not only in machinery and agronomy, but in politics. It's not hard to see that those installations are supposed to be the forerunners of collective farm centers."

Some of the men at the other tables were getting interested in the conversation. Two came over and sat down. They were young men, not much older than Franz. He wondered how they felt about all this.

"Well," he said, "the government takes a lot of interest in training young people in the country. They can go on to any of the schools and universities."

"Yes," one of the young fellows said, hesitantly, "that's true to a certain extent. If a worker's son is willing and able to learn, he can get government scholarships. What a lot of people don't realize is that these privileges are open to the children of workers almost exclusively. For children of farmers, lawyers, or small businessmen, it's very hard to get admitted to a university. The government spokesman says this in so many words; they intend for the future leaders of the German people to be mainly of proletarian origin. That's why workers' children are so generously favored."

"So, I suppose what it really means is that the state functionaries hold a sort of monopoly of education, and want to keep it to themselves and their families?" Franz suggested.

"That's what our present rulers are working for all right," was the reply. "Let's of boys and girls are living away from their families because this class system compels them to study in the Western Zone or in West Berlin, where of course there's complete freedom in this respect. Class background doesn't matter. No matter how you look at it, you'll find that nothing goes in the Eastern Zone unless it serves the purposes of a Communist society. Any theory or practice contrary to the almighty Soviet state religion is sooner or later stamped out by the security people."

Franz was interested to see how soberly and objectively this young man saw the situation in Eastern Germany, and he wanted to know if there was any difference from the conditions in other countries of the Soviet bloc. The elder man answered his question.

"Yes, there's a big difference. Eastern Germany borders directly on the western world, and we have the island of Free Berlin. When people can't stand it anymore, they can catch the first train, slip through an inspection or so with their papers, and get into West Berlin. There are a lot of people there, resting up from their troubles. This gives us a great advantage compared to the Czechs or the Poles. It's one reason the propagandists are having so much trouble with our young people. They refuse to be absorbed. They see the falsity of Russian propaganda for themselves, every time they get to Berlin. This makes it a lot more difficult for the Soviets to bend the youth to their purposes than in the other countries of the Eastern Bloc. Of course, here as anywhere, there are a few young fanatics who support Soviet policy."

Franz asked the old man, "But you think they're in the minority?"

"Yes, I do," was the answer. "I'm sure of it."

Franz did not reply. There was an awkward silence.

Perhaps the men felt they had been talking too much? The old man was frowning and looking at Franz narrowly. The younger man's glance seemed distrustful. They were probably frightened. "You needn't look at me so suspiciously," said Franz quietly to the elder. "I'm not on their side. But we should be more careful what we say in public. Well, I have to go now. Good-by, and thank you."

Franz paid his bill and continued, rested, on his way. After a long hike, he reached the village of Ostwalde where Mr. Reinhardt had said Franz's parents were staying. It was nine o'clock in the morning. Franz had been walking all day and through the night, and he was dog-tired. But he had been irresistibly impelled to keep going. After his long exile and ultimate escape, he glimpsed the end of his journey before him. There was the little village, lying in the valley before him, surrounded by fields and meadows.

Franz stood lost in thought. So, this was the final goal of all his struggles. How could he slip in unobtrusively? He was unfamiliar with this particular village. Ostwalde was a hundred miles from his old home. He reflected that no one would recognize him here. No one would notice a young man coming through or stopping somewhere.

He struck out across the fields, leaving the main road, along a trail leading past cherry orchards. Before long he began to see buildings. There was a long row of houses on each side of the village street. Almost every house was fronted by a little garden, with sheds and stables to the rear. The village seemed very quiet. A few sheep were peacefully grazing on the green common. Now and then a dog barked. Mr. Reinhardt had told him exactly where the house was, near the far end of the village. On the way, he passed a good-sized structure, identifiable as the local administrative and police headquarters. In front of it was posted a large production graph. Franz paused a moment to study this exhibit. He noticed that the farmers of the vicinity had been active in all branches of agriculture. According to the figures, crops had increased year by year. Products were itemized, from milk and cream to beets and potatoes. Familiar propaganda phrases appeared in big letters. For example, "First Work Harder, Then Live Better." Or, "Steady Production Gains Raise Our Standard of Living." He had seen enough.

This is exactly like Russia, he said to himself. You might have seen the same thing on a Soviet collective farm, the same slogans. Everything done according to rule. The Soviets were making themselves at home; they gave orders and expected to be obeyed. National individuality didn't bother them. Let the other people adopt our ways, they seemed to think. Then they'll soon be prosperous and happy. Anybody who objected because an enemy of the people and was liquidated. It doesn't look very promising, Franz thought to himself as he walked on slowly. Soon he found the house. He recognized it easily, a whitewashed and ivy-trellised cottage. In back there was a shed and a little stable. The front walk led through a little flower garden. Franz recognized his mother's handiwork. The walk was freshly graveled and edged with whitewashed stones. Franz stood in front of the garden gate and hesitated. It was perfectly still. Should he enter? What if no one were at home? I hope they recognize me and don't die of fright, he thought. Well, I can't stand here forever, I'll have to go in sometime. Slowly he walked through the little garden. He thought he heard his mother coming to the door.

"Who is it?" said a clear voice.

Franz didn't know what to say. His mother's voice sounded somehow apprehensive. How often had the Russians knocked at this door? How often had it been opened fearfully to admit unwelcome visitors? Now it was he who sought admittance. I'll have to answer, he decided.

"It's all right, mother. It's Franz. Don't be frightened. I've come back."

The key was turned from within. The door creaked open. His mother stood in the doorway.

"Oh, my boy," she said, "you've come at last! It's been such a long time. I thought I'd never see you again." They embraced. Neither spoke for a time. Each was thinking of all that had happened since Franz had left his home.

"I'm so glad to have you back," said his mother at last. "You've grown much bigger and stronger. We can use your help. Thank God for bringing you home to us. You're the only one I have left. Oh, ever so many people have been crushed by grief and disappointment," she went on, "and have taken their own lives. Sometimes, when things were at their worst, I've been tempted. But I wasn't sure what had become of you; that gave me strength to go on. And now you're here!"

She led the way into the kitchen and made Franz sit down to breakfast.

"Where's father?" Franz asked.

"He's out in the field. He'll be so glad! He's had a hard time since you've been away. He was arrested twice, and they questioned him and mistreated him. They took the farm away from us, and he had to give up his life work, raising horses; they gave us an hour to move out. Even here, we've had trouble. It's been very hard on him. We must try to give him new strength and hope."

When he had finished his meal, Franz thought he would go and find his father. "I don't want to wait until tonight. How do I get there? Is he working by himself?"

"Yes," said his mother, "you can go straight on from here. It's about three miles. You can find the place easily, because there are a lot of birch trees." She gave him directions.

Franz went at once. He didn't know the neighborhood, and looked about him with interest. People working in the fields paid no attention to him. He passed a potato patch after some time, and in the distance, he saw a fence with rows of white birches behind it. That must be the place, he thought.

When he got closer, he saw a man mending the fence down at the far end of the pasture. It was his father.

Franz ran eagerly towards the enclosure, where a few cows and horses were grazing. His father was wearing a green hunting outfit, as he had been accustomed to do, and a gray hat with a little feather.

He looks just the same, thought Franz. He's dressed the same, too.

"Good morning!" called Franz, when he was about ten yards away. His father turned and rose slowly from his work.

"Good morning, young man. What do you want?"

"Is that any way to talk to your son?" Franz asked soberly, and went on: "You don't seem to recognize me. Have I changed that much?"

"Why it's - no, I can't believe it." He stared at Franz, motionless. "Yes, it's really Franz. Come here, my boy! - This is a surprise. I think I'm going to have to sit down."

Suddenly he became very animated. "So, you're here at last. That's wonderful. Now I'm glad I've lived so long. You'll make it all worthwhile. I've lived for the day when you might come back. Now you're home safe and sound."

"I hope it's going to be all right," Franz answered his father. "Let's finish here and then go home and talk things over. It would be better if nobody saw me. I might get arrested."

"But what for? What's wrong?" his father demanded.

Franz outlined the story of his escape and explained that he was going to have to register with the police sooner or later for identification papers, and went on:

"I can't very well explain to the burgomaster that I'm a fugitive. He would have to report me."

"All right, let's go home now. We can talk, and there'll be time for this tomorrow."

"Fine," Franz agreed. He felt very light-hearted, careless of the dangers ahead. Quickly he helped his father hitch the horses to the cart. They got on and drove home. Franz's mother opened the yard gate. The horses were quickly unhitched, stabled and fed.

"Come inside," said his mother. "Go into the sitting-room. I've made some tea."

Willingly the men accepted the invitation and settled themselves comfortably.

"I see you saved the paintings," Franz remarked. "That's wonderful." He noticed a picture of one of the horses his father had raised in the old days. "There's Mephisto, the dark sorrel I learned to ride on." He had been a handsome but willful creature. He had a way of stopping short and trying to throw his young rider. Franz remembered him clearly. He thought it was probably his own fault that the horse had been so wayward. He noticed that the furniture in the cottage had been salvaged from the wreck also. Everything else had been lost. He felt very fortunate to be home again, at least. Too many had perished, far to the east, and never seen their loved ones again.

Parents waited in vain for their children. Brides mourned their husbands. The exiles lay in their mass graves or languished in some labor camp far away in the trackless wastes of Siberia. Thousands lay buried under the frozen snows. When the thaws came, the stench of rotting corpses was plowed into the earth. The Russian campaign had been a frightful chapter in German history, disastrous in its consequences to victor and vanquished alike. Franz's father was speaking.

"Well, there's a great deal to talk about, but maybe we had better begin by deciding what should be done."

"Would it be possible to leave here and go somewhere else to live?" Franz suggested. "No one would know who we are."

"I think it will be safer right here," said his father. "We've only been here a year, and nobody knows much about us as it is. I can have a talk with the burgomaster. I can tell him you've been living with relatives back west, in order to finish at school, and have only just returned. He'll be sure to accept that."

Franz's mother agreed. "I think that would be the best plan," she said.

"We can talk about it some more," said Franz. "Maybe I should sleep on it. Possibly I could get a job somewhere around here, and learn a trade. Then I could come to see you on weekends."

"Before long," Franz's father went on, "I'm going to have to start taking it a little easy. I'm not as fit for this heavy work as I used to be. And I'm not very ambitious to sacrifice myself for the Communist state. My health hasn't been so good."

"Well, I could stay here and help out if you intend to keep the land," Franz replied.

"That might be the best idea for the time being," said his father.

Franz said good-night after a while, and went up to his room which his mother had prepared for him. He fell into bed, dead tired. He had had little rest in the last three days, and he was feeling the strain.

A long, loud cock-crow waked Franz next morning. He jumped out of bed, washed in clear cold water, dressed, and sat down to a hearty breakfast. It was a beautiful Sunday morning.

"Why don't you go to church with us, Franz?" said his mother.

"Oh," Franz replied, "people would only stare at me. I'd better not. Maybe after I've been around a while."

"All right, do as you think best."

The villagers had swept the street in front of their houses, and the church bells were ringing, clear in the crisp autumn air, summoning the faithful to prayer. People left their houses singly and in groups, dressed in their Sunday clothes, on their way to church.

Franz and his father and mother stayed at home in the afternoon and made themselves comfortable in the sitting room. After giving an account of his adventures, Franz asked his father:

"And what's been happening here at home while I've been gone?"

"Well," his father answered, "people are sometimes very hard to get along with; especially the Russians. Right after their invasion, I was appointed manager of an estate that had been taken over by the Russian military government. I had a good opportunity to get acquainted with Russian farm practices. They planned everything very carefully. They figured out what they meant to plant and how much, and held me strictly to account. Within the first few months, a lot of trained Bolsheviks came back to this country from Russia. They proceeded to take over the key positions in civil administration and in the economy, with the help of the Russians, since they were all men who saw eye-to-eye with the Soviets. You can imagine. A number of these political agitators came in to carry out the agrarian reforms in our neighborhood. It was a big propaganda campaign. Big public meetings were held. On the billboards, great posters proclaimed the Soviet farm program. They had slogans like 'The land belongs to the workers and peasants,' 'Down with all landlords,' and so on. Then the workers on the estate were assembled in the meeting hall. The head organizer outlined the program and asked for discussion. A few of the men tried to argue with the agitators. It seems to us, they said, that the reforms shouldn't be carried out without some preparation. We haven't got far enough along yet. What's a dozen acres of land, anyway? We can't make a living on that. Give us bigger allotments so we can have regular farms. And where are we supposed to get the stock? The Russians took it all away. Questions like that.

"And the speaker told them that it was not for nothing that he had spent several years in the Soviet Union and been instructed in matters of this kind. He explained it something like this:

"'Comrades,' he began, 'our model for the reconstruction of a democratic Germany must in all areas be the Soviet Union. Only from the Soviet Union can we learn how the enemies of the people are to be defeated. The Soviet people has shown us how, from small beginnings, by rational planning, great and lasting achievements can be won. The Russians, too, at the end of the First World War, had to start from nothing. By their own efforts they have built an industrial state able to match itself with the most advanced countries of the earth. And was not this possible only because the proletariat had assumed the leadership in economics and in politics? Why, then, should not the same thing be possible in Germany or any other country?'

"But it turned out," Franz's father went on, "that some of the workers couldn't see it that way. They objected to the Russian example, and answered: 'This isn't Russia, and we have to adapt ourselves to German conditions. Why not let us go on in our own way? The reforms won't help without the necessary means; we'll only be worse off than before. What are we going to do about plowing and seeding? First the Russians take away all our livestock, and then they urge us to follow their example and work our fool heads off. We're expected to make good those losses out of our own hides, and then we're asked to emulate Russian examples.'

"Then the organizer played his trump card. 'Fellow workers,' he shouted, 'it is time something was done about these disrupters and alarmists. These elements are trying by their vacillation to bar our way to a better future. We will tolerate no opposition on this question. Our security agencies will ruthlessly smash the forces of reaction. I personally will see to it that these die-hards can no longer raise their voices against the interests of the working people.'

"Officers of the Soviet security service appeared in the room immediately. No one spoke. Discipline was restored. People were quick to grasp that all protest against the new regime was useless. The newly appointed Communist burgomaster stood up on the platform and took the floor.

"'After what our Comrade has said, I trust it is perfectly clear to everyone present that the land reform will be carried out as we have proposed, and as is unquestionably in the interests of the toilers, in spite of all reactionary resistance.' The burgomaster looked confidently around the room and continued. 'Now we will put the question to a vote as it affects this village. After the vote, we will proceed to elect an executive body to be responsible for carrying the program into practice. Will those in favor of the reform please raise their right hands.' Almost everybody raised his hand. The burgomaster, the organizer and the Russian security officers looked approvingly around the room at their well-trained charges. After a short pause the burgomaster continued.

"'Those opposed.'

"Nobody raised his hand, nobody spoke.

"'The assembly of this place,' the spectators heard the speaker saying, 'has unanimously resolved that a democratic land reform shall be carried out. We may now proceed to the second point on the agenda, the election of an executive committee.'

"Then the burgomaster's clerk monotonously read off a list of names. The nominees were unanimously elected by the meeting in the same manner. The speaker appointed another time and place at which to meet with the members of the committee for further deliberations, thanked all those present for their attendance and, there being no further business, declared the meeting adjourned."

"Well," observed Franz, "so you had a chance right away to see what is meant in the Soviet Union by true democracy."

"It took longer than it seems when we look back on it now," his father demurred. "When the Russians told us that all German institutions were henceforth to bear a democratic character, we actually thought that the idea of democracy was, in itself, indivisible. But in the course of time the Soviets demonstrated by their methods that they meant something entirely different by democracy from anything we could have imagined. Their way of governing became more and more dictatorial and more and more remote from the democratic. I had an opportunity once to discuss the point with a Soviet major, a man of very good education. He had been an agronomist in civilian life. So, we were colleagues in a manner of speaking, and naturally we talked shop. The Major was also well informed about Communist institutions and Marxist-Leninist dialectics. To my question why the Soviets did not behave as dictators with a clear conscience, and describe their practices as dictatorial, the Major replied that the Communists derived their claim to the attribute 'democratic' from their Marxist doctrine. That doctrine, of course, proclaimed the workers' dictatorship. The Communist promise was that they, the Communists, were the only party that could claim the right to call itself the workers' party. From this point of view, it was not difficult to arrive at the conclusion that this party had the actual majority of the people behind it, and as such could also claim the right to call itself democratic. Though heaven knows that makes a very big difference, for even in a modern society, the pitch makes the tune. The point where minds refused to meet was when the question of the <u>how</u> of democracy came up."

"I see," said Franz. "The Soviets make it very easy for themselves. They pull out their Moscow bible and quote chapter and verse to prove their democratic character. They do this at will, because it suits their policy just now. It's a sort of courtesy to the western allies. They used to scorn to call themselves democrats."

"I don't think," his father objected, "that it can be a courtesy. It's simply a tactical ruse, or who knows, it may even be some kind of commitment."

"That seems unlikely," said Franz. "Why should the Soviets feel committed to the western powers? A lot they care about agreements with former allies. You know how Hitler used to act. All dictators are without conscience or compunction in that respect."

Franz's father answered, "It's not quite that simple. In the first place, the Soviets, by agreements they made with America during the war, obligated themselves together with the other great powers to become guarantors of world peace after the joint victory over fascism. The Soviet Union, in fact, promised the U.S.A. to drop all plans of world revolution after the war, in return for the assistance received, and to pursue a policy of conciliation and moderation. And the Russians know very well that they have every reason to be wary of the United States. The atom bombs dropped on Hiroshima and Nagasaki just before the end of the war was a clear warning, intended to show them that they must reckon with the United States."

"That may be true," Franz conceded. "But what always puzzles me is the fact that the Soviets really believe their party is the only true one. They seem to ignore the other socialistic parties in the countries of the west, which have actually proved stronger than the Communists in the industrial and working-class countries. After all, that makes the Soviet thesis of the absolute dominance of their party over the entire world proletariat meaningless. The facts, in the free countries, refute the best points of Soviet propaganda."

"Don't forget," warned his father, "that there are strong

Communist parties wielding great power in the countries of the free world, too. These organizations are legal in character, and in genuine democratic elections they have been able to win a good many parliamentary seats. They have even been represented in cabinets. This places them in a position to pursue a potentially successful policy of obstruction if their supreme masters in Moscow demand it. These facts may be unpalatable to the west, but they are indisputable; something will have to be done very soon in these free countries to counteract the snow-balling of such Communist forces. It's like a tumor in the democratic body politic. The western powers cannot stand by idly while Moscow's fifth column aggressively bores from within all over the world."

"But," Franz asked, "what do you think the western powers should do to stop Communist penetration into the free world?"

"By themselves, of course, the western powers can't do much," Franz's father replied. "It depends a great deal on those countries which are direct targets of Russian attack. The question is whether the threatened nations will have the energy and the will power to meet the danger and deal with it. Without some willingness to sacrifice, the problem cannot be solved. In the last analysis, the taxpayers of the United States cannot be expected to constantly make financial sacrifices for foreign aid without getting something out of it. A nation lacking the ability to help itself will not benefit no matter how much American assistance is rendered. On the contrary, assistance on such a basis would be detrimental to the west, and beneficial to the Russians. It should never be forgotten that Communism is a sort of ideology, or religion. Consequently, the struggle between the free world and Russia will have to take place largely in the intellectual arena. That is strikingly clear when the activity of Moscow agitators is observed everywhere. Wherever they go, want and poverty are their best allies, conditions which are a big advantage for the agitators.

"The Communists feed on discontent," he continued. "That is one of the oldest lessons of history. It was the same in ancient Greek and Roman politics. Panem et circenses, or bread and circuses, as the Romans put it. It is easy for Communist agitators to stir up discontented workers in the free world, because as citizens of a democracy they can utilize freedom of speech and press for their subversive plans. Their technique is based on continuous criticism. In countries like France and Italy, the Communists have nothing to lose. They can promise the workers mountains of gold without committing themselves to any risk. If they should actually win an election by democratic methods, they would not hesitate to proceed in exact accordance with directives from Moscow. The same methods being practiced here today would be applied. They would turn the country upside down not only politically but socially. All liberty and legal safeguards would disappear almost automatically."

He continued: "The people in those countries seem to know that this is true. For despite intensive propaganda, the Reds have not yet succeeded in obtaining a decisive majority in the countries of the free world. Nevertheless, I think the west is very ineffectual in opposing the Stalinists on the propaganda front. Youth should be made aware of the anti-human and degrading aspects of this system, since it is particularly receptive to Communist ideology, because most young people are eager for progress and enlightenment. Owing to their inexperience, they have no adequate basis of comparison for refuting the arguments of the Communists. If the west is to resist Communism, it must have an exact understanding of the ideals and aims of the Soviets. The youth of our own countries must be made aware of the threatening danger before mankind is swallowed up in a twilight of aimless, monotonous slavery."

Those words brought Franz and his father back to the gray reality in which they were living. It was a paradox. The country was as attractive as ever, and nature bedecked in seasonal beauty was oblivious to political upheavals. The people of Eastern Germany found themselves in a great geographical prison. They were unconfined, but under durance, forced into a way of life to which they had to submit irrespective of their political choice.

For young people born and raised in the midst of Soviet society, such conditioning would have been at least tolerable. But to those with a yearning for democracy and self-respect, life in a dictatorial society is perpetual torture. Those who were young might well ask themselves: Why should I spend my lifetime in this hall of coercion?

Franz looked out of the window and watched the birds, happily twittering their melodies. The sheep were grazing peacefully in the rich fields. Everything looked about the same as before he went away. If only the cruel features of the new state had not changed man and his behavior and reactions so basically. The crops in the broad acres seemed to be thriving as of old. But a keen observer could not have failed to notice that now instead of spacious fields small, limited areas of only two and four acres had been planted. This fragmentation was a result of the reform imposed by a powerful invader. The great, seemingly endless seas of grain had disappeared from the East German countryside and replaced by a patchwork-quilt pattern. Where formerly there had been the solid color of yellow wheat, there was now a mosaic of all sorts of crops--poppies, rape, vegetables and corn of all kinds. Thus, had human planning transfigured an entire landscape.

Castles, except for a few scenic points of interest, had disappeared from the eastern part of Germany. The debris had been used for building materials in the many mushroom settlements on the outskirts of villages and towns. In one respect, the people had benefited to an extent by the introduction of the reforms. Despite the cruelty of the method, the acute refugee problem was, as a result, somewhat diminished.

The problem of refugees had assumed formidable proportions in Germany after the end of the Second World War. In 1945, there were twelve million displaced persons wandering on the roads in Germany. The Russians had simply chased them off the territory east of the Oder. They had to try to find food and shelter somewhere else in Germany. In a devastated and starved country, this was impossible without foreign aid. This circumstance may have been one of the reasons why the Communist authorities in Eastern Germany adopted such drastic measures. The greater part of the German population passing through the country in refugee torrents undoubtedly came from rural districts. The immediate division of the land enabled the Communists to get the refugees out of the camps and off the roads. A man acquired a home, a plot of ground, and a place in the process of production. Opponents of land reform had to admit that this was, for the time being, a remedy. The crowds of transients could not possibly have been left to their fate. Establishment of camps did not solve the problem. The only solution was to integrate the refugees into normal life. But the point always being made by those opposed to the Communist reforms was the inhumanity with which the Russians were carrying out these experiments. Why, people kept asking, are we not allowed to settle so important an internal question ourselves? Why are plans being carried out in disregard of the most elementary human rights? For example, as many believed, families who had held a large farm estate ought to be allowed to keep enough acreage to earn a decent livelihood. Legally and humanly, this would have been entirely proper. But complete expropriation and expulsion, without any compensation, of thousands of respectable families--that was shameful. It was cold-blooded and calculated class warfare. The class enemy was to be cut off from any opportunity to exist by utter expropriation. The Soviets knew what they were doing; they were striking the iron while it was hot. Once they had destroyed this social class, it would be an easy task to smash the remainder of the peasantry at leisure in a very few years. Meanwhile, the Communists were, of course, dependent on the poorer class of independent farmers, and could not have afforded, for pressing economic reasons, to quickly liquidate them. But the citadel of hostility to Bolshevism was being destroyed.

The Soviets never tired of proclaiming that they were rendering a great service to mankind. For, according to them, the representatives of the big German landowners, next to the capitalists of vast industry, had been the chief instigators and aggressors in both world wars. Certainly, a great many well-known people in Germany had risen from that group. But this did not seem to entitle the Soviets to such a sweeping, ruthless policy of coercion; and, after all, the Soviets did not confine their attentions to their former enemy, Germany, but used the same technique of terror in all the countries they occupied, even Poland, Russia's ally, which would not have consented to those high-handed proceedings except under duress. So, the inference was plain that the Soviets ruled by might instead of right. They used their power unscrupulously to their own advantage. Thoughtful people saw the reforms which the Russians were carrying out by these methods as the germ of collectivization, the formation of a classless society, and the socialization of all means of production. These were, of course, the Soviet objectives, but most people did not yet perceive them, for in their treatment of their victims the Communists showed themselves to have a diabolic understanding of human nature.

They pretended not to have the slightest desire to concern themselves with the internal affairs of a subjugated country, and liked to pose as good Samaritans, lending aid wherever there was need. Many households were happy enough about the farmland, pasture and timber suddenly allotted to them free of charge. And for a little while, all went well. The peasants exerted themselves to raise stock and place the neglected fields into production. But whenever a certain amount of progress had been made, the Soviets would tighten the screws. The peasants were required to increase their output and their tribute to the government every season. Farmers or homesteaders who failed to meet their quotas faced arrest as enemies of the people and economic saboteurs, and were subjected to endless questioning and other forms of persecution. The class struggle was beginning to assume an intensified form.

Now the characteristic feature of all the countries of the eastern bloc was that despite the Herculean efforts of the population, the standard of living fell rather than rose. This was because the Russians had converted the conquered territories into tributary provinces of their empire. They proceeded in much the same way as had the Roman proconsuls in Syria and Africa. For it must not be forgotten that under Stalin, a special form of Bolshevism had developed--Stalinism. It upheld the theory of Marxist and Leninist ideas, but its practice had become crueler, more brutal and more despotic in character: the only term to adequately describe it was Machiavellian. The conduct of this man in the Kremlin merited no better name. His methods were sinister and medieval. Though he called himself humane and progressive, his actions showed him to be a damnable liar.

Franz's first weeks in East Germany passed quickly under these powerful impressions. When he had become somewhat accustomed to his new surroundings, he began to look up some of his former schoolmates. Many had emigrated westward, but a few were staying on in the Soviet zone.

One day Franz told his father he was going to visit his friend Horst, whose parents had a grain and feed business in town.

"Regards to Horst's parents," Franz's father and mother called after him as he left the house. He had to walk about two miles to the station. Some farmers from the neighborhood were waiting for the train. An hour later, the old locomotive came chugging in. German railroad facilities were inadequate everywhere, the Russians having torn up nearly half the rails. Franz climbed aboard, and after an hour's ride, though it seemed much longer, he reached his destination. He had no difficulty in finding his friend's home. It stood by an old mill, secluded on the outskirts of town. A little stream murmured nearby. There was nothing in the immediate vicinity to suggest the ravages of war. The place was like an island of peace, ringed with woods, meadows and gardens, a charming springtime landscape.

A couple of foxhounds lay panting on the doorstep. Franz reached the gate and clapped his hands twice; the dogs came running up, the front door opened. Horst's sister, Inge, was coming toward the gate.

"What can I do for you, sir?" the girl asked.

"Hello, Inge," said Franz, "don't you know me? I can't have changed that much."

"Why, Franz! No, I didn't know you. We all thought you must have been killed. It's good to see you again!"

The two warmly shook hands. At the girl's invitation, Franz walked through the garden into the house. His friend's parents welcomed him, but with astonishment at his sudden reappearance.

"Where's Horst?" Franz asked at the first opportunity.

"He had to go downtown," was the reply, "but he'll be back in an hour or so. And where have you been all this time? How did you get along? I suppose your father and mother were surprised to see you."

"Yes," Franz answered, "it was quite a reunion. You people have been lucky; this place doesn't seem to have suffered very much from the war. Everywhere I've been, I've seen towns and villages in a terrible state of destruction."

"That's right," Horst's father replied, "we've been fortunate in that respect. But it's hard to say how long our luck will hold. The future here looks dark and uncertain."

"Why should that be?" Franz asked in surprise. "You have your own place, plenty of everything, and such beautiful surroundings."

"It looks that way," said the head of the house, "but it's a deceptive picture, all this natural peace and abundance. Difficult years lie behind us, and still more difficult ones ahead. So far, of course," he went on, seriously, "the authorities have needed us to cultivate the land and repair the damage done by years of neglect, but I keep feeling that the days of our private business are numbered, under the Red occupation. They'll kick us out as soon as they think they can do without us, I'm certain of that. We really ought to get out now, before it's too late. But we're too stubborn. We cling to what we feel belongs to us. Irrationally, people keep on trying to hold on to, and even add to, what has come down to them from previous generations. Now, all of a sudden, everything's different. What was right yesterday is wrong today. But in spite of everything, we stay in this country, ruled by treacherous and conscienceless despots. Why do we remain? Just the habit of being here--home, love of country, duty. And what do these ideals mean today? They are despised and trampled underfoot."

The old man must have experienced Russian methods in the last few years, Franz thought. He tried to cheer him up.

"Well, sir," he began, "you really aren't so bad off here, compared to lots of people in the satellite countries. You've had suffering and hard times, but in Germany at least it's still possible to escape to the west by way of Berlin. Surely that's something to the good."

"I know," the grain merchant replied, "but there's no escape from the slow torture we're subjected to while we're here. It's a gradual process. Things might go on for another ten years before we're finally liquidated."

"We must remember," Franz pursued, "that after such a vicious war as we've been through, there would have to be a difficult postwar period too. The beast in man is still in control. We are still suffering from the consequences of the war. A better time is sure to come. People must have learned something from experience. Reason will triumph at last."

"Young people are much more optimistic than we can be," answered the elder Horst. "The worst thing in the postwar history of Germany is going to be this unnatural partition. That is going to work out very much to Europe's disadvantage unless some satisfactory solution is found soon. No one knows which of the two titans--Russia or the United States--is going to win out. Right now, they are quarreling over our country, and it is not hard to guess which nation has the sympathy of the majority of Germans. We belong to the west, and given our cultural evolution, it could not be otherwise. But we will not be consulted. If one knows how long the country was going to be split in two like this, it would be easier to make up one's mind to give up everything and start over again somewhere else. However," he continued, "as long as this uncertainty remains, here we are, working and hoping for the best."

Horst's daughter, Inge, was in the kitchen, preparing some refreshment. The garden gate opened. Through the window, Franz could see his friend Horst approaching. He crossed the garden, opened the door, and saw Franz, whom he instantly recognized.

"Well, well," said Horst with enthusiasm, slapping Franz vigorously on the back, "this is a surprise. They can't keep a good man down. This calls for a celebration." Horst hurried off to the cellar to find something worthy of the occasion.

"You be careful," Franz warned him. "You might have trouble drinking me under the table after all the practice I got in Russia."

"I can believe that," said Horst, "but we'll have to pour a little libation anyway; eh, father?" he added. "If this isn't reason enough, I don't know what is. I hope Inge will bring us something to eat now."

"I'm coming," she called from the kitchen and entered, carrying a tray. The boys made themselves comfortable in the large chairs, ate, drank and chatted about their experiences since they had last met.

"What's happened to the rest of the gang?" Franz wanted to know.

"Well, a lot of them finished school this year and find themselves out in the cruel world," said Horst.

"None of us thought it would be like this, did we?" Franz remarked. "The teachers do the best they can, but there's nothing like real life to test you out."

"That's right," said Horst. "What are your plans now that you're back in Germany?"

"I'd like to learn a regular trade," Franz replied. "That ought to be the most dependable thing. I could get along anywhere. Right now, I'm farming with my father. I find it pretty restful after all the excitement."

"I think that's the best thing you could do," the old gentleman put in. "What kind of trade did you have in mind?"

"Well, I've thought about being a mechanic," Franz answered him. "Do you happen to know of anything? There are supposed to be some big shops in town where they're hiring."

"Oh, all of those are nationalized. They were taken over right after the war, and the owners fled to West Germany," was the reply.

"Would that make any difference?" asked Franz. "I saw an outfit like that in the Soviet Union, the whole thing, with political education and everything. Couldn't I go to somebody in charge and give your name as a reference?"

"I do know the foreman in a diesel repair shop," the older Horst answered. "If you're interested, you could go there some time and say Mr. Altbauer sent you. I think he'd probably do something if he could."

"That's very kind of you," said Franz gratefully. His friend's father wrote down the address for him. The boys continued their conversation about their former schoolmates.

"Quite a few of the fellows came to the conclusion, in

school and in the youth organizations, that Communism was the answer after all," Horst told Franz. "They accepted the promises and ideological claims of the regime. Axel and Rudi are functionaries in the local youth organization. You wouldn't know them, to hear them talk and argue."

"I see," said Franz. "I wouldn't have expected that. What do their parents think of it?"

"Rudi told me once he had had some bitter quarrels with his parents," Horst replied, "but finally he went over to the Communists. He told me that a movement which gave young people a chance ought to be given consideration, and that the government deserves support. He thinks international Communism has a great future, and that there need be no scruples about becoming committed to it. He's a typical organizer. It's the same with Axel, except that he had less trouble with his family and was more diplomatic about it. You know both of them; they don't mean any harm. They feel they're still fighting for freedom. You might look them up some time," and Horst gave Franz the addresses of the two young men.

"I'll do that, the first chance I get," Franz told him. "I'll be very much interested to hear what the two of them have to tell me about Russia and Little Father Stalin. Of course, I'll lie low and allow myself to be instructed. It ought to be fun. But I really thought better of those two than that they would join up with such an outfit for better or for worse. We ran the 400-meter double relay twice with Axel and Rudi for our school, remember?"

"Certainly, I remember," said Horst. "We won the junior championship in 1945. That was a good contest, with fine organization and good sportsmanship. Remember when Axel saved the situation with his finishing sprint at the last meet? Sports are about the only thing all of us still have in common."

"Well, that's something, anyway," said Franz. "Whatever came of the boys in the saddle club? They were all good fellows."

"Most of them got out into the Western Zone," Horst told his friend. Some are dead, and a few are in business around here in a small way, not doing too well either. But we can't make anything like the showing we used to, though there's plenty of interest; we just don't have the means."

"Well, as far as practice is concerned, I had plenty in the Caucasus. I got to be a regular acrobat on horseback. They have wonderful horses, all right," Franz conceded.

"I'm sure they do," the other agreed. "They helped themselves to the best we'd been able to produce over the centuries."

"I'll tell you something, Horst," Franz retorted, "we Germans ought to be careful about talking like that. You know that we were the ones who attacked the Russians first. We needn't be surprised at the way they've treated us since the war. You should have seen the devastated fields, towns and villages, from Berlin to the Volga. The scorched earth policy took a terrible toll. We're paying for our political stupidity now. I don't mean to defend the Bolshevists, but you have to understand these people; they have every reason not to trust us. Things like that are not so easily forgotten. We could have known just exactly what would happen if the Russians beat us. But most of our compatriots were afraid to look things in the face. I'll have to talk that over with Rudi and Axel. Maybe they'll show me the right road to salvation," Franz concluded ironically.

Horst's mother interrupted them.

"It's getting late, Franz. You'd better stay here with us. Get some rest. You can see about everything tomorrow."

"That's very kind of you," said Franz, thanking her.

A short time later, they all said good night, and as soon as Franz's head touched the pillow, he was asleep.

The author during a cross-country competition.

The author with his prized stud.

The author at the jumping phase of the competition.

The author during a cross-country competition.

The author is pictured second from the right as a mechanic at VW.

Franz Haeussler, 1959

The author riding in winter at his farm.

The author swimming in the Grand River.

The author during a cross-country competition.

*The author is pictured 5ᵗʰ from the left in
the backrow VW coworkers.*

*Author as a six-year-old on the right during
a pony ride at the Baltic Sea.*

The author jumping a home-made obstacle.

The author practicing his dressage movements.

The author as a nine-year-old with his uncle and cousin.

The author breaking a Trakehner stallion.

*The author as a six-year-old with his
father in a pre-WW1 hanomag.*

The author posing with one of his horses.

The authors father driving horse and buggy.

"Schloss Goetschendorf" authors childhood home (1932-1942)

Author on his Anglo-Arab horse (2003)

Author with a young Trakehner stallion.

Chapter VI

Next morning Franz was up and about early. After a hearty breakfast he took leave of his friends and embarked on an exploration of the streets of the town. It was a place of some importance on the interzonal highway connecting the exclave of West Berlin with the zones of occupation of the western powers. An unbroken stream of traffic, maintained communication between West Germany and its Berlin outpost.

"<u>Donnerwetter</u>," said a man in work clothes admiringly, waiting with Franz at a crossing. "Just look at that job there!"

He was pointing at a heavy Krupp diesel truck, a triumph of West German industry. It was followed by a big Mercedes bus carrying a crowd of tourists. The onlookers gazed in astonishment at the smart clothes and elegant appearance of the travelers. This bit of highway was like a little window through which Franz caught a glimpse of the other world.

The light changed, and Franz strolled on. He paused in front of a bank building. Looking at a great portrait of Stalin, he thought how the aspect of a street, or of a city, was changed by signs and placards. Were the travelers from the west supposed to think that these slogans reflected the political attitudes of the population; or were these passengers from the other world perfectly aware that the propaganda represented the views of a tiny minority? They would have to draw their own conclusions. Stalin's portrait was flanked by the slogan: No Marshall Plan Wanted - We'll Build Our Own Economy. Another poster accused the western powers of deliberately sabotaging German unification. So, it continued along the entire street. Everywhere, former private business had disappeared. Stores of the government trade organization dominated the business section. Franz recalled seeing merchandize centers like these, with their pegged prices, in Russia. Curious, he entered a food market. He noticed that the stands were doing a brisk trade, in spite of the high prices. Franz overheard two housewives discussing the cost of butter and meat. One was saying to the other:

"Actually, most of the people standing in line here can't afford to buy at all."

Franz ventured to interpose. "But everybody's paying cash, or there wouldn't be any sales made, would there?"

"Of course, young man," said the woman who had spoken, "that's just it. People are paying because they have no choice. Take my husband, for instance; he's a boilermaker. I can't expect him to go hungry, doing heavy work like that. So, we simply do without other things, like clothing and furniture."

So that's it, Franz thought. At least, people in the East Zone were able to concentrate on one consumer area and satisfy the need, whereas in Russia the majority of the population were still on very short rations in every sector of the market. Franz did not quite understand why the Russians, in those early postwar years, were allowing the people in East Germany to enjoy a better standard of living than their own workers at home. Perhaps it was for the sake of propaganda effect in the west.

Franz moved over from the food market to the dry goods department of the same big government store. Here prices were still much higher. He saw fewer purchasers. Franz was interested to observe a few Soviet officers standing in front of the counters with their wives. People with no intention of buying were free to examine the merchandise and admire or deprecate the achievements of Russian industry. A Russian lieutenant wanted some blue fabric. A saleswoman had piled up many rolls of material for his inspection. The Russian felt one roll after another between his fingers and exclaimed over their poor quality. The clerk said calmly that this was all there was. When her rather difficult customer had been voicing his criticisms a few minutes longer, the section manager noticed him and came to ask whether there was anything he could do.

"Do you call this merchandise?" demanded the Russian. "I want something really good."

"I'm afraid I can't help you, sir," the manager replied. "You might try a larger city, where they would have more variety to choose from."

The Russian officer took himself off, muttering something about fascists and saboteurs. The manager seemed relieved when the street door closed behind him. There were quite a few women in the store. They showed a good deal of interest in nylon stockings, which were of good quality and readily negotiable. Franz noticed a graph illustrating business volume posted over the main entrance. Franz concluded that

the government trade organization as a whole was a subtle tool
of Soviet exploitation. About sixty per cent of the proceeds of
all sales was diverted into the Soviet reparations fund. In the
establishment of this fund, Russian advisers had been on hand
to teach the tricks of their trade to the German management.
The enormous profits drawn by the Soviets from this undertaking were based on the correct assumption that German
consumers were exceedingly eager for the goods to be offered
them, although, at fantastic prices, in the state stores. As the
regular ration cards could be made to last only half as long
as they were supposed to, the majority of consumers could
not resist the temptation to go on buying in the unrestricted
state stores, and that was the point of the whole thing, since
the receipts flowed back into the treasury. The Soviets were
giving an inch and taking a yard. In this underhanded way,
the people were being bled white, and had to pay until their
pockets were empty.

At the same time, the Soviets were so shameless as to
pretend that all proceeds were being applied for the benefit
of the public. They said nothing about the lion's share that
was being devoured by Russia. Franz had seen enough, for the
time being, of the Russian economic system in Germany. He

left the store and walked on. A few doors away, he found the "German-Russian Friendship" headquarters. Here there was another heroic portrait of Stalin. Beside it, he read: Eternal Friendship with the Glorious Soviet People.

That's a good one, Franz thought to himself. The Russians must think the Germans have very strong nerves, to offer them friendship in this manner. What did they think they were doing? Had the years of hatred and fighting left no trace? The suggestion was so ironical and shameless, it was almost inconceivable. In all seriousness, a stripped and plundered nation was being offered eternal friendship. Were the Soviets drunk with victory and power politics? Were the Bolsheviks to destroy the honor and pride of a nation, too? In organizing this friendship club, had they forgotten that they had driven twelve million people off the land, and that only a few years earlier, they had forcibly evacuated half of eastern Germany? They could not have forgotten, and yet they expected the vanquished to consent to this self-abasement. Did the Russians imagine that there could be real peace or friendship on these terms? In the flush of victory, did they not realize that some-day they would reap the harvest they were then sowing? Had they learned nothing from history? They were treating the peoples of Europe no better than the Nazis had done. They did not deserve the name of liberators. The people who had actually suffered enslavement were the true witnesses, with ample testimony to refute all propaganda. Franz was unable to resist the words of invitation written on the poster at the door of the House of German-Soviet Friendship: Become a Member and Learn the Truth.

I'll have to look into this, he thought. I wonder what they're going to try to tell me about the Soviet paradise.

Franz opened the door of the building and stepped inside. A clerk sitting at a desk looked up inquiringly, and Franz explained that he was very much interested in the aims and activities of this organization and would like to get detailed information.

"Yes, of course," the clerk said. "Naturally you wish to know exactly what we are doing before joining the ranks of our mass organization."

That's it, Franz thought--mass organization. A familiar expression in Russia; everything was masses and organization there. The individual was nothing. The mass, the we, was everything.

The clerk was droning on monotonously. "Realizing that

the international solidarity of the working class can only strengthen world peace, we have made it our special task to create the closest of friendly relations between the German and the Soviet peoples."

Franz put in, "You say the German people. Do you mean all of Germany, or only the population of the East Zone?"

"I mean all of Germany, of course," replied the functionary.

"But West Germany has a different economic and social system," said Franz.

"That makes no difference," said the clerk. "There is a peace movement there, too, supported by the workers, who understand that the Soviet Union is on their side, and on the side of world peace."

"But there is a deep division between the two countries now," Franz suggested. "People can't be expected to forget the terrible war period at a moment's notice, and pretend that nothing ever happened between Germany and Russia."

The official answered, "That is the typical argument of the class enemy. You forget that the last two wars fought between Germans and Russians were simply imperialist wars of aggression. Now that German imperialism has been smashed, that is no longer possible. We have rooted out the militarists and erected a peace-loving workers' and peasants' state on the site of the annihilated imperialism. Our strength is the international friendship of all the workers of the world who accept the leadership of the Soviet Union in the preservation of peace."

"So, you are working for friendship, peace and international understanding," said Franz, summarizing, and went on. "Then why is it that your methods are anything but friendly?" he burst out. "Why do you maintain prisons here to force non-Communists to follow your line? Why did Tito and Yugoslavia get out of the Communist alliance? I'll tell you why. He realized that the Russians, by policies of exploitation and extortion, were bringing the conquered countries to the edge of disaster. What becomes of unity in your Communist world, when your camp of world peace is splitting up so soon after the victory? Tito saw the path in which the Russians were leading us all would end in ruin. He had the courage to free himself of dependence on Moscow."

The clerk had turned pale. The girl at the next desk had stopped typing and was staring at Franz, horrified. The clerk took a step towards the young man and hissed at him: "Listen here! Don't let me hear you saying things like that again.

That's the speech of a fascist provocateur. Only outright enemies talk like that."

Franz had cooled off a little, and realized that he was
being very foolhardy. He resolved to correct his mistake and
tried to smooth over the incident.

"I'm afraid I got excited," he apologized. "I beg your par-
don. Thank you very much for your explanation. I understand
what you are trying to do. I will think over carefully what you
say. Please don't be offended. I'm certainly not a provocateur.
Good day."

Franz left the building with alacrity and merged with the
stream of passers-by. He breathed a sigh of relief. He had been
lucky that time. How could he have been so careless? Franz
know that for less than this, many a man had been sentenced
to years at hard labor. He hoped the official would not report
him. He knew from his Russian experience that people often
got out of very embarrassing situations by profession of guilt
and repentance. Anyway, he was going to try to be very careful
from now on, and he hurried on his way to the shop to which
his friend's father had directed him.

Soon he reached the plant. It was a former arsenal that
had been converted into a public commercial enterprise.

As everywhere, the entrance of the building was hung with streamers bearing the usual phrases urging higher productivity and over fulfillment of quotas. Franz did not stop to think about them. He approached the guard at the door and asked to see the superintendent. A few minutes later Franz found himself in the office stating his business.

"All right," was the prompt reply, "I'll speak to the foreman. We need young fellows willing to learn and work hard. You'll hear from us by letter."

"Much obliged to you," said Franz, and took his leave. That had been easy enough. Franz felt there was nothing more to do in town, and started on his way home. He was stimulated by his new experiences.

When he got home, his father asked him how he had found things in the city.

"There seem to have been a lot of changes," Franz told his father. "In outward appearance, it might be a provincial town in Russia. Of course, it only looks that way. On closer inspection, it's all compulsion and pretense. People seem constrained, somehow."

"Did you visit your friends from school?" his father asked.

"Yes, I visited Horst. But I didn't have time to look up

Rudi and Axel. Horst said they were Party functionaries now, and devoted to the Red cause. I looked around for a job as an apprentice, too."

"What for?" said Franz's father in surprise.

"Well, I think it would be better if I learned a trade. I would be more able to take care of myself. You can get work like that anywhere. I don't know whether I am always going to be living in the Soviet Zone, anyway."

"Surely you don't mean to go abroad again, after your long exile?" said his father.

"It isn't that I want to," said Franz. "Sometimes you have to do things whether you want to or not. I think conditions under the Reds are more likely to get worse than better. I'm young, I have my life before me, and I'm going to have to choose whether to remain in the land of oppression and violence, or to enter the free world outside, even if that may not be the easiest solution. I would rather escape to the western world, where free human development is still possible."

"But my boy," his father objected, "you're dreaming. You can't want to leave home in these unsettled times. Besides, I need you. Still, I don't want to interfere with your future. Aren't you interested in stock raising, and agricultural pursuits?"

"Of course, I am," said Franz, "but how am I supposed to get started? There aren't any places of any size around here anymore."

"You could stay in the east and study to become an agronomist."

Franz said, "Father, it won't be long before we have the same situation here as in the Soviet Union. Private interests in the economy are being thrust aside. The estates are already nationalized. The peasant farms will follow in a few years. As yet, it all seems to be in the nature of individual enterprise, but present development and plans clearly show what will happen if we follow the road laid out by the Russians; there will be big state properties, so-called production combines. A big agricultural machinery industry will be needed. Of course, it hasn't come to that yet, but the preparations are being made."

"Yes," said Franz's father, "but the Soviets will need young people to carry out the plans."

"That's not for me," Franz answered. "I've looked things over, and I don't want to lend myself to such purposes. I think it would be wrong for me to participate in such projects. I would be working for the world revolution against my own convictions. I would be working to do the same evil to men of the free world that has been done to us. I can't summon any enthusiasm for such ideals. What would be the good of material gain and luxuries of life if I couldn't approve of what I was doing?"

"That may all be true, my son. But sometimes we have to hunt with the pack. Remember that with all these disagreeable things, a place of material security is open to you. Becoming a Bolshevik is the price you have to pay."

"I don't want to pay that price," Franz said to his father. "Liberty is more precious to me than the opportunities and so-called security that the Communists can offer to young people."

"Well, you've known the bitterness of exile. The path of idealism is a thorny one. You can live in a Communist state well enough if you make up your mind to it, and see things as they really are."

"I don't suppose I'll ever be able to do that," Franz replied. "We shall have to remain in subjection here, and obey orders from Moscow. I happen to prefer freedom and privation to slavery and plenty."

"You will have to make your own decision," said Franz's

father resignedly. "But be sure to think the whole thing through. Consider the advantages and disadvantages carefully."

Franz avoided discussing the subject with his father thereafter. What the old man said might reflect the wisdom and experience of his years, but Franz viewed the matter with the optimism of youth.

Time passed on. The work on the farm had to be done. All day, father and son labored in the fields that afforded the family a modest livelihood. The harvest time was approaching. The grain would have to be cut in primitive fashion with the scythe, since no one now could afford modern machinery.

Dark storm clouds were gathering on the political horizon in that autumn of 1948. The significance of the Marshall plan was being debated. An absurd currency reform deepened the division of Germany and hence of Europe.

In the proposal of the U.S. Secretary of State, the Communists saw an ambitious maneuver by American capital to regain the territory overrun by the Russians.

Propagandists in all countries of the eastern bloc played the same tune. But the oppressed peoples of eastern Europe felt new hope that the hour of deliverance from Moscow's clutches was at hand. This hope was to prove illusory. The ruler of the Kremlin had no intention of giving up what his armies had gained by bitter struggle.

The battle for Germany raged with increasing violence. The cold war between the two rivals for world hegemony threatened to become a hot war. At that time, many people in East Germany still hoped that western policy would succeed in rescuing that country, at least, from Russian power. They thought in terms of a restoration of the status quo in Central Europe. The monopoly then still held in the atom bomb by the Americans was a reassurance and an encouragement to endure. Some people in these countries even longed for the day when the murderous weapon would be used. Better a terrible end than endless terror, they said. Others, more far-sighted, inclined to be sober and objective, said that all these understandable expectations were only wishful thinking. They stated in so many words that Europe had ceased to occupy a place of importance - let alone leadership - in the world. By the end of the Second World War, these few had realized that the greatness and glory of the European nation states were a thing of the past. Still others refused to recognize this precisely because the civilized nations of Europe, almost overnight, had become stakes in the game of world politics. It was soon to prove that the victorious countries of western Europe would fare no better than the conquered and oppressed peoples of eastern Europe.

Ever since 1945, Russia and the United States had been determining the course of world history. The Soviets experienced a great ascendancy in world affairs during the first five postwar years. All their efforts were bent to displace their American rivals from Europe.

In the conquered countries, the Russians took a firm stand. The peoples of the eastern world were not to carry on any exchange of ideas with those of the west. This, of course, was absurd, especially as the German as well as the Polish people were thoroughly western in orientation, culturally and in many other respects. All that was now to be changed. The Communist rulers had given orders that the conquered peoples must accept the new religion. Anyone who objected would feel the wrath of the Russians. A cruel, barbarous Asiatic policy was being forced upon the nations of East and Central Europe. From Vladivostok to the Elbe, all countries marched in step and fought for the same cause. This deliberate and forcible regimentation of peoples in defiance of national religions repeatedly roused the hatred of the impotent victims. Instead of living in the enlightened and progressive twentieth century, they felt they had been thrown back into the darkness of the Middle Ages. There were witch hunts, as in medieval times. Stalin's spies and agitators kept the provinces in fear and terror, condemned to hopeless bondage. That was the quintessence of the Stalinist method. Communist society was literally to be created by this generation. In despotic pose, Stalin demanded precise execution of his plans. Many complained, by no means reconciled to do without the comforts and pleasures they were enjoying. They had no desire to sacrifice themselves for the ambitious aims of the ruling clique. The masses of people in Russia, as well as in the countries of the eastern bloc, desperately wanted consumer goods, but they had to be content with promises. For the ordinary citizen, it meant hard work from morning to night, with scarcely enough to eat. In East Germany, the situation was especially critical because of the presence of West Berlin. The shop windows of the western world were to prove a great stumbling block to the Soviets in the cold war.

Everywhere in East Germany it was rumored that great events had taken place in Berlin since the institution of the Marshall Plan. Money and labor had regained some semblance of their former value. Through the sound purchasing power of money, the forces of commerce and industry were enabled to develop vigorous activity. All the products of the West European market found their way to West Berlin, where Germans and all others beyond the Iron Curtain were able to see what reconstruction really meant in the west. These convincing facts were undermining Soviet propaganda. The scale of living being publicly demonstrated in West Berlin had a tremendous influence on the temper of the East Germans.

Russian propaganda did everything in its power to convince the Germans that the Marshall Plan was merely a grandiose fraud on the part of the Americans. It was directed, according to the Soviets, against the national independence of the German people, and degraded its victims into being colonial slaves of America.

But people were not misled by this propaganda outcry. They traveled to West Berlin and saw for themselves that the Communists were lying. Seeing that talk did no good, the Reds attempted to master the situation by stratagem. They blockaded all roads giving access from the western zones to West Berlin. This city was a sore spot in Stalin's enormous empire, a source of terrible danger that had to be dealt with. The plan was cruel, cold-blooded and murderous. Two and a half million people were to be starved and frozen into submission. By that time, the Germans realized that they must look to the western powers if they were to have any chance of recovering their freedoms and their rights. In those critical weeks, the solidarity of all democratic peoples of the western world came to life. The statesmen of the west were now aware that only mutual defense could be an effective bulwark against the rising tide of Bolshevism. Those weeks and months in which the west resolved to oppose Soviet expansionism will never be forgotten by any who took the cause of democracy seriously.

The last and decisive action came when the United States and Great Britain undertook to operate the air lift. This was a triumph of western technological superiority over the inhumanity of the Soviets. Stalin had lost a decisive battle in the cold war when he realized that his plan had failed and was compelled to end the blockade.

In those heroic days, the East Germans enthusiastically supported the frontier spirit of Berlin. Over the radio, they listened to the inspiring speeches of the Mayor, Ernst Router. This man made a substantial contribution towards restoring Germany's good name abroad. He attracted the sympathies of the oppressed people of East Germany. He became the symbol, the bond between man and man, ruthlessly exposing the lies of the Communists and proving himself one of the great fighters for the good cause in the world.

By 1949, the formation of a civilian army had been started in East Germany. Stalin intended to be prepared for every eventuality. Armed units of considerable size were to be seen drilling and marching. True, the soldiers wore police uniforms and were referred to as a police force, but everyone knew this was the precursor of a Communist combat group, to be trained on the Russian model and by Soviet instructors.

During these crucial weeks and months on the cold-war front, Franz had become absorbed in farm work, helping his parents to bring in the grain and potato crops. The family was sitting at the table one midday when there came a knock at the door. A man entered and introduced himself as the local Party leader.

"Comrade," he said to the head of the household, "I come to deliver an order from the burgomaster. It shows precisely what quantities of products you are required to furnish from this year's harvest."

"Thank you," said Franz's father shortly. "I will study it after dinner." The official then took his leave.

"Let's see what they've cooked up now," said Franz. His father handed him the instructions.

Franz spread out the chart on the table and studied the figures closely. After a short time, he turned to his father.

"I told you so. There is no point in trying to accomplish anything here under the Reds. According to this, you are supposed to deliver more than half our crop to the state. That's about the average--sixty percent of the harvest. That's what we have to surrender to the government for a petty leasehold. The same applies to eggs, milk, beef and pork. Where are we supposed to get seed for next year? How are we supposed to supply all this milk and meat? Next year they'll raise the quotas. If we comply, we'll be ruined financially. If we don't, we'll be arrested as saboteurs and be maltreated by the police. A fine prospect. You work all season for the benefit of a few political adventurers. Finally, you realize that all your trouble was for nothing. Something has got to be done. A few more years like this and you'll find yourself broken in health. Can't we think of something? We should try to start over somewhere else, instead of working ourselves to death here for the good of the Soviets."

"Take it easy, Franz," said the father. "Things will work

out. Before long I am to receive a small pension. After all, the land is my property. They won't take it away from me when I retire from the heavier work. I think the best thing for us to do is to make delivery to the government as required. Then no one can say anything against us. When we have done that, we'll place the acreage at the disposal of the state. Let them do what they like with it. My title is illegal anyway. The rightful owner was expropriated just as we were. We'll get through the winter all right. Then we'll see."

Franz went out and got to work sacking the rye and the potatoes and carting them off to the receiving station. This went on day after day, week after week, until most of the family's crop had been delivered to the authorities. The small barn behind the house looked sadly empty. The pitiful remnant of the grain harvest was heaped in one corner. The last of the pigs were driven from the pen. Franz reported to the local official, "Look here, Comrade Link, what about this? We can't deliver any beef, and we're short of milk too. I understand we can turn in pork instead, is that right?"

"That's right," Link replied, "equivalents can be substituted. We have a sort of conversion table. Go and speak to the secretary. He can make the changes in the list."

"Thanks," said Franz, thinking to himself: The devil takes their lists and requisitions. That evening, discouraged, he told his father how matters stood.

"So far, everything is taken care of," said Franz, as the two of them stood by the pasture fence. "We still have to deliver the last of the pigs, and then the show will be over. The pigs will make up for our deficit in beef and dairy products."

"All right," said the old man, indifferently. "We're going busted anyway, so the sooner the better."

"Don't worry, father," Franz tried to cheer him up. "We'll get away from here, and things will be better."

"Yes, you're still young," said the old man, "but when people have been knocked down and stepped on as my generation has been, they lose hope."

"Father!" said Franz in a shocked tone. "How can you talk like that? I've always known you as a firm and strong-willed man."

Twilight had overtaken them. The autumn wind rustled over the upturned potato field. In silence, the two watched a horse and foal grazing in the fading light. Golden-yellow leaves drifted down from the trees and were scattered over the pasture by the wind, giving it an appearance of rippling waters.

"That's life, my boy. It's late autumn. The death agony of nature has begun. Everything on earth must perish. Do you see that yellow leaf, up there?"

"Yes, I see it," Franz replied.

"I, too, shall soon leave the ranks of the living, in obedience to the law of nature." The old man was feeling a presentiment of death. The present was drab and cheerless, and the future looked very black. Franz tried to find words of encouragement.

"But just look how that colt has grown through the summer," Franz said. "It embodies the renewal of life, teaching us that we need not despair. Good will triumph at last over the evil in life. We must have faith that the good, the true and the beautiful will always be able to hold their own in the world. Looking at that colt, we can forget all our troubles. How did you manage to save the mare from the Cossacks?"

"Dumb animals are sometimes smarter than we think," his father replied. "When a soldier tried to lead her away, she roared up and came down with her forefeet on his head and shoulders, and he collapsed senseless in the stable doorway. I took the opportunity to get her into hiding. I've always loved those horses. Their spirit and endurance transferred themselves to me whenever I rode them. Now I can't protect them anymore. Death is the only thing left for them too."

"Oh, no," the son protested, "we can find them a good home somewhere around here. It would be too great a shame to destroy them."

"I couldn't do that," said Franz's father, "but I should hate to turn them over to the Communists."

"But that would be the best thing that could happen to them," said Franz. "They'd be well cared for. It would be better than seeing them hitched to the plow on some grain farm. I can speak to the manager of the stables. He'll take them in."

"That's all right, my boy," said his father. "All the same, they remind me of the old days--the whole world that is being so cruelly uprooted and destroyed. These two Arabian horses are all that is left of my life work. It seems impossible that it should all be over. Do you know what I mean?"

"Yes, I know only too well," Franz answered him, "but we are powerless against the events taking place about us, and condemned to silent obedience. Nevertheless, we are victorious--at least in the spirit of freedom. Stalin's empire, too, will begin to crumble. A state founded on terror and falsehood cannot survive the man who built it. We need not look far historically to see that. The recent fate of our own country confirms it. That is why liberty is more than a mere ideal to me. It will always be a wonderful to live as a free man in a free country."

Both were lost in thought for a time. "Let's go in," Franz's father suggested at last. "It's getting late." Franz agreed. His mother met them at the back door.

"A man was here from the town hall," she said. "The burgomaster and the political director want to talk to you. Perhaps you can go over tomorrow. It's too late tonight."

"Yes, I'll see what they want in the morning," said the father. "I wonder what it is this time?"

Father seems to be feeling better, Franz thought. He'll have a chance to rest up in the winter months.

The next morning Franz accompanied his father to the town hall. The required quotas had been delivered, so it was with comparative calm that the two entered the police head- quarters where the burgomaster had his office. The burgo- master, after a curt greeting, announced that the Kabel family would have to vacate their house in one week without fail and move at least fifty miles away.

"Who's responsible for this decision?" Franz inquired.

"It's an outrage!" Franz's father burst out.

"Calm yourself," said the burgomaster, coolly. "The action was taken by the district committee. The only appeal is to the district magistrate. I can tell you nothing. I am strictly an executive official, and have nothing to do with the substance of the order. My only suggestion is that you communicate with the magistrate."

"Thank you," replied the old man, and left the building, accompanied by his son.

"What does it mean?" asked Franz excitedly. "What reason can they have for dispossessing us without warning?"

"Oh, you know what people are like. Someone must have had a grudge against me and turned me in. It would have been enough to say I belonged to the camp of the reactionaries. This will make the second time I've been expelled. I'm already fifty miles away from my old place. How long can that go on? Life isn't worth living in this country any more. Your mother will be horrified. She's suffered enough already."

"But what are we going to do now?" Franz asked his father. "Aren't we at least going to try to get this straightened out?"

"Of course, we are," said the old man. "We'll go to the magistrate--that is, if he'll see us. That's all we can do."

Next day, Franz and his father boarded the train which carried them to the nearby town. They hurried to the office of the magistrate. The district magistrate had considerable authority in the Communist administration. He was not a mere underling. He had authority to make independent decisions within his sphere. He had more latitude of discretion than most of the petty functionaries in the all-powerful party organization.

The two men reached the district headquarters. It was a large, square brick building, covered on the outside with propaganda posters proclaiming the virtues of the regime. On demand of the police officer on duty, Franz and his father showed their papers. They were admitted to the waiting room.

"One moment, please," said the receptionist to the old man. "The Magistrate will see you in a few minutes. Kindly be seated."

"We can wait," Franz's father replied. They both sat down.

The Magistrate, whose name was Meier, happened to be a resident of this same town - contrary to the general rule. Franz's father had known him before the war. Most individuals occupying positions of prominence in East Germany in these unsettled postwar years were either Communists or former inmates of concentration camps. Many of the latter represented themselves as political prisoners when the Red Army released them, even if they were nothing of the kind. They simply seized the opportunity to fish in troubled waters. So, it was not uncommon, in the confusion that prevailed in Germany after 1945, for ex-criminals to turn into innocent victims of fascism and acquire all the privileges of citizenship. No one dared to say anything against them, as they had the complete backing of the Russians. As a result, large groups of the population often found themselves at the mercy of gangster officials. Comrade Meier was not one of that type, he was an honest German workingman and former democrat, very popular at least among the workers of the district. He acted as a brake on the headlong rush of the Bolshevik mob. Wherever revolutionary hotheads threatened to do irreparable damage, Meier's calm self-possession and sound common sense had their effect. In fact, by his superior character and politically blameless past, he gained the respect even of his many Russian colleagues, and he took great pains to deal with all disputed matters as humanely as possible. When necessary, Comrade Meier did not shrink from joining the Russians in their wild drinking bouts. The Russians, in turn, were deeply impressed with his capacities in that respect. No matter when a representative of the Russian command might choose to visit Comrade Meier's office, he was sure to find plenty of vodka at hand, and Comrade Meier was vigilant in seeing that the glasses were never empty. He gained considerable influence with the Russian military government. He was the kind of man the typical Russian understood and liked. Many Germans whom the Russians arrested summarily for a trifling offense were set free through the intercession of this official. Franz's father knew all this, so he had some hope of escaping from his difficulties through Comrade Meier's assistance.

The receptionist opened the door and invited the two men to enter. Father and son quickly rose and went into Meier's private office.

"Now, then," began the Magistrate cheerfully. "What's the trouble now? I haven't seen the delivery report. Just a moment."

He rapidly shuffled some papers.

"Well, I see your quotas have all been met. What brings you to my office?"

"Comrade Meier," Franz's father began, "I've been ordered

to get out, bag and baggage. This is the second time that has happened to me, I've put a lot of work into my new home, and I think somebody must have entered a false accusation against me."

"That's very strange," said Comrade Meier. "I know nothing about it. I wonder who signed the order? It must have been Otto. What do you suppose he had in mind?" He rang for the receptionist. "Young lady, please ask Comrade Lehmann to come in here a moment."

The man who had been summoned came in and was introduced as Comrade Otto Lehmann. The Magistrate then asked him whether it had been he who signed the eviction order.

"Yes," Lehmann replied animatedly. "I signed it on recommendation of the local political director. I acted in accordance with the law. The accused is a former militarist, and as such to be excluded from the community. So, I approved the recommendation and signed the order."

"Comrade Lehmann," said the Magistrate, "I see that your action was entirely correct in principle. But in this particular case I feel I should intervene. The accused has been evicted once before. In other words, he is already at a distance from his former sphere of activity. He has proved himself a useful member of society. He has regularly met his obligations, and never conducted himself in an improper manner. We must try to be reasonable. It will do no good to go off half-cooked. We shall make ourselves unpopular if we prosecute inoffensive citizens like criminals. I propose to cancel this order; I am not going to fall in with the envious machinations of some local functionary. Such ridiculous proceedings are injurious to the good name of socialism." Turning to Franz's father, he went on, "Comrade, I shall dictate a new order at once for the authorities in your village. The matter is closed. You may stay on."

Assured that there was no objection to their remaining in their present home, Franz's father thanked the Magistrate, and both the visitors departed, much relieved. At the door of the building, they reclaimed their papers from the policeman on duty.

Identification papers were needed everywhere in the Red empire. Anyone who ventured to move about without them, let alone to undertake a journey of any length, risked arrest as an agent of the western powers. Inquiries followed at leisure. Only when the accused was proved innocent would he be released. Franz had seen enough of this sort of thing in Russia.

Franz and his father recovered their papers without difficulty and were free to go their way. When they reached home again, the old man sat down, tired, on the sofa, and told his wife how he had got out of trouble again for the time being.

During the following days, whenever father or son met the local political director, they noticed that he seemed to be avoiding their gaze. Franz mentioned this to his mother.

"I don't see how it's possible for fellow Germans to lend themselves to such underhanded and despicable practices. I wouldn't have believed it. I saw something of betrayal among the German prisoners in Russia, too. One would denounce another as a Nazi, or militarist, or perhaps saboteur. The informers got better treatment from the Russians and all sorts of privileges. Prisoners lived in terror of the informer's displeasure. Now I see the same thing here at home. Are people like that everywhere, or only among Germans?" Franz went on to ask his mother.

"There are some people like that in every nation," his mother replied. "There is some bestiality and some envy in everyone. Hard times bring it to the surface. Many become ruthless and make their way over the dead bodies of their fellows. This is not peculiar to the Germans. When the Nazis overran Europe, Quislings were to be found everywhere, ready and willing to sell out their country's interests."

"On the other hand," said Franz, "there should be plenty of reasonable people among the Communists--men of education with whom one could arrive at an understanding. Even in a country under proletarian rule, there must be individuals of intellectual capacity far beyond that of a Party apparatchik. Could you imagine, for example, that a man like Goethe might arise in a Communist society?"

"That remains to be seen," said his mother. "According to what I understand, in the Soviet Union the monopoly on education so often denounced by the Communists has been broken. There certainly was such a monopoly on education under Czarist rule. But the new proletarian society needed scientists, and after the revolution in Russia that monopoly broke down of itself. No doubt the masses have been benefiting by this increasingly."

Franz felt inclined to disagree. "It would seem, though," he replied, "that present developments under Stalin have been approaching dangerously close to the educational situation under the czars. A new Stalinist elite has grown up in Russia, and occupies a privileged position in society. Much depends on one's father's occupation. It is generally admitted that the officials and the Heroes of Labor receive special preference so far as educational opportunities for their children are concerned, and that is very nearly the same thing as monopoly."

"Well, my son, I suppose that groups of that kind are continually being renewed and enlarged. I mean that the upper stratum is constantly recruiting new forces from deep within the Russian nation. The ablest of the workers are constantly selected and upgraded. I've read a good deal about socialist competition in Russia," Mrs. Kabel went on; "it is supposed to enable the women to take a hand in the economy. I should think that would add substantially to industrial production, wouldn't it?"

"Yes," said Franz, "and so it does. But just think, mother, you would practically be doing a man's work from morning to night. As an engineer, for example, you would be spending nine hours a day in the factory; or you might be working as a mason on construction jobs. That's what the Russians mean by equal rights. Lots of people think only of the positive aspects, and overlook the fact that the duties imposed on Russian women by their emancipation are out of all proportion to the rights allowed them."

"Don't you think the rights and duties of Russian women are fairly balanced?" his mother asked.

"Well, you would find out soon enough if you were a woman in Russia and taking part in the show. At first the only work Stalin expected from women was in typically male occupations. Quite a few Soviet women gained major reputations in scientific fields. But when he put Russian women into the armed forces, he may have overlooked the close connection between emancipation of women and the problem of population. In the English-speaking countries, of course, there are equal rights for women, too. But that's entirely different from what is meant by equal rights in the Soviet Union. In the western states, women received the same constitutional rights that men had, but they were not on that account thrown indiscriminately into the common labor market, like their Russian sisters.

"Then in a few years," Franz continued, "it turned out that the Stalinist emancipation policy had committed a fundamental error. The birth rate in the USSR was declining rapidly. The authorities finally noticed this. Thereupon the dictator instructed his propagandists that Soviet women were once more to be honored as mothers. As a special incentive, unusually prolific mothers were awarded the title of Heroine, or granted decorations, and held up as public examples of the ideal of Soviet womanhood. These measures may have helped solve the population problem in the USSR, but to Russian women they meant obligations heavier than ever. They had to be really adaptable to do heavy factory work and be mothers and homemakers at the same time. That is why many Russian women today live under a crushing burden of daily routine no better than slavery. How can a woman find time for study or cultural pursuits? Stalin was demanding too much. The hardiest people in the world couldn't have stood it."

"But one reads so much about day nurseries and government institutions to lighten the task of roaring and caring for children," said Mrs. Kabel.

"Yes, they exist all right," said Franz, "but what about the mothers who don't wish to have their children brought up on those principles?"

"All this is very interesting. You should talk it over some time with your old history teacher, Dr. Schmidt. I am sure he would be delighted. Perhaps we'll ask him to dinner someday soon," she suggested.

"That would be nice," Franz agreed.

CHAPTER VII

The political director's vicious attempt to destroy the home and livelihood of the Kabel family had been a severe blow to the old man. Franz took his place in settling with the burgomaster about the formalities involved in the transfer of title to the state. Towards the end of the winter, the condition of his father's health became very serious. He was admitted to the local hospital, and had to undergo a serious operation, which proved fatal. With the family breadwinner gone, Franz went into town and looked up his friend, Horst Altbauer, whom he found in the front yard of his home.

"Hello, Franz!" Horst called out. "What's new? Say, you aren't looking very cheerful!"

"Horst, I need some help." Then tonelessly, he said, "My father died yesterday."

"Oh, I'm sorry to hear that. What can I do?"

"Well, I suppose I'll have to get a coffin. I thought you might know of a place around here. Would you go with me and help me make the arrangements?"

"Why, of course. We'll go at once. That shouldn't be too difficult. Wait a minute and I'll get the car."

The two young men climbed into the car and drove to a coffin maker's shop on the other side of town. He told them he had several coffins ready. Franz asked about the kind of wood.

"Well, now," said the craftsman, in a businesslike tone, "we don't have much of a selection these days, young man. Those times are past. We used to have everything in stock from a plain board coffin to a lead casket. We had a particular clientele. I'm afraid all I can offer you now is ordinary pinewood."

"All right," said Franz, "we'll take one. Have you a man to go to the hospital with us and see about things?"

"Yes, certainly. That's included," said the coffin maker.

"How much is it?" Franz asked.

"Two hundred fifty marks," was the reply.

The bill was paid immediately. With the assistance of the man assigned to them, they loaded the coffin on the back of the little truck and drove off.

A few minutes later, the vehicle stopped in the driveway of the hospital. Franz got out and stated his business to the nurse on duty. She led the way to the mortuary, where Franz caught sight of his father's body. His heart contracted. The face was scarcely recognizable, and only the long, heavy hair looked real. He stood motionless for a while beside the remains. Tumultuous thoughts crowded in upon him. He considered the days when his father had coped so well with life's obstacles ... the two wars he had survived. And how much he had done for Franz. What pains he had taken about his son's upbringing. Very early he tried to pass on to his children a knowledge of the world, and protect them from the snares and pitfalls that beset man's path through life. He had taught them what road to travel that they might not perish in a heartless and inhospitable world.

Franz clearly remembered his dad's vigorous presence from his own childhood days, returning in dusty boots from the work in the fields to be welcomed by his last and youngest son. The elder three had already been lost, somewhere on the plains of the east. Their bones lay beneath the black Russian earth. How he must have felt when the last of his children, too, had disappeared without a trace. How much this man must have suffered and endured! Perhaps he had had an easy death. Perhaps it had been a release; a release to which he had looked forward with increasing eagerness as the tide of injustices and humiliations had risen to sweep away his life's work.

Not a few blameless men had chosen to take their own lives in similar circumstances, but that would have been contrary to his Christian philosophy. He held on to the end, and gained his reward, thought Franz sadly, looking at his father's pale and bloodless countenance. In his contemplation, he had not noticed that his friend Horst and the assistant were waiting impatiently for him to awaken from his reverie.

"I'm sorry, Horst," he apologized, "we'd better hurry."

"Well, I didn't want to interrupt," his friend replied.

"That's all right," said Franz. "Thanks."

Carefully the two boys dressed the dead man and laid him on a clean white cloth. They spread the shroud smooth beneath the body, took it by the corners and lowered it into the coffin. They covered the body, and the man from the shop nailed down the cover of the coffin professionally. Two sturdy orderlies carried the coffin outside and deposited their burden in the truck.

Horst took the wheel and drove back to the village with

Franz. The bereaved wife was waiting at home, and Franz and his friend spoke words of comfort to her. "Yes, his troubles are over," said Franz's mother. "Perhaps he will be reunited with his sons in the other world. Oh, when will it be my turn?"

"We must have courage, mother," Franz said, feeling himself gripped by a strange numbness and lassitude. He asked his friend Horst to stay for the funeral.

The last rites were very simple. The sorely tried widow and her son stood at the graveside. They said their last farewell to the dead. Horst and a few neighbors were the only other mourners. The pastor had ended his funeral sermon, in the course of which Franz had once more seen his father's life pass in review. Vague scenes and portraits of former days rose before his mind's eye.

How men had changed, and the times with them. In this old man, a representative of a past epoch seemed to have gone to his grave. But the words and spirit of his teaching had a permanent ethical value. Such things were of more than temporal significance. The minions of Bolshevism had perhaps laid waste the traditional home of such ideals. They had perhaps trampled earthly possessions and amenities underfoot, but the spirit of a free people they could never destroy. That spiritual inheritance would continue to be held in honor by future generations.

Franz was overwhelmed by the tumult of his thoughts.

What had these satanic forces done to his country? They had not only done physical and material harm. That would have been tolerable; but they had tried to kill the spirit of the people. They had not yet quite succeeded. But a third of the land was in their power. By their fiendish methods of reeducation, they were trying to bend the youth of the country to their false and inhuman purposes. If only the majority in the west knew how serious the threat to their democracy, their freedom and their way of life really was. They would be profoundly shocked, and would turn aside from the luxuries of life, willing to make any sacrifice in order to avert this terrible danger.

This is not the time for such reflections, thought Franz, struggling with the misgivings that rose at times in his own breast against his hatred for the totalitarian regime.

How was it possible for the most precious creature on earth, for man, for all things human, to be thrust into the background and ignored, for the sake of an all-embracing materialism, with no living content but quotas, plans, machines and production. These things were the idols set up by the Bolshevik to be worshiped by contemporary mankind. This materialistic world had no room left for the free development of the individual.

Submergence of the individual was a threat in the western democracies too; but there, people had thus far preserved liberty and a free way of life. So long as these values remained realities and did not degenerate into empty phrases, the world might still have faith in a free future for humanity.

His mother's touch wakened Franz from his meditations and brought him back to actuality.

As they walked homeward, Franz said to his mother, "I'm going to go to work in town as soon as I can. I wouldn't know what to do with myself all day here. I need to keep occupied. The foreman at the machine shop told me the other day that there was an opening."

"You must do as you think best," said his mother. "You're old enough to make your own decisions."

Next morning, Franz took the train again. He went straight to the repair shop and reported to the foreman. He was put to work at once. He enjoyed it. All mental anguish seemed automatically suppressed. Franz had deliberately subjected himself to this sudden change. Fresh from the farm, he threw himself into the machinery of the Communist industrial process. That evening, tired out, he rode back home to the village.

There were about two hundred people employed in the shop. Diesel engines were dismantled, overhauled and reinstalled in trucks and tractors. There were about twenty other apprentices. Most of the men were industrious German workers, little interested in Communist politics. They were content to be able to follow their regular trade. Everyone was required to be a member of the central state labor union. The apprentices belonged to a junior auxiliary. Franz was hardened to the annoyances of over-organization. He took pleasure in his work, and was generally assigned as helper to one of the journeymen. He was moved around fairly often. The foreman would give him first one assignment and then another, so that he would learn all of the jobs as soon as possible. In rest periods, when the workers would sometimes discuss political questions of the day, Franz held himself aloof and pretended to be a complete ignoramus in such matters. He noticed, though, that most of the men were extremely unfriendly towards the practices of the regime. Franz occasionally worked with mechanics who had spent some time in Russian captivity. They told of the primitive conditions in which the majority of workers in the Soviet Union were still languishing, despite propaganda boasts of progress. Franz knew nothing of all this himself, or rather, he knew only too well that it was best to seem to know nothing. As a beginning apprentice, he was kept busy familiarizing himself with the details of construction and operation of diesel engines, having had no previous experience in this field. When he reached home at night after nine hours of hard physical labor, he was tired enough. But his new interests confronted him with new problems for solution every day. In time, his sorrow at his father's sudden death became less bitter. The work had helped him to forget and master his grief.

Once a week he was required to attend the shop school. In addition to vocational subjects, there was a good deal of political instruction. What was meant by political instruction under the Bolsheviks was simply Soviet indoctrination. On every day when school was held, a representative from the German-Soviet Friendship organization would appear to discuss current political and economic questions with the students. Representatives of Soviet youth organizations came, too, and tried to recruit the boys into these mass movements. As a rule, some functionary would give the apprentices a talk on the aims and objectives of the five-year plans in the countries of the people's democracies. In all their remarks, the speakers strongly emphasized that to a class-conscious worker, no other orientation was possible. Franz listened in patient amazement. He was especially interested by the motion pictures which the Friendship organization people would exhibit. These showed nothing of the vast wastes of the Russian landscape. The young people were shown the palaces of the land of Communism. For example, they saw impressive views of the Moscow subway, cathedrals, amphitheaters, and beautiful scenery of the Crimea and the Caucasus. Usually the motion-picture shows were followed by lengthy discussions. These were a systematic incitement to class struggle and an invitation to accept Stalin as a demigod. On the other hand, however, Franz noticed that the educators sometimes had a pretty hard time of it. Many of the boys were reluctant to be convinced. Clearly, some of their homes were still ruled by the spirit of tradition, and this often made it very difficult for the Bolsheviks. A typical representative of the new Red youth intelligentsia was a young party functionary whom Franz and his fellow workers knew as Anton Wolf.

Anton Wolf was perhaps thirty years old. He had been a prisoner of war in Russia, and years of intensive training had made him a confirmed Bolshevik. His position as an organizer carried a very good salary. He had a new car and lived in a neat cottage outside of town. Comrade Wolf had got hold of the property through his Russian connections.

In any country with a dictatorial form of government, it had always been necessary for the all-powerful one to recruit and develop his praetorian guard for the purpose of maintaining his authority in every town and province. Most people in the East and Central European countries had not realized what the political course mapped out for them by their leaders would be after the Red Army marched in. They had a completely false conception of Communism and Bolshevism. Many thought in terms of some sort of leveling of all classes and individuals. But even in the foremost Communist country, the Soviet Union, great changes had been taking place in this respect ever since the beginning of the proletarian revolution. But the stormy events that had taken place there in the past thirty years were quite unknown to the majority of those who now suddenly fell into Stalin's hands as defenseless victims. Nor could the ordinary citizen have been blamed for this, for people had been too busy with their own troubles during that period to have taken a lively interest in foreign politics.

This had been especially true in National-Socialist Germany, where the people were caught in a political squirrel cage that kept them oblivious to developments abroad. Furthermore, Germans had no public opportunity to interest themselves in any other ideology than the Nazi one in any way. So, it was not surprising that, in 1945, most people were quite unaware that Russian Communism had changed since Lenin's death into a battlefield of power-hungry party leaders. When finally, Stalin emerged victorious from among the rival camps, the whole country lay prostrate, terribly weakened by a world war, two revolutions - the bourgeois March Revolution under Kerensky and the Bolshevik Revolution in October of the same year - and the ensuing civil war and political struggles for power.

When Stalin had sufficiently consolidated his power, he was able to devote his energies to the practical realization of his ideas. Any other nation would have been reduced to despair and dispatched its cruel dictator in short order. But in the Soviet Union, Stalin pointed the new political direction at once, with epoch-making effect. Leaders of all Communist parties abroad were obliged to submit to him. Stalin regarded struggle as the progenitor of all things. Back in 1905, he had played a prominent part in the revolution against the Czar, as also in the socialist revolution of 1917. He had known hardship and privation in the czarist dungeons. He ruthlessly used his years of experience in illegal party activity against his adversaries. Thus, bred in perpetual struggle, he gave his enemies no quarter. He had no use for the conciliatory policies of the right-wing Social Democrats, whom he opposed no less bitterly than he had the representatives of czarist feudalism before the revolution. With all his cruel methods, Stalin was a man possessed of far more than average human energy. He had the iron will for extraordinary achievement and accomplishment. To build an empire was the greatest and most magnificent of human undertakings. He mastered unusual situations by unusual means. He placed enormous demands upon the Russian people. The exploited masses, exhausted by war and famine, were called upon to transform the condition of society in the largest country of the world at an unparalleled rate under his lash. But this was not all. The economy was also to be radically changed, though in this sphere Stalin only partially achieved his goal. He was so fortunate as to be able to carry out his plans, by methods of brutal violence, among the urban population of Russia, but even he was frustrated by the stubbornness of the Russian peasant. True to the teaching of Karl Marx, Stalin undertook to revolutionize social relations in the Russian villages. The great feudal lords had been expelled immediately after the revolution, but there remained a multitude of large and medium-size peasant holdings. The state of affairs was anything but that of a classless society. Yet Stalin's aim was to abolish the contradiction between town and country. He intended to create a perfectly gray and uniform mass. To do this, he had to eliminate private economy completely from Russian agriculture. This was the reason for Stalin's immense economic experiments in collectivization of the Russian peasants. The richest peasants were systematically liquidated by simply requiring them to furnish such quantities of agricultural products as they could not possibly deliver. The regime counted upon their inevitable failure. The proprietors were imprisoned or simply driven off the land. This was leveling by sheer coercion. "Grain factories" resulted. But the stubborn self-will of the peasants did not allow them to be converted into farm proletarians so easily. A police apparatus, carrying out one wave of arrests after another, was necessary in order to break down the open resistance of the Russian peasants at last. Collective farms were successfully administered by managers and agronomists, the workers performed their appointed tasks just as they were obliged to do in city factories, and wages were paid in the form of money or agricultural products. But such changes, destroying a centuries-old economic system virtually overnight and substituting something unprecedented and ultra-modern, necessarily had their drastic consequences. These took the form of famines, in which many thousands perished. The whole job was done too quickly. The war years through which the Soviet state had passed prior to these reforms had sapped social and individual morale to the uttermost. But Stalin pushed his program through regardless. He promised no rosy future to his own generation. He was too great a revolutionary for that. Lash in hand, he dared to require the rising generation of Russia to sacrifice its own well-being on the altar of the Soviet fatherland. Anyone who supposed that a fair division of consumer goods, with the aid of accelerated production, would soon meet the human and material needs of the Russian masses, was much mistaken. Despite his complete subjugation of Russia, Stalin never dreamed of satisfying the human wishes of his subjects. He intended to create a world power. For this he needed a strong army and a powerful heavy industry to supply it with modern weapons. He smashed all opposition. Enormous concentration camps appeared in the vastness of Russia, in the arctic territories and in the warm regions of the Asiatic steppes. These convict armies, millions strong, provided the state with a reservoir of cheap slave labor to count upon in planning. Stalin needed such armies to carry out his ambitious program. They built the canals, they planted timber bolts in the steppes, they labored to develop the barren areas of Russia. Thousands might perish, but all that mattered was that the plans should be fulfilled. The victims were in any case enemies of the regime and deserved no better. Thus, Stalin and his police system were killing two birds with one stone. All forces of opposition were found out and tracked down by informers and secret agents, and at the same time the victims were an inexpensive means of carrying out economic programs.

One might have thought that mankind could dispense with such systems of government in the twentieth century. In fact, the Russian people could have been governed otherwise, and would have been much better off under some other system, whether capitalist or socialist. Above all, however, the Russian people yearned for humane treatment. They, too, hated such barbarous and medieval exercise of governmental power. It was only their inexhaustible patience that had enabled Stalin to succeed to such an extent. No other European people would have been capable of so much endurance and self-sacrifice in the first place.

But there is a limit to even the greatest patience. The history of the two Russian revolutions of 1917 plainly showed the world what a grim reckoning the Russians can exact of their tormentors. Fury, long pent-up, had been discharged and expressed itself in the wildest excesses. Modern dictators should have learned from history and drawn the proper conclusions, but people seem to learn little from the past, and commit the same errors again and again. It is conceivable that the slaves who built the Pyramids for the pharaohs were no worse than the captives in concentration camps under modern dictators; but after thousands of years of progress in technology and civilization, the great powers should be ready to rule by persuasion instead of violence and coercion.

The Communists never tired of advertising that they were working for human progress and happiness. But Stalin meant this in an extramundane sense. He was developing an antihuman, abstract communism, not geared to the spiritual and material interests of his subjects. The Stalinist period in Russia was one of petrifaction and dehumanization. This was the tremendous sacrifice demanded of the people. The dictator did indeed, by these methods, make the Soviet Union into the strongest military power on earth, and the greatest world power of all next to the United States. But what did he make of the Russian people in the process? One could not help wondering whether Stalin's disciples, the inheritors of his policy, would succeed in continuing on this road, which led only to conquest of a position of absolute world power. Or would they be content to hold the territories gained by their master?

If the Soviet Union should be governed in the future by men less firm and resolute than Stalin, it might be assumed that world Communism had reached its zenith. The point is that Stalin's successors would not have only external fees to deal with; the entire world picture had shifted since World War II, and the constellation within the Communist world had changed basically, too. Not only had the East European satellite countries been added to the Soviet Union, but the center of decisive events had shifted to Asia. What had occurred in Russia in 1917 was happening in Asia in 1949--the victory of Communism in China, the most populous country on earth. Would Stalin's successors ultimately be able to maintain their primacy over the Chinese? Would that nation, three times as numerous as that of Soviet Russia, continue its adherence to the Moscow party line, which would dictate to them how Communism was to be attained?

The example of Tito was significant. Here, in his former pupil, Stalin had found a grim political antagonist who successfully withstood the whole of world Communism and went his own way independent of Moscow over lordship. Even an autocrat such as Stalin had not ventured to take military action against the dissident Tito and crush him. Stalin, no doubt, was unwilling to commit himself to that extent. His status in international politics had suffered considerably as it was.

While the Russians were exploiting the satellite countries

more thoroughly than feudal barons their domains, Stalin was trying to create a worldwide impression that his East European allies were true sovereign states whose governments really represented the will of their peoples. His propagandists repeatedly proclaimed the free and equal status of these puppet states. Tito demonstrated to the world the meaning of true freedom and independence of Moscow.

Ostracism was the strongest measure the Russians could bring against him. Why have they been behaving more respectfully and cautiously towards other nations in recent years? Have they given up their plans for world revolution? They have no such intention. If, since Stalin's blunders in Berlin and in Korea, they have followed a more careful policy, Pravda has not, therefore, ceased its barrage of invective against western imperialism.

The Soviets had clearly recognized that the international balance of power did not merely consist of a Communist eastern bloc and a capitalist western bloc; they were perfectly aware that the calculation of forces involved a third quantity, the majority of peoples of Africa and Asia, many of whom had succeeded in winning complete independence from their colonial masters after World War II. The most notable examples were India and Indonesia. Here the Soviets saw their big opportunity. They had no fear that these nations would join in military alliances with their former rulers under NATO (North Atlantic Treaty Organization) or SEATO (Southeast Asia Treaty Organization), and they felt that Russia would be the logical source of economic aid to these underdeveloped countries. The Soviet Union was able to do this because it was free from any onus insofar as the former colonial peoples were concerned. The latter seemed to provide an ideal soil for Communism to take root.

There had been many who believed that the Communists would never succeed in gaining a foothold in such countries as India or Thailand, because the inhabitants were so much in the grip of religion that the Kremlin ideologists would be unable to convince them of the truth of their doctrine.

But now the revolution in China, as had been the case in Russia, demonstrated that even deeply religious peoples could be swayed by Marxist materialism to the point of accepting the concept of the socialist state notwithstanding ideological difficulties. Certainly, the Communists in each instance selected the right moment in history in which to fight their decisive battles. Revolutions of such tremendous scope were carried out either in the confusion of war, or in the misery of postwar periods. It was obvious that the propagandists needed the support of the masses if they were to effectuate their plans and then seize the reins of power, but they could influence the people in abnormal times only. In wartime, hunger and discontent ripened increasingly among the belligerent populations. Without such a situation, the Bolsheviks could never have accomplished their revolution in Russia. Now, in the newly freed underprivileged countries, international Communism saw its great opportunity to intervene and hoist its victorious banners over new subcontinents. They did this not by military might alone but by economic expansion, dangerously threatening the American program of aid to underdeveloped areas.

Superficial thinkers might have asserted that the Americans need not fear such competition, that the Soviets did not even have enough food and goods for their own people, hence they could never become serious competitors of America in the world markets. They failed to take into consideration that the Soviets had forced a low standard of living upon their own masses, thus enabling them to build up an enormous heavy industry, through which they could export large shipments of munitions and other capital goods. The Russians, with a definite objective in mind, did not hesitate to underbid world prices in the hope that the countries in urgent need of basic materials would be won to their side. If these ends were to be achieved, it would be at the cost of Russian workers who would labor and starve for these ends. Now that the world revolutionaries in the Kremlin have gained a measure of power in international affairs, it means that the free peoples are in great danger.

The specter of the Yellow Peril, so vividly placed before the peoples by General Ludendorff, seemed to take shape and assume a grim reality. The worst danger consisted in the fact that such giant governmental structures were always directed by a dictatorial group immune to any international restraint. This group might at any time make decisions that would radically change the shape of the world overnight. It was subject to no control by the governed, and accountable to no one, unlike the elected leaders of the free western democracies.

In the United States and in Great Britain, the governments could not have unleashed a preventive war because the voters, through their representatives in Congress and in Parliament, would not have permitted such action. In those countries, the people were intent on enjoying a high standard of living. Responsible statesmen in the western world spent most of their time trying to explain to their constituencies that defense taxes were a necessary evil--necessary if they were not to risk being overrun by the Soviets. To obtain the necessary funds for this purpose, the democratic governments were obliged to engage in time-consuming debates with the opposition parties even after they had patiently explained matters to the electorate.

In the Soviet Union, such obstacles did not exist. There, the leaders soberly examined the world situation, dispassionately weighed the pros and cons of any measure, and acted accordingly. Such a dictatorial system was more flexible in action than a cumbersome government apparatus conducted by the methods of democratic procedure. It was not without reason that the ancient Romans, in critical times, would choose an exceptionally valorous and experienced citizen as dictator for a limited period. Though they were republicans from deepest conviction, they did not hesitate when necessary, to adopt every possible means of achieving victory. In our vaunted modern world, statesmen have had no choice but to observe the lessons of history and obey the precept _si vis_

<u>pacem para bellum</u>. If you would have peace, prepare for war. This issue was imperative, namely, whether humanity was to learn anything at all from history. If the two aggregations of power persisted in the arms race with their superweapons of mass annihilation, the nations of the world would drift towards certain catastrophe. It needed no prophet or pessimist to foresee such an eventuality. But whose was the primary responsibility? How could this grave dilemma be resolved?

Chapter VIII

When the Allied Powers had smashed Nazism in the year 1945, Stalin thought the moment had come to deal the death-blow to what remained of the capitalist system in Europe. The Americans, on the other hand, took things easy, and imagined that with the downfall of fascism, most evils had been banished from the earth. They concentrated all their energies on reconversion, though some experts warned against trusting the promises Stalin had made to America during the war.

The coups d'état staged by the Russians, as directors behind the political scene, showed even the most skeptical that the Soviets were serious about their plans for world conquest, as the warning voices had prophesied. When least expected, they launched their political offensive on the rest of Europe, though the military shocks had only recently been absorbed by the sorely tried western nations. The act of political violence so skillfully put on by the Soviets in Czechoslovakia was to be the dress rehearsal for their last great push against Central Europe. Stalin had clearly seen that 1945 opened the most favorable period for Russia to take the political offensive.

Meanwhile, Soviet diplomacy was going full steam ahead. The Americans tried everything to induce the Russians to withdraw from Germany and Europe. The first civilian soldiers were already marching in the Eastern Zone. True, in outward appearance this militia strongly resembled a police force, but the initiated know that in event of withdrawal of the Americans and the British from western Germany, the units would be used for Stalin's plans of European conquest.

At that time, the Soviets were still agreeable to a reunification of Germany under guarantees of neutrality. Thus, the defenseless western remnant of Germany would be at the mercy of Stalin's civilian army. Had the Soviets succeeded in carrying out this intention, probably the whole continent of Europe would have been a windfall for Bolshevism. What prevented this was NATO. The Communist parties of France and Italy would have made a decisive contribution. Such a development was frustrated primarily by the prompt and resolute action of American foreign policy, demonstrating by such examples as the Marshall Plan and the Berlin air lift that America was determined to oppose Stalin's expansionism. People in Western Europe were realizing with increasing clarity the true character of the Communist democracies. The persecutions and purges carried out by Stalin in the countries of Eastern Europe were warnings to those in the free world who still believed that indigenous Communist movements could come into being independently of Moscow leadership.

The unique example of Tito showed that such tightrope-walking, if possible, at all, involved terrible risks. For in every Communist country there was a group of jealous Stalinists to see that their hero's wishes were enforced. An army of trained propagandists kept drumming their ideas into the heads of the masses. With monotonous repetition, they hammered their political phrases into men's brains. The special objects of their attack were the youth, who were to be imbued with mass thinking. Through them the Bolsheviks hoped to conquer the future.

It should be remembered that Franz had become aware of the German-Soviet Friendship Organization and its party functionary, Anton Wolf, the day he had first gone to the School for Apprentices. In addition to the "educational" talk by Wolf, the organizer also exhibited a slide film on the cities and regions of the USSR. After he had finished with the slides, he read a few paragraphs from Stalin's book, <u>The History of the Communist Party of the Soviet Union</u>. Then Comrade Wolf proceeded to deliver a pep talk to the apprentices from the shop.

"Young men, my friends," he began, ingratiatingly, "why have I shown you all this, and why do we now proceed to discuss this subject? It is because we should become better acquainted with that glorious people, our neighbors. True friendship includes mutual respect and understanding. Such is the purpose of the Soviet Union. It restores our independence. It assists us in building a Communist state, and in smashing the capitalist enemies of our people. For we must not fail to construct a socialist society. In this we can be sure of the support of the Soviet Union. Its ways are a guiding example to us. But here in Germany, it is difficult to pursue a true socialist policy of international friendship except in the Soviet Zone, because in the western part of our land, a reactionary and capitalistic policy is being fostered. Such a policy can only be harmful to our people because it leads to seizure of power by the militarists and fascists. But on our side, and that of the Soviet Union, stand the great peace movements throughout the world. They are in accord with us, and working for the same ends. Anyone who still rebels against the Soviet Union does not deserve to live in our society and enjoy the material advantages our system offers him. Hence, when you join in German-Soviet Friendship activity you demonstrate that you are a true socialist. Are there any questions on this topic? Speak your minds freely." Then Comrade Wolf concluded: "I am here to help you in every possible way."

Franz waited for the discussion to get started. Several boys raised their hands. One asked:

"Are there ties of Soviet friendship with the German people only, or with other nations also?"

The agitator replied, "The Soviet Union has friends everywhere. There is an overall organization which concerns itself with details of administration and propaganda."

Another young man asked, "My father is still being held in Russia as a prisoner of war, so how can I be friends with the Soviets?"

"It is the fault of the fascists that your father is there," Wolf answered. "In joining our Friendship organization, you will be doing your share to prevent a repetition of such catastrophes."

"But it seems to me," the questioner persisted, "that in their invasion, the Russians behaved in such a manner as not to merit our respect, let alone our friendship."

"By talking like that, you only help our enemies," said Anton.

"I don't care," the boy replied, excitedly. "Facts are facts. I will not join your organization."

Franz raised his hand and was recognized.

"You mentioned," he said, "that the Soviet Union was going to restore our full sovereignty. I think that's a lie. Why are we not allowed freely to elect our government, as is our right? Why do you want to force an alien way of life upon us, unsuited to the character of our nation?" He continued, "What excuse do you have for liquidating socialists and capitalists who take a position against the Moscow policy of coercion? Why do you conduct big sham trials in the states of the eastern bloc, with democrats and anti-fascists as victims, people who enjoy great popularity in their own countries and on the international level? I can imagine why you do this. These people are hounded because, on orders from Moscow, the opposition in the people's democracies is to be crushed and the capitalists eliminated rather than permit any progress towards socialism independently of Moscow. These dissenters are blamed for the mistakes that have been made. Then," said Franz, "it is easy to accuse these helpless people of espionage and sabotage. I would never join your organization," he concluded.

Comrade Wolf seemed to hesitate. It was too much. What Franz had said was close to a public indictment of the regime. The official's voice trembled with anger. Wolf turned and addressed himself to Franz:

"How dare you talk such rot about the aims of the Soviet Party? You're much too young, ignorant and inexperienced to evaluate the situation. If you don't mend your ways, I warn you, we will deal with you as you deserve."

There was a roar of protest, and the director of the school looked in to see what the trouble was.

"What's going on here?" he demanded. "Can't you conduct your discussion in a disciplined manner?"

When order was restored, another of the boys took up the debate.

"So, this is what you mean by freedom and democracy. You must have it all your own way. And if anyone speaks the truth, you call him a fascist or an ignoramus. Fellows," he turned to the others, "are we going to stand for this?"

"No! Never! Throw him out!" the boys chorused.

Despite a warning, there was more disorder. Wolf tried to say something, but the apprentices drowned him out. Shaking his head, he left the room with a parting remark: "Other methods will be tried on you. You're nothing but a bunch of fascists!"

"Get going. We don't want you," the apprentices shouted as the door closed after him. In a moment the director of the school entered. Silence fell.

"This is disgraceful," he exclaimed. "Have you taken leave of your senses? Don't you realize that Wolf will incite the city government, the party and the police against us? As director, I'm responsible for your behavior. Do you want to get me into trouble by your hot-headed and thoughtless conduct?"

"No, of course we don't," the boys answered.

One of the apprentices spoke: "Well, what should we have done when Wolf tore into us like that?" he asked. "Are we supposed to sit here and listen to that stuff? We tried to tell

him what we thought in a quiet manner, but he got excited
and called us fascist provocateurs."

"That's all very well," the director retorted, "but you must
realize that we lost the war and have to take orders from the
Russians. Be very careful of what you say. This will have to
be made clear to you in political indoctrination. I should like
to get the whole thing settled without any Russians or the
police interfering. When the youngsters reported to school
the following week, they found that a new director had been
appointed. He began talking to them quite grimly:

"What got into you boys last week, anyway? You're living
under Soviet protection and enjoying its advantages. After all,
this is the first time that we have been free of exploitation by
monopoly capital. Don't you realize that? If there were no
Soviet soldiers here, we would fall prey to exploitation again.
Have you no class consciousness at all?"

One of the boys raised his hand.

"Well, what is it?"

"I think we shouldn't be forced to be friends of the Soviet
Union by high-pressure propaganda," said the apprentice.
"Why can't you convince by sound logic that you're right? If
you do, we'll support you. But if we're not convinced, then

how can we agree? You just said that if it weren't for the Russians, we would be exploited by the monopoly capitalists."

"Yes," the director replied.

"But how do you know that the Russians have our national interests at heart? Perhaps we prefer the system they have in West Germany? Forced friendship is worse than none," the boy concluded.

"Have you lost your mind? Don't you see you're working against your own interests?"

"Seeing is believing," a red-headed apprentice answered back; then he asked the Director: "Were you ever in West Berlin? Did you see the shop windows? People can buy anything they need, and the prices are nowhere nearly as high as in our state stores. There is more of a feeling of happiness and freedom there than here. I know some people there myself. And you try to tell us that they are being exploited, and that our life is heaven compared to theirs? I'm sorry, but we can't swallow such hypocrisy."

The youngster sat down and looked around. He felt that he had made his point. The class waited anxiously to hear what the new director would say to him. Within a few moments he proceeded, with logic, to reply to the apprentice's accusations.

"You are too young, my boy, to form an opinion. You are permitting yourself to be misled by the superficial impressions you have formed about West Berlin. In that sector, thousand are unemployed, and desperately in need. And why do you think the West Germans have an abundance of merchandise? They are not getting it for nothing. They will pay for it by sacrificing their national independence. In short," he emphasized by tapping his fingers, "the West Germans are being intensively Americanized. Possibly, under Adenauer," he continued, "they will someday be used as shock troops against East Germany. That is the price the West Germans must pay for their new American way of life. We Communists are against this; we are struggling to defend and preserve our national interests. That is why we in the eastern part of this country have rejected the Marshall Plan."

"That's very clever," said Franz, slowly rising from his seat, "but you have not convinced us. Why do you reject West German policy? Do you actually believe that we would be better off if we went along with the Russians? They've taken much from us, and given practically nothing in return. And you want us to believe that they are our best friends. Of course," Franz went on, "we lost the war. But what is the lesser evil--the predicament we are in or Russian domination? It's impossible to believe that the lesser evil is the Russians, although they pretend that they want to establish our national independence together with democratic freedoms. I think," Franz emphasized, "they want to use us for their political purposes."

"That's true," several apprentices exclaimed. "They are using us shamelessly, and want us to believe that they are offering us real friendship. That's the biggest joke yet."

The bell rang, which meant that the discussion period was over.

Week after week, training at the shop school became increasingly intensified. The Communists were trying very hard to indoctrinate the young people of the district because they believed they were pliable enough to accept Communist ideas. However, they were not sure of the experienced older generation whose minds could not so easily be changed. In addition, political agitators became increasingly active in the state enterprises. Even after quitting time, they pressured the people to attend political meetings. Too frequent absences from these meetings was likely to be interpreted as lack of sympathy with the regime.

Every person in a factory was a statistical entity. The political interests of every employee were constantly being investigated by special government agencies. An army of officials served the authorities by checking up on everyone's thoughts and utterances. The value of a person in the Red empire was always judged by his political activity. An official or technician might be an expert in his field, but if he was not schooled in the Marxist and Stalinist theories it was impossible for him to advance economically. Neutralists, as they were called, were, in some degree, aiding the enemy by failing to participate actively in the building of a new society.

For two years Franz worked in the engine repair shop; one more year and his apprenticeship would be completed. He was obliged to probe deeply into the intricacies of Communist theory. The political director of the shop had observed how Franz resisted theoretical indoctrination in Marxism-Leninism-Stalinism, hence he personally drilled him in ideological exercises. However, Franz had somehow avoided having to join a Communist mass organization, his excuse being that with his keen interest in athletics, it was necessary for him to practice steadily to be prepared for participation in the forthcoming competitive games.

Through this interest, Franz came into contact with athletes from Russia and the eastern European countries, exchanges which were financed by the government. The Russians realized that sports were an excellent means of utilizing the younger men for military and political purposes. For Franz, they seemed the only means of forestalling his decision to become a member of a Communist organization or not. Once he had been accepted for an industrial occupation, he felt he would know what to do next. With this in mind he continued to postpone his declaration of joining the party despite constant pressure from the political director.

The strain on Franz became nerve-racking for the director would repeatedly ask Franz:

"Why aren't you an active member of our political group?"

"I am bearing it in mind," he would reply. "I still have a great deal to learn. Besides, I have to pass my journeyman's examination, and I have a lot of work to do on our sport club's newspaper. These things," he added, "are keeping me very busy."

"Yes, I know," the director would reply, "but do not delay much longer. Remember, one must, without undue delay, declare what side he is on."

"Oh, I'll make the correct decision, all right. You can be sure of that. But before a person joins the organization," said Franz, "he should have developed intellectual maturity." So, Stalin's zealous young director had to be satisfied with Franz's excuses for the time being.

Despite his important and well-paid position, the director was in constant fear of his life, for he could be a victim of the next big purge, which might be initiated by Stalin without notice. If this happened, many old-time party stalwarts would be among the victims, for they looked the lightning-like reactions essential to escape the bloody attacks of the suspicious pioneers. Every little despot was obsessed by a deep-seated fear of liquidation, a powerful motivating force which prevented the dictatorship from disintegrating.

Befitting a powerful totalitarian state, the Soviets had begun to exploit the cult of personality. The Russians had learned this lesson quickly, as the time interval between the people's former deification of the czars and their present exaltation of Stalin was comparatively very short. Under the Russian yoke the masses were forced to adopt this ludicrous idolatry. A typical example was the spectacle of Stalin's birthday celebration. An impartial observer might have doubted that he was in the twentieth century, instead of imagining that he was witnessing a provincial town festival under one of the Roman emperors. Such a parallel would surely occur to anyone who was familiar with the works of Pliny, Cicero or Tacitus.

In the government-owned diesel repair shop where Franz worked, feverish preparations were under way for the Stalin observances. The workers tore down the old streamers which were not militant enough for this occasion. All the sign painters in town were working overtime lettering new slogans honoring the glorious career of the Red dictator.

An enormous portrait of Stalin was placed at the entrance to the plant. Above it was the inscription:

> WE THANK STALIN, THE LEADER
> OF THE CAUSE FOR WORLD PEACE,
> FOR HIS GENEROUS AID

Heads of important committees were busily engaged in giving instructions. The Comrade Director had almost completed a speech which he intended to deliver to the shop employees previous to their attending the political demonstration that evening.

"Comrades," cried a lively, bouncy leader who was in charge of the contingent, "we will fall in here in four ranks and march in close order to the courtyard. There we will join the main detachment. Otto and Rudi, you will carry our standard."

The young workers lined up obediently. The leader took up his position at their head. The unit reached the factory yard and found its place in the waiting column.

The plant superintendent was standing on the platform like a general, reviewing the disciplined ranks. Franz and his friends were kept waiting another hour before the army of workers had been properly assembled, and they were getting restless.

"Gustav, you big ox, you've got more strength than I have. Why don't you take this thing for a while?" demanded the young fellow with the red flag.

"I'll do that just for you," replied the other, and grasped the big pole in his powerful fists.

"Pfui!" muttered Franz. "This is just like the army. Hurry up and wait."

A murmur of protest went through the ranks of workers.

"Shut up!" the agitator called out hastily.

At last the superintendent began to speak. The platform had been adorned with a red banner displaying a large portrait of the hero of the day. Plant guards had taken up positions flanking the platform.

"Comrades, friends, fellow workers," the speaker began, "today the working class of the whole world is celebrating the birthday of its heroic leader. We will not be behind others in this celebration, and will demonstrate by our conduct that we know the true significance of this occasion."

He paused briefly. "Stalin is the Lenin of our generation. May his indomitable spirit and youthful strength long be preserved to us, that he may continue to lead us through the confusions of the time towards our common goal. In honor of Comrade Stalin, let us pledge ourselves to work a special ten-hour shift next Sunday. Comrades, I ask your concurrence."

The political director and some of the workers began to clap vigorously, and the whole force joined in the applause as one man. Anyone who dissented at such a climactic moment would have signed his death warrant. The clapping seemed to be expressing the impotent rage of a people forced to accept this indignity. Gradually the ovation subsided.

"Thank you, comrades." The superintendent went on: "I

am happy to announce that the employees of this plant have unanimously adopted the Sunday work proposal."

The superintendent gave his lieutenants their marching orders, and the mass set itself in motion. The Heroes of Labor and the activists of the plant were in the front as they marched, with the band following them. Now the head of the column had reached the reviewing stand. On either side of the rostrum there were grandstands occupied by local representatives of Soviet military commands. Divisions of workers were marching upon this point from all over town. Having arrived in the square, the processions were deemed up by the crowd, so that all traffic came to a stop.

Representatives of mass organizations delivered inflammatory speeches against the western powers at street corners. Worker delegates from various contingents telegraphed greetings to Comrade Stalin. Voluntary pledges by shops and factories flew like hailstones. Everything was well organized and went off without a hitch. In the evening there was a tremendous display of fireworks. Somewhere in the distance, a carillon was heard intoning the Internationals. And then followed the Soviet national anthem. A garishly lighted picture of Stalin stood in the market-place. The size

of this portrait was overpowering. Just before the great occasion, special rations of meat and liquor had been issued. The
Red leader's functionaries governed on the same principles as
the provincial proconsuls of ancient Rome. They knew that
the strategy of divide and rule had not been improved upon
down through the centuries, and giving the people bread and
circuses was being emulated by Stalin's chieftains in the countries of Eastern Europe. When the nations had been starved
and sweated long enough, they might be allowed an increase
in food occasionally.

Franz had endured the frenzy of mass demonstrations
without complaint. In fact, he had actually succeeded in view-
ing the whole proceedings with a tolerant eye. He had become
adjusted to this sort of carnival in the toilers' "paradise," the
Soviet Union. There, too, it was a point of honor for the Party
to hold great torchlight processions and mass demonstrations
about twice a year. Then if there were a few voluntary pledges
of labor, the organizers could rest on their laurels for a few
months. After all, they had to have something positive to report
to their immediate superiors if they were to keep their posts.

It had grown late. Franz decided not to attempt the long
ride home.

"I'll look up my friend Horst," thought Franz.

His friend's house at the edge of town was soon reached. Franz saw a light in the living room.

It's a good thing they're still up, he thought. At his knock, Horst's sister opened the front door.

"Oh, Franz!" said the girl. "It's you."

"Good evening, everybody," Franz said as he entered. "How's it going?"

"Not so good," was the answer. Horst was sitting in the living room, staring disconsolately into space. He didn't seem to have noticed his friend's arrival. Franz stopped, astonished.

"Why, what's got into you? Why is everybody looking so serious? What's happened?" he asked, shaking Horst by the shoulder. "Inge, I wonder if you couldn't get me something to eat? I've been marching and demonstrating all day and I am very hungry."

"You're the old demonstrator, aren't you?" the girl retorted. "And they marched father away yesterday. The political police, I mean."

"So that's it," exclaimed Franz. "I'm sorry. What do we do now, Horst? How did it happen?"

"Franz," Horst answered, "you can imagine what a

position this puts us in. Father's been locked up because he's supposed to be mixed up with western elements. The whole family's under suspicion. The people's court will pass sentence any day," he finished ominously.

"But, Horst," said Franz excitedly, "you must know whether they can arrest you on this charge, too! I should think they would have done it at once, if they were going to. Why don't you wait a while and see what the court decides?" Franz suggested.

"You're quite an optimist," Horst replied. "You know how the Communists work these things. They'll put on a big show for the whole town. They'll work on my father with all their techniques of inquisition, until he's ready to sign a confession. They'll soften him up all right. I'm wondering whether there's any point in my staying here."

"Horst," said Franz, "if I were in your place I'd wait for the verdict. You can't know for sure what the intentions of the authorities are. If your father is convicted only--I mean without confiscation of his property--then, if I were you, I'd try to hold on to the place and save as much of it as I could. You could sell a lot of the stuff. What I mean is that escaping to the west would be easier with money."

"That's probably true," Horst replied. "But the authorities will nationalize the business anyway. Since they haven't been able to pin anything on father, they're going to frame him. They always figure out some way to get what they want."

"I agree with you there," Franz answered. "Has your father been taking trips to West Germany, or West Berlin?"

"Sure, he's been to West Berlin lots of times. Who hasn't? As a matter of fact, we have some funds on deposit in the west, just to be on the safe side," Horst admitted. "But that's got nothing to do with spies and agents!"

"Well," said Franz, "these people know how to make their victims admit anything they want. They'll work on your old man until he makes a public acknowledgment of guilt and signs the statement with his own hand. I saw all these coercive methods used when I was in Russia. If the Germans aren't up to the job, they'll bring in Russian specialists. It's just a routine assignment to them."

"So that's our reward for generations of hard work," Horst said. "They force a man to drag his own carcass through the dirt and make him testify against himself. That's a fiendish kind of justice."

Inge brought some food. The young people ate in silence.

They knew they were powerless against organized terror. There was only one way of escape--fleeing to the west. But Horst was still too much attached to his home. He loved the family estate deeply and was unable to reconcile himself to breaking away completely. Franz's situation was different. Right after the invasion, he had lost everything except his life. Once he had completed his apprenticeship, he would find it easier to turn his back on the Reds.

"Anyway," said Franz when they had finished, "we've got all that demonstration business behind us. Don't worry too much, and get some rest." With a deep sign, Franz lay down on the couch in the living room and was fast asleep.

CHAPTER IX

Meanwhile, Horst's father, Mr. Altbauer, had been taken to the new secret-police prison. At first, he had been placed in a roomy private cell. Hours passed. The older man waited patiently. In the middle of the night, he heard footsteps approaching. Two guards appeared. One of them opened the door of the cell.

"Mr. Altbauer," said one, tonelessly. "Kindly come with us."

Horst's father got up stiffly from his stool and walked in front of the two guards through the long, deserted corridor. Now and then he saw a bare light-bulb hanging in front of a cell door, giving the scene a dim and ghostly aspect. The prisoner and his guards had reached the interrogation room.

"I'll call you when I want you," the Russian NKVD

major, sitting behind a desk, said to the two officers, who vanished instantly.

The major spoke excellent German. "Mr. Altbauer, we are going to settle this matter as expeditiously as possible. As you know, you have only to sign a paper. That is all we require of you. Be so good as to sit down." He seemed quite gracious. "May I offer you a cigarette? Now then. By your signature, you confess yourself guilty of crimes dangerous to the state. On several recent occasions, you have met with one Patow. This Patow is known to us as a liaison man acting as intermediary for American news services and their agents in East Germany and in Berlin. You are accused of having transmitted messages to Patow that jeopardize the cause of socialism and the prestige of our state. Let me emphasize again that any postponement of your confession can only hurt you. On the other hand, a prompt and open admission will improve your position. What have you to say?"

Breathlessly, Horst's father had listened to the accusation. What is this man saying, he thought? This is incredible. What a contemptible fraud.

At last Altbauer spoke. "But I know myself to be completely innocent. What you say is strange and unfamiliar to me. It's true that I've been in West Berlin a few times, but that was only to see some exhibits. I didn't do anything wrong, and I don't know anyone named Patow."

"Well, that's delightful," said his interrogator sarcastically. "Of course, you are completely innocent. I thought as much. We'll see about that." He pressed a button, "Take him away. Second section," he told the guards.

Mr. Altbauer was put in a small, dark cell. He felt dog-tired. But he couldn't sleep. What was that? He listened. There it was again. Boom-boom, tock-tock-tock-tock, boom, boom! There was no use trying to sleep. The tapping went on all night. Sometimes it clattered like a windmill on the roof of the cell. Then it stopped for a few minutes, only to begin again louder than before.

The prisoner was left to himself all next day, with nothing to eat. The noise went on incessantly through the day and the following night. About dawn of the second day, the cell door opened and Altbauer again found himself face to face with the NKVD officer.

"Well, what about the confession?" he asked coolly.

"I have nothing to confess," cried Altbauer. His nerves were already ragged from the maddening noise.

"What about Patow in Berlin?" the interrogator resumed. "Why don't you tell us about it? Don't make things hard for us."

"I don't know anybody named Patow," Altbauer repeated. "Leave me alone. I know nothing about all this."

As he spoke, a half-dozen tough-looking citizens burst into the room and started roaring at Altbauer in chorus.

"You do know Patow! You do know him!"

They kept this up for several minutes, until they had yelled themselves hoarse, then went away, leaving only the officer who had been questioning Altbauer. This was evidently the key point of the accusation. They were working on Mr. Altbauer night and day just to make him admit to having met "Patow" in Berlin.

"Well," came the inquisitor's voice, "why don't you confess? You can get everything you want by just doing as you're told."

Horst's father kept stubbornly silent so was led back to his cell. Days passed. Blows and ill treatment were his daily lot. After a week of this punishment, the victim was ready to obey orders. Through isolation and repetition, plus other methods of violence and terror, the jailers managed to extract a confession from Altbauer.

Next day the local people's court handed down its decision.

The old man was sentenced to five years in the penitentiary, including confiscation of his property.

In his distress, Horst sought out his old friend.

"Now what's happened?" Franz wanted to know.

"What you might suppose. My father was given five years. They've also seized the property. Now I'll have to get out of town," said Horst.

"That's terrible," said Franz. "Life isn't worth living in a country where there's no justice. But why don't you come home with me for a while? Nobody knows you in the village. Besides, the conviction didn't involve the rest of you, did it?"

"No," Horst replied. "But I'd like to know how they got father to confess. He said things in court that would make you think he was actually a criminal."

"That's the Stalinist system of forced confession. It's a technique of theirs in the Soviet Union. The German Communists have adopted it, I suppose," said Franz.

"Look here," Horst went on, "I've got a couple of trunks full of things I managed to salvage from the house. Could I bring them over to your place? Would you keep them for me? You might have a chance later to ship them after me. I can't stay here much longer."

"Where do you intend to go?" Franz asked. "I'm going to be leaving too, one of these days. We'll have to keep in touch."

"That's right," Horst answered. "Let's go, then. Mother and Inge have left for Berlin already. I hope they got through."

The two youths hired a cab and picked up the trunks at their hiding place. Before long, they reached Franz's house, where they unloaded and stored the salvaged things. Horst stayed overnight, and next morning took leave of his hosts. The young men bade each other farewell.

Horst walked to the station and bought a ticket to Berlin. Through trains in Soviet Germany were always overcrowded, the Russians having dismantled the double track. The situation was especially acute along the approaches to Berlin. He got a seat in a crowded express compartment. Farmers and businessmen were among the passengers. Everything seemed normal. People were conversing about crops and prices. Suddenly, when the train was still some distance from Berlin, the talk ceased. Everyone know the train was about to reach the main police inspection post, and that there would be nerve-racking procedures. A specter of apprehension seemed to have passed through the train. Each passenger was stealing himself for the ordeal. But everybody felt he was going to get a glimpse of the free world. That made it all worthwhile.

The train arrived at the transfer point of Falkensee, where all passengers had to change to the metropolitan line. Each one had to pass the police inspection post before he was allowed to board the cars which would enter West Berlin. Many travelers had the good fortune to be allowed to proceed unmolested, after their papers had been examined. Individuals were singled out for more thorough investigation. Horst took his place in the waiting line.

Now if only I can get over this hurdle, he thought.

Carefully, he took his papers out of his pocket. He wasn't carrying much luggage. A small grip contained everything he needed for the present. However, he had a considerable sum in currency sewn into his underclothes. The boy knew he would get at least three years in prison if the police should find the hidden money. Taking large amounts of cash into West Berlin was strictly prohibited.

Horst was not old enough to keep calm and cool in such situations. His heart seemed to beat louder and faster as he drew closer to the barrier. The waiting crowd was beginning to get restless. At the end of the line, a couple of workingmen started arguing with the police.

"Aren't you ashamed of yourselves, pushing your own people around like this?"

"Shut up," said the policeman gruffly.

"I won't shut up," the other retorted. "It won't hurt you to hear the truth for once. You'll be sorry when the time comes. People will get fed up with you one of these days. You'll see."

The man was losing control of himself. He was talking himself into a mounting passion, and began hurling vile insults at the police officers. The inspector in charge intervened.

"Arrest that man," he ordered.

Two policemen seized the troublemaker and marched him off, said boos and catcalls from the bystanders.

Horst had meanwhile reached the first of the inspectors. He showed his papers.

"All right," said the official. "Report over there for baggage inspection." Horst had to step out of line. His grip was opened and searched.

"Now wait here," said a policeman shortly.

"Why?" asked Horst innocently. "I've been passed already."

"I said wait here," the man repeated with emphasis. Some

other young men were waiting with Horst. When all the in-
coming passengers had been processed, the police loaded the
boys on a truck.

Where are they taking us now, Horst wondered anxiously?
He was not long kept in suspense. The truck stopped at a
guard station. All were ordered to get down and line up inside
the building. A sentry guarded the door.

The boys were thoroughly questioned and taken individually into another room. Horst's turn came.

"So, you're going to West Berlin?" he was asked.

"Yes," Horst answered.

The official asked what business he had in Berlin.

"I'm going to see a girl friend of mine," said Horst
carelessly.

"All right, tell her I said hello. You can go," the official
decided.

Relieved, Horst left the room. But the performance was
not over. He was now to be thoroughly searched. This was
the crucial test.

A policeman expertly frisked each of the boys in turn. Still
the authorities were not satisfied. The whole group had to
strip down to their underclothes and undergo closer scrutiny.

If they find the money, Horst thought, I'm done for.

All of a sudden, he felt a wave of fright. His heart was pounding violently. But the money had been very cleverly stitched into his long drawers, which were just a trifle too large for him, and nothing was noticed.

"All right, got dressed," said the inspector. The boys were reloaded on the truck, after being required to sign a statement. This bound them to observe complete silence about what had happened, under penalty of imprisonment. The truck took them back to the station, where they were to board their train. The place was deserted. Horst had to wait a long time before the next metropolitan train arrived.

On another platform, Horst saw some policemen sorting and packing confiscated valuables. He knew that these things were going to be put on sale in the state stores. How many refugees from the East Zone must have left their last few treasures here!

Horst's train approached. It would take him to freedom, but to a world of fresh uncertainty, too, he reflected as he climbed aboard.

At this moment, Franz had just finished his lunch and was about to resume work. During the afternoon he thought more than once of his friend Horst, and out of curiosity he passed by the old Altbauer place on his way home. All the furnishings had been removed. The mill and the rest of the property would no doubt be administered by some class-conscious worker. Franz found the whole scene very dismal. Now that Horst was gone, he had few real friends left here. He decided that he too would seek an early opportunity for flight. First, though, he wanted to take his examination. So, he kept quiet and waited patiently. He worked in the repair shop during the day and studied his lessons at night.

In the Communist empire, it was not enough to be an accomplished craftsman. Any young man who expected to make the grade had to be well up on current political events and on the history of the international working-class movement. Franz was preparing himself for a classroom discussion to be held the next day. All he knew was that some young Communist leaders were to be present. The best he could do was to inform himself as minutely as possible on current topics. Such discussions had been held in the shop from time to time. Franz knew the majority of the workers were hostile to Communism, but only a very few dared to answer their questioners in public.

The difficulty was that the agitators were supported by Russian bayonets and that they were in a position to avenge any inconvenient criticism. So, the problem was to find indirect expressions to demonstrate that these Communist policies were not favored by the majority of workers. This was difficult to accomplish because the Communists in the satellite countries, paralleled with their actual dictatorship, had created a sham democracy which included a sham legislature. In East Germany this fraudulent body was called the National Assembly, or <u>Volkskammer</u>, a political showplace for foreigners. Some of the more naive observers became victims of these Soviet tricks, since seats were held not only by Communists but also by representatives of other parties. However, all parties and other mass organizations drifted in the wake of the Communists.

All this was well known, so Franz was not surprised to learn that the theme of the next educational session was to be real and formal democracy. The main speaker and discussion leader would be the state chairman of the Party. The workers had assembled in the tractor shed. The distinguished guest was standing at the back of the speaker's platform, chatting with the superintendent about quotas and production. The meeting was opened by the chairman of the shop youth group.

"Friends," he began, "today we are privileged to welcome Hermann Rosenfeld, of the State Committee, to our midst. Comrade Rosenfeld, who is state director of agitation and propaganda for the Socialist Unity Party, is going to speak to us on the meaning of real democracy. As you know, comrades," he continued, "we in this country, unlike our western compatriots, live under a true democracy; theirs is merely artificial. Comrade Rosenfeld will explain why this is so, and why we alone can call ourselves real democrats."

"He must be crazy," one worker remarked to his neighbor. "It's the other way around."

"That's adding insult to injury," said an engineer indignantly. "If they call this true democracy, the future looks pretty bleak. The discipline is worse than in the Nazi army. How do they expect us to believe that stuff?"

Meanwhile, Comrade Rosenfeld had deliberately taken his place on the platform and was beginning his lecture.

"Fellow workers, I am aware that there are many in this audience who believe that we are not living in a real democracy; who say that this is a dictatorship, and that American democracy is the genuine kind. First of all, I should like to tell you something of what American democracy is like. So far as

the American people are concerned, it is more or less a matter
of indifference whether the Democrats or the Republicans
are in power. That is why no revolutionary social charges
take place over there; the aims of the government may vary,
methods may change in the course of an administration, but
social relationships remain unaffected from one election to
another. The monopolists constantly retain their influential
position. Through the enormous concentration of capital, a
small group rules over the people. This group controls public
opinion and hence national policy." He paused briefly. "Now
what is the significance of the great power of money in the
hands of so few? It is a dictatorial power, wearing a democratic
fig leaf. The same kind of democracy is to be found in the
capitalist countries of western Europe. Through the Marshall
Plan, the American economic potentates engage in wholesale
exportation of capital. By virtue of their money, they will
soon exert a tremendous influence in West Germany, and
control its political affairs. This is only one example of what
the Americans are doing all over the world to make their ideas
victorious over Communism."

Then Rosenfeld raised his hand significantly. "And
what about real democracy in the Soviet Union? There the

government is chosen and supported by the workers and peasants. Who will deny that the workers and peasants are the majority of the population? Every four years the toilers in Russia elect their representatives to the two houses of the legislature--the Soviet of the Union and the Soviet of Nationalities, representing the constituent Soviet republics. Thus, the government looks for its mandate to the masses of the people, and not to influential financiers and newspaper magnates. This is democratic popular sovereignty. Thus, we live, not under a false but under a real democracy."

The superintendent thanked the speaker and invited all present to participate in the discussion. Comrade Rosenfeld stood on the speaker's platform in an attitude of ease, ready to answer all comers. The speaker knows in advance that none of the workers would dare to challenge him. All feared the state security agencies, mention of which had deliberately been omitted by Comrade Rosenfeld in discussing the significance of Soviet democracy.

The first to ask for the floor was a middle-aged engineer who had seen something of the world and was politically sophisticated.

"Comrade Rosenfeld: You stated that under American

democracy there is absolute domination by money, and that all must submit to this domination. I was a prisoner of war in America for three years, and believe that while there, I learned something about the financial situation. In the first place, I deny your contention that democracy in America is merely nominal. Such freedom as exists there can rarely be found elsewhere."

The silence was almost painful as the engineer continued. "Do you know that everyone in America is equal before the law? That every person has a fair chance under that law, to accomplish the objectives for himself that already have been achieved by prominent businessmen. There, no one can force a worker from his job nor prevent him from going elsewhere to obtain more for his labor." There was a brief pause. "With the money he earns and saves, he can do whatever he pleases. If the people do not approve of the political measures or financial policies of the government, they have a free press and radio or television through which they criticize the party in power, demanding a change of administration."

"Furthermore, an American citizen is free to go anywhere he likes. That is to say, he can live anywhere he wants to without any special hardship. On the other hand, look at the difficulties a Soviet citizen encounters should he desire to travel to some country of the western world. In the first place, the average man would be denied permission from the State Authority to follow such private inclination. That, I believe, is the main point--whether people are in fact free or not, to say nothing of the enormous difference in the material standard of living between the Soviet Union and the United States, the paradox being that the working masses in the Soviet Union should be better off, considering that Communism is completely dominated by a materialist doctrine. But the materialist doctrine and its consequences are used for other purposes. Instead of creating an abundant standard of living, the Soviet leadership prefers to strengthen its influence in the world by means of power politics. For this the masses in the Soviet Union pay a heavy price in hard work and privation. Moreover," he continued, "they have no opportunity to pro-test through the press and radio against arbitrary proceedings on the part of the government. The people are compelled to follow the line laid down by the Party, and anyone who deviates from it is in trouble with the police. Yes, Comrade Rosenfeld, I must insist that we cannot build a democracy on a foundation of terror; in attempting to do so, we have already left the realm of freedom and entered that of dictatorship. Now if it is asked which of the two forms of government is the right one for a European nation, I must reply that we cannot mechanically impose either of these two systems on our nation with its great traditions and diversity of cultures. Instead, we must try to regain our former position of leadership in world economy by the outstanding quality of our products. If the European countries east and west of the Iron Curtain remain under the political and economic tutelage of the United States and the Soviet Union, then in a decade or two they will have completely lost their national independence and identity, and degenerate into satellites of the two world powers. We in the eastern part of Europe have already come perilously close to this condition. Other European countries have been making attempts at economic rapprochement, but national antagonisms are proving to be very serious obstacles. Despite these contradictions, there is no alternative to political and economic union, as in a United States of Europe. That is the only way to keep our national individuality. If we fail to bridge these incompatibilities, we shall be swallowed up by Russians on the one hand and the Americans on the other.

"The age of colonial powers and nation states is coming to

an end. All Europeans must collectively look to their national identify and their national cultures if they are to weather the storm. So, the question, as I see it, is not, for us Germans, Poles, or Frenchmen, whether the true democracy is the Russian or the American kind. On this point, I take a definite European position. The Occident has been threatened by alien influences many times in the past. But the danger of such a threat has never been as great as now. For today, thanks to the two opposed ideologies, we have a line of demarcation. On either side of the Iron Curtain, underground movements are maintained for the purpose of undermining and destroying the established order."

"But the Soviet Union defends the national independence of all peoples," insisted Comrade Rosenfeld.

"In what way?" asked the engineer. "Don't you see that all of us in the states of Eastern Europe have the same form of government? We are all unilaterally oriented eastward, and dependent on Russia. That's the very danger I've been talking about; the national aspirations of small countries are simply disregarded by the Russians, who are trying to impose their own way of life."

"That's right," cried a number of voices, "the Russians should let us go our own way. He's talking sense. We agree."

The workers enthusiastically applauded the engineer's remarks.

"So, at last somebody had the nerve to speak up," commented an old foreman.

"Yes," said one of the workers, "it's high time these Soviet leaders found out what people really think of them. That's all to the good."

However, the agitator stuck to his promise that the Soviet system was the right one for the working people of all countries. To the question why there had to be such a uniform administration of the people's democracy in the Eastern European countries, he replied that the working class would make its way in the world only under a strong, united, energetic leadership.

"Otherwise," he continued, "the class enemy would be given too much opportunity to subvert and overthrow our system. If there are those among the masses who cannot or will not understand this, our security agencies will have to convince them."

"That's what you really mean!" many exclaimed fiercely. "Now you've come to the point. Your talk is only the language of force."

At last the meeting was adjourned by the manager of the tractor shop. Such incidents were not infrequent. They became a common occurrence in the eastern countries. So long as the workers did not question the fundamentals of Stalinism, they were allowed to argue as much as they liked. This lent the dictatorship a faint aura of democracy.

Towards the end of the year, when Franz had completed his apprenticeship, he was notified to report for examination in a few weeks. There were four parts to the examination--practical, oral theoretical, written theoretical, and political. The examination was to be judged by a board. A week before, Franz and the other apprentices started working on the practical assignments. They were allowed ample time to do their jobs, but they worked late into the night on their projects. A room had been set aside in which they could work undisturbed, as much care and precision were required.

"What are you going to do when you're a journeyman?" Franz asked Gunther, the young fellow working alongside him.

"I don't know exactly. I haven't made up my mind," he replied. "I may stay here at the shop, or I may transfer to a tractor station out in the country. That ought to be a lot more pleasant."

"Perhaps you're right. I'll have to give it some thought. I might go too. But then we would have to contend with the field work and help to collectivize agriculture. We would have a hard time staying out of the Party then," Franz objected.

"Oh, don't worry about that," said Gunther. "We'll think of something. We always have."

By arduous labor, the boys finished their projects on time, and on the appointed day they appeared before the examining board. Each in turn was expected to demonstrate his project assignment and explain how he had completed the job. The chairman was an elderly engineer who casually conducted the proceedings, dispelling the nervousness felt by some of the apprentices.

After the technical questions on diesel engines and other equipment, the board began to test the political knowledge of the examinees. A political instructor called the boys in individually and plagued them with questions about the teachings of Marx, Engels, Lenin and Stalin. Some of the boys had taken this subject lightly, thinking: As long as I know my work, I'll be all right. But the political instructor saw to it that these were failed mercilessly, and they had to repeat the examination until they were proficient in this department.

Franz had survived the rigors of examination day, and had just completed the last ordeal, when he met Gunther in the anteroom.

"Well," said Franz's friend, "how did it go?"

"I sailed right through," was the reply. "I didn't attract any special notice, either way. How far have you got?"

"All done except this damned political part," Gunther answered. "What kind of questions are they asking, anyway?"

"Better brush up on Stalin's writings," Franz suggested, "like the <u>Short History of the Communist Party of the Soviet Union</u>. Just review the whole thing once more. If you set your mind on it, and can give a clear and fluent account of these things, the instructor will have to pass you. If you know your way around the great man's works, the rest will take care of itself."

"Thanks for the advice. I've got another couple of hours to do some studying, so I guess I'll take advantage of it."

Next morning the two friends met on the job.

"I won't keep you in suspense," Gunther said immediately. "Everything went off all right."

"Fine," said Franz. "I've made up my mind, Gunther. I'm not staying here. Let's both go out to some tractor station.

Country life will do us good. I'm going to speak to the manager today, get released, and then treat myself to a short vacation."

"I like that idea," Gunther agreed. "I'll go along with you to the office. We'll ask the boss for letters of recommendation. It will be much better if we can go out together."

"Well, it won't be much of an adventure," said Franz, "but I'll be interested to learn how Germany is to convert the former peasant properties into collective farms, Russian style. We young workers are supposed to bridge the gap between town and country. The machine and tractor stations are just a preliminary to the socialization of all means of production on the land."

"That will probably take quite a while," Gunther remarked, "before the Communists break down the opposition of the farmers. If it wasn't practical in the Soviet Union, it won't have a chance in Germany. You don't know how stubborn country people can be."

"I don't care if they are stubborn," answered Franz. "We'll tend to our business of repairing tractors and keep our heads above water. As long as things are still in the preparatory stages, they'll leave us alone out there in the sticks with their political education. But that's why I want to take some time off. In two weeks, we'll meet again in the great outdoors."

"All right, see you then," Gunther said cordially.

Franz lost no time in settling the formalities with the management of the shop. When he bid the director goodbye, he received a letter of recommendation addressed to managers of tractor stations.

"I hope," said the director, "that you will prove that there is no distinction between town and country, that you will become a productive worker, aiding in the construction of a Communist society."

Franz again thanked him and hurried to the railway station. He boarded the waiting train which took him to his home nearby. His mother was surprised to see him, and asked if everything was all right now.

"Don't worry," Franz reassured her. "I got along all right in Russia, and I ought to be able to take care of myself in my own country."

"Try to be careful. You young people are much too hot-headed," she warned him. "Think over each step thoroughly before you take it. Here's a letter from your friend Horst. He finally made it to the west."

"That's interesting, he's in Berlin. I can visit him on my vacation. After all, I've never seen the show window of the western world."

The express train was approaching the inspection station on the outskirts of Berlin. The passengers had been talking and complaining about economic conditions in the East Zone. Franz noticed that they now gradually fell silent, that a feeling of apprehension was in the air. Most of the travelers could not boast of clear consciences so far as the authorities were concerned. Some intended to escape to West Germany, others meant to resume or maintain contact with acquaintances in West Berlin. This was the ideological as well as the geographical boundary between the two worlds. Not only were all externals different on each side of the frontier, but the mode of living was particularly subject to changes of the times. On the eastern side of the Curtain, people were following a way of life that had been forced upon them. In the western part of Germany, including Berlin, they could behave freely and naturally. Western mankind had already forgotten the rigors of war and was devoting its energies to the task of reconstruction.

The boundary station was reached. Franz got out. All

passengers had to line up and wait their turn to go through the check-up procedure. Some of the women had much baggage with them, raising the suspicion of flight. These were subjected to a thorough search by Soviet policewomen, but it turned out that these travelers were farm women from the vicinity. Many of these peasants were abandoning their farms, for they had been bullied by the Reds to the point where they realized the futility of remaining in the eastern part of Germany any longer. Surreptitiously, they had left their homes, hoping to peacefully earn their bread in the free world.

Many citizens of the Russian satellite countries were unfamiliar with the doctrines and aims of the Communists. They became aware of the real danger only when they saw that the authorities were deliberately imposing impossible production quotas in every area under their control. The farmers, driven into a corner, had only two alternatives. They could drop everything and flee to the west, or they could go to prison, leaving their properties to the tender mercies of a planned economy. All at once, an idea had smashed the work of many generations. Even the strongest were obliged to surrender at last to superior force. A few fled at once; many followed later. A wave of arrests broke over the country. Some impression of the extent of such police campaigns might be gained by the impartial observer at the transfer points affording entry to the western world.

Franz was not carrying luggage or other goods. To the police officer's question about his destination, he replied, East Berlin and was allowed to pass through the police inspection without challenge. Beyond the German officials, there were Russian sentries. Franz conversed with the young soldiers in their own language. When asked how it was that he spoke Russian, he replied that he had taken a keen interest in their country and its language. They let him through without objection. Once past this point, he boarded a Berlin municipal train. He rode to West Berlin without hindrance and found the dwelling of his escaped friend Horst. At his ring, the lady of the house opened the door. Franz introduced himself as Horst's friend and was invited to step in. Horst appeared in the hallway to meet him.

"Hello, Franz, it's good to see you," Horst greeted him. "Come on in and meet my Uncle Anton."

Franz was presented to a distinguished looking man in his middle fifties, a high-school history teacher. Tea was served.

"These are troubled times," Horst's uncle remarked, at

one point, "and Europe has become a wasteland. Our country especially is cut apart by the front lines of the cold war. One really needs to be an ideological acrobat to follow the swift changes in the political climate nowadays. In the first half of this century, I suppose we in Germany have experienced every form of government to be found in modern times. Until 1916, we had a constitutional monarchy. Then until 1933 we lived under a republic. That didn't agree with us either. So, for the next twelve years we tried dictatorship. This proved to be an even bigger mistake. And now we have got to the point where we have two rival forms of government at the same time. Anyone who doesn't like eastern-style dictatorship can move over to the free democracy of the west. And those to whom the western way of life doesn't appeal can try their luck in the eastern world; if that doesn't suit them either, all they have to do is go to Berlin. Here we have a divided world and a divided Germany compressed into one city. The foot-loose have only to walk across the Potsdamer Platz to escape the influence of Moscow or Washington. It all depends on which influence they want to accept or avoid. If it weren't so terribly serious, it would be funny. Young people particularly must find it an acute problem."

"Yes, indeed," Franz agreed. "Especially those of us who have to live under Red rule. Sooner or later every one of us will have to face the question: East or West? Young people in the western world don't have the same problem because they didn't experience the change so abruptly in their formative years. Boys and girls in the west have been able to go on unhindered according to the old rules. But what about those of us who live in the eastern world? We too were brought up in a humanistic or occidental spirit. So, everyone is confronted with the question whether he can actively support the ideas of Communism for the sake of material advantage. Every informed young person knows that international Communism intends to bring the rest of the world under its sway. In other words, the conditions we now have in the Soviet Union are to be duplicated all over the world by every means of force and stratagem. Can a well-brought-up young man allow himself to be converted into an instrument to promote Communism? One of the most sensible ways to escape that menace is to take refuge in the west, where people live as free citizens and earn their livelihood with a clear conscience."

"Don't forget," Uncle Anton interposed, "that people will cling to their homes as long as possible. Many will endure the terror and persecution rather than go into exile. But of course, the worst thing of all would be if the two post-war world powers should change their tactics--if the cold war should suddenly become a hot war. Then many young men would have to fight and die against their own convictions. Considering this, it would certainly be better if each individual were to go where his belief calls him."

"I don't think there's going to be a hot war," said Franz.

"Why not?" the older man asked.

"It's possible, of course," Franz replied, "but the Soviets have other ways of fighting. They are feverishly, and lot people starve and toil till they're bled white. But the western powers are underestimating Russia just as they underestimated Hitler. The Americans are proud of their superweapons and their industrial potential, forgetting that the chief weapon of the Soviets is not armed force but the religion of Communism. They have developed a new principle of warfare. The Soviets need their big armament program only to obtain the respect of world opinion, which a world power necessarily requires. The big armies are only a diversion. The western powers concentrate on isolating the Communist bloc from the rest of the world by means of a system of treaties with like-minded nations. This is a step in the right direction, but geographical and military isolation alone is not enough. Many people in the west have as yet failed to understand the innovation in Soviet warfare. In addition to the regular army, the Soviet Union and the satellite countries are training an army of agents, which they term the apostles of Bolshevism. After finishing their training, they are sent out primarily into the underdeveloped countries of the globe. When they arrive at their respective destinations, their mission is to win people over to the idea of Communism and stir them up against the U.S.A. Naturally, the Russians always select the worst-defended and strategically most important objectives, where they can easily win victories for their ideas.

"Although the Americans have been pouring their dollars into the underdeveloped regions so as to compete with the Communists, such measures can succeed for a brief period only. Take the example of China. If the masses there will not, by hard work and sacrifice, take a firm stand against Soviet Russia, then no amount of dollars will change their viewpoint in favor of the west. The only thing that could help would be the erecting of self-sustaining bulwarks against Communism. Nevertheless, in those teetering countries, a sound economy can be developed if American aid is given rationally and productively.

"The Berlin air lift and the firm defensive stand of the west demonstrated that the free peoples of the world are united and resolute, a big plus in their favor. Such action repudiates Lenin's thesis that the western democracies are mutually antagonistic. The first rule for all anti-Communist nations is unity. In this sphere, after their confused separatism following the war, the western countries have regrouped themselves and stand united against the Russian menace. But this is not enough. The free peoples have not yet succeeded in finding any adequate answer to Soviet strategy in the ideological theater. The west must prove its ability to match or overcome these Russian weapons, arriving at a crystal-clear statement of the aims and purposes of its policy. These western ideas must be energetically followed through into those parts of the world which are especially exposed to Soviet propaganda offensives. In addition to economic experts, the west must send educators into these countries, a combination the Russians will be unable to withstand. If the various peoples who have not yet taken a definite position in the battle lines of the cold war can be won for western ideals, then the Moscow world revolutionaries will find that the wind has been taken out of their sails.

"This struggle demands strong nerves and untiring political activity, if the ideologists of the Kremlin are not to win the hearts and minds of the uncommitted nations. Everywhere, the fifth columns of Communism are now gradually working their way forward and do not care what methods they use. They will make the most fantastic promises, and spend enormous sums to land weight to their cause. After a certain area has been permeated and honeycombed, a carefully planned coup d'état is staged, and there is one more Red statelet in the world. Soviet practices follow the standard Moscow pattern. Aside from social and economic measures, strategic requirements also receive consideration. Conquered without firing a shot, the satellite is built up as a strong military base. So, by the use of their insidious strategy, the Soviets take one bridgehead after another. There is apparently no stopping them, and they will persevere until they have gained the balance of world power. It may be assumed that the Soviets, using this type of warfare, hope for many more successes, particularly since the west has so little with which to oppose them."

Horst interrupted to ask his uncle a question: "How would

you account for the growth and influence of the Communist parties in Italy and France? I can understand how the Reds get adherents for their doctrines in comparatively unsophisticated countries, but I don't see how they have obtained such a foothold in countries like France and Italy."

"That's not so difficult to understand," his uncle answered. "The Communists there deliberately conceal their real intentions from the voters. They don't inform the unsuspecting electorate that even if they were to get into power, they could not possibly pursue a sound national policy. The Communist parties in the western countries conceal from the people that Stalin has demoted them to more receivers of instructions from Moscow. People in Italy would have just as bad a time as those in Poland and Rumania if the Communists headed the government."

"Lots of people living under the Russian heal in Eastern Europe," Franz put in, "are still hoping for a victory of freedom. They think that Americans will give them military aid to help them throw off the yoke of domination. Do you think their hour of liberation will ever come?"

"That's hard to say," Anton, the history teacher replied. "Notice this: the Russians know very well that the Americans are not like the Nazis. I mean that the western powers will not unleash a military preventive war. In a parliamentary democracy, the president or prime minister cannot start a war of aggression, because the system is too slow and cumbersome. Besides, the people desire ever-increasing prosperity, which is incompatible with war. Because western policy has committed many blunders, Bolshevism has become so strong that a war against it would entail tremendous risks. However, if the Reds found themselves faced with a unified intellectual and material front, the time would have come when the west could talk to the Russians about the status of the satellite countries. On the other hand, revolutionary countercurrents might become active in the captive countries. We must give time a chance to work, and give the submerged peoples every possible aid. But liberation by a hot war is impracticable at present."

"Do you believe," asked Franz, "that the acceptance of the Marshall Plan and the formation of the Federal Republic of Germany represented progress towards opposing Russian expansionism in Western Europe?"

"Well," Anton replied, "that was the most sensible thing the Americans could have done. Economic recovery of Germany will be a stumbling block to the Russians in

Europe. Western Germany is anti-communistic, and has the biggest heavy industry on the continent. The American policy has shattered the Russian dream of conquering all Germany. We have seen that the Soviets, despite the attempts of their agents in West Germany, have been unable to gain any significant political influence. At the same time, we must not overlook what the consequences of a West German policy would have been without the Marshall Plan; the Soviets would have taken over all of Central Europe. With the marginal states seriously infected with Communism, the peninsula of Europe would have been an easy prey."

"Let's stop talking politics," Horst suggested.

"What do you intend to do now that you've got out of East Germany?" Franz asked.

"I'm going to fly from here to West Germany and get some kind of a job. We can still keep in touch. You'll be sure to get to West Berlin every now and then, so you can pick up my letters here."

"Good," Franz replied thoughtfully. "I'm going back to the East Zone, but not for long. After careful preparation, I too shall have to leave home, to go the same way you are going."

Franz took leave of Anton, and took a short walk with Horst along one of the busiest streets of West Berlin. Here the glitter of the western world was displayed to eastern visitors. The two friends gazed curiously at the merchandise in the shop windows, studying prices and comparing them with what they knew about wage levels. People seemed uninhibited and freely expressed their views on matters of public interest. This was a different kind of life from that he had endured recently. This was real freedom. The districts of East Berlin looked gloomy and menacing when compared with the brilliant show windows they were now admiring. At last, Horst accompanied Franz to the station.

"My friend," he said, "I know how hard it is for you to have to go back, but keep your chin up. We'll meet again one of these days."

Franz turned and boarded the waiting train. The knowledge that he was returning to the East Zone greatly depressed him.

Chapter X

The return journey from West Berlin was uneventful for Franz, and the next day he was home. One morning his friend Gunther called for him, and they set out for the tractor station to which they had been assigned. They completed the first leg of their trip by rail, and disembarked at a little village named Gumtow. At the police station Gunther found out what road to take.

"It's quite a distance from here; about ten miles," said the officer. "The road is still on the drawing board. I guess you'll have to walk. Go on to the end of the village, then take the path across country, keeping to the right."

"Thanks," said the boys as they started out.

"This looks good," said Gunther. "Far from civilization, in the middle of nothing. Do you suppose they have political education and commissars out here?"

"They will have, soon enough," thought Franz. "At first we may get a rest from them. But afterward we'll get plenty of indoctrination out of Stalin's writings."

The lane would through green rolling country. Now and then the boys passed a bit of woodland. Cows grazed peacefully in fenced pastures. Crickets chirped in the grass, followed by the call of birds.

Towards noon the boys saw the end of their long hike approaching. At the edge of a wood stood a long red-brick building. There were numerous vehicle entrances, identifying the building as a sort of garage. Close by there was a typical North German farmhouse. The owner had been forced to leave the house by the Russians in 1945. Now it was being used as an administration building by the Communist land reformers. A great deal of agricultural machinery was standing nearby, which had been brought here from expropriated farms. Some workmen were busy putting up a fence. In front of the building, the boys saw the usual giant transparency, reading: "Through Stalin's Teaching We Will Construct Socialism in the Countryside."

"There you are," said Gunther. "We've just beat our way in through the wilderness, and what do we get: political slogans."

"I could have told you that in the first place," said Franz. "This station is being installed on the Soviet pattern. Such machine stations are supposed to be the centers of political life in the country. They are intended to be nuclei of Communism in German agriculture."

The boys reached the building, and reported to the manager's office.

"Just a moment," said the secretary. "The Comrade Director will be right back."

Franz and Gunther soon found themselves face to face with a powerfully built man of medium height who introduced himself as Comrade Schlenk.

"The head of your shop told me you were coming," said Schlenk, showing Horst and Franz into his office. "Our problems out here are not simple. We more or less have to make something out of nothing ... to break trail for a new system of cultivating land in this section ... to apply the discoveries of Soviet agricultural science. We are also going to have the job of carrying out one hundred percent mechanization of farming to break down the contradiction between town and country. But above all," Comrade Schlenk spoke in a tone of warning, raising his right index finger, "I want you to be on the lookout for enemies of the working class. There are many of them left in the villages, and they devote their energies trying to block Soviet progress in the rural areas to achieve the victory of reaction. Your task will be agitational in character. You must try to convince the local inhabitants of the desirability of our social system. You won't have any difficulty once you begin to know the people and the neighborhood."

Comrade Schlenk had warmed to his subject. He felt himself to be something of an innovator. The left lapel of his jacket was decorated with the insignia of the Party and the German-Soviet Friendship society. He showed the boys where they were to work. Instead of a shop, it was a shack. The floor was bare earth. Modern tools were lacking. All they found there was two work-benches and vises. In front of one bench there was a crude homemade injection nozzle testing machine.

"Here's your shop," said Schlenk. "You'll be able to fix it up a bit. More machinists will soon be coming in. The major repair work is done in the plant."

"But," Gunther asked, "how can we change diesel engines without tackle?"

"You'll have to manage with levers and jacks. Your bunks

are in the administration building. Today you can just take a look around. You don't start work until tomorrow."

Franz and Horst reentered the converted farmhouse and found the room to which they had been assigned. It was large and square, and might once have been a former occupant's guest-room. In their room, the two boys found a few miserable remnants of furniture, which had been supplemented with two cots. A couple of high windows, however, afforded an agreeable view of the spreading fields and meadows.

"We'll have to forget about motion pictures and other amusements. But we shall lead a healthy and natural life for a while. I don't think I'm going to be here very long though," complained Gunther.

Next morning the boys began their work. There were about fifty tractors at the station, including some ancient Russian models with steel tires. These machines ran on fuel oil and needed a lot of attention. The mechanics and drivers were trying to get the engines started.

Franz swore. "We'll kill ourselves trying to crank these jobs. Come on, Gunther, let's tow them to get them started and then warm them up a while." With the help of the mechanics, the boys got the machines running. The tractors were supposed to go into service that afternoon.

The manager of this installation worked closely with the chairman of the producers' cooperative. This was an institution which the East Germans had taken over from the Russians. The organization of producer groups on the land for better distribution of labor and its products was known in Russia as collective economy. The Germans changed the terminology slightly, but the meaning and intent were the same.

During the next few weeks, a few journeymen checked in at the tractor station from the surrounding towns. More frequently, the force was compelled to work extra shifts, a practice common to Communist countries of the Stalin period. At harvest time, especially, the mechanics would work in the fields on Sundays, ostensibly by their own choice. Actually, Sunday work was a systematic and calculated policy of exploitation on the part of the government.

In the eastern states, the work plan was the very basis of the economy, and it had to be fulfilled and, if possible, overfulfilled.

To execute a prompt over fulfillment of plans, the Communist leaders would draw up alleged resolutions which, in most cases, the workers would have to adopt unanimously. If they balked, they might be accused of obstructionism.

Everybody was aware of the dangers inherent in such an accusation in a police state, and acted accordingly. So, the mechanics at many tractor stations worked Sunday after Sunday, in the collective farm fields from early morning until late at night. The main point of such demonstrations was their propaganda effect. Communist newspapers were always happy to report such socialist construction exploits to their readers.

But the mechanics received no extra pay for working long hours on Sunday. It was supposed to be volunteer work, performed out of conviction and enthusiasm. The men submitted reluctantly to their tormentors, who extorted this extra labor from them by the threat of police action.

Most of the people felt that the war was over. For many years they had been exploited inhumanly and had no desire to sacrifice themselves for the new group in power. Hence, quotas were not strictly enforced on the collective farms and in the tractor stations, even though these institutions were specifically Soviet in character.

The labor battalions of large urban enterprises would also be forced to show up for country work on Sundays. At the tractor station where Franz and Gunther were employed, the masons from the city pledged themselves to erect the new buildings for the station within a given time. Whole truck-loads of government office workers were hauled out into the rural areas. They would serve as helpers in the construction of new buildings, or would be deployed to gather the harvest. Everything was thoroughly regimented and organized. The police apparatus kept the economic functionaries up to the mark by continual intimidation, and spurred them on to greater efforts, which encountered much passive resistance among the population. In the countries of the eastern bloc, a sharp antagonism developed between the people and the government. Pressure generates resistance. All idle talk about international working-class solidarity and fraternity was ren-dered meaningless by these oppressive and coercive measures.

Through the summer, Franz was responsible for a fleet of tractors. Poor quality of steel often caused serious trouble which interfered with the performance of the equipment. Injector and pump components of diesel engines suffered es-pecially. Very often the vehicles would arrive in defective con-dition from the factories. The fleet consisted of twelve trac-tors and two reapers. The machines were distributed among three localities of the neighborhood, and had to be overhauled at regular intervals. When necessary, the mechanics would replace worn-out parts. Each morning Franz would mount a tractor and drive from one location to another, talking to the farmers and tractor operators and repairing their machines.

In the rural areas of East Germany and eastern Europe, hopeless confusion prevailed during the early 1950's. Until 1945, the lands had been cultivated on the principles of bourgeois capitalist economy. Now, since their occupation, the Soviets had socialized all enterprises comprising more than 250 acres. Still, the system of administration had remained strictly private up to 1950. Until that time, the farmers retained a certain amount of freedom, provided they delivered their forced quotas punctually to the government agencies.

In 1950 all this was changed. The first five-year plans were proclaimed, with the objectives of creating a socialist society and an integrated collectivity of producers. This, of course, meant an intensification of the class struggle in the countryside. The last stronghold of private enterprise in the economy was to be stormed. Thousands of landholders deserted their properties to escape the wave of political arrests. The concentration camps and prisons of the Red dictators were filled. Dramatic scenes took place at the frontier posts, the outlets for the exodus of refugees into the western world. Whole villages stood deserted. The farms came under state administration. Equipment was concentrated at central points. Districts were placed under the supervision of agronomists, who worked hand in glove with the directors of the machine and tractor stations. The state functionaries found themselves under mounting pressure, confronted with tremendous tasks they had never been confronted with before.

Thanks to Soviet assistance, the class struggle in the eastern zone was waged successfully. But the problem of production was yet to be solved. For example, the collective farm workers evinced little interest in the Plan, mainly because of the low wages they were receiving from the government. The masses saw the futility of the whole operation, and lacked incentive, which is only born from personal, individual interest. But in those days the workers were being forced into a definite economic collectivity not to their liking. The Red leaders, despite their knowing what was happening, continued their ruinous policy.

Franz weathered the first harvest under the Red sickle with little anxiety. The young men now at the station were recruited into special crews for the exhausting labor of potato digging.

Franz and Gunther, as usual, drove to the fields in a truck to service the many tractors. One morning, a strange scene awaited them. The broad acres of the potato field were dotted with people who had been brought there in trucks from the surrounding towns.

"Well, what do you know about that," said Franz, laughing. "Look, just look at all the girls! We'll have to do something about this."

After a squad of tractors, assisted by the digging machines, had turned over the potato field in record time, the imported townspeople were counted off into working groups. But the boys and girls kept drifting together, stopping to talk. With Franz's help, Gunther built a bonfire. It was not long before some of the girls gathered round the flames. Potatoes were tossed into the fire, to be eaten freshly roasted. The young people chattered gaily, ignoring the exhortations of the functionaries, who were trying to get them back on the fields.

"What do you expect?" asked a big, strapping girl, excitedly. She was a clerical worker in the administration of a neighboring town, and was annoyed at becoming involved in this expedition on her day off. "We've been slaving all week in the office, and now I'm being refused some needed rest."

The boys heartily agreed. More and more of the harvesters gathered around the fire. Forcing the workers into the fields became hopeless, so the Red leaders had to make the best of a bad bargain.

By the end of the season, the station management had completed the construction work. The state chairman and high party officials congratulated the staff. Several activist mechanics were honored. Others received bonuses. Franz got a short holiday and visited his mother, who received him joyfully.

"A letter came for you from West Berlin, perhaps from your old teacher," she said. From the handwriting Franz knew it came from his former Latin teacher at the Neubeck school. He began to read:

My dear Friend:

Like so many others, I have been forced into exile at last. By all sorts of pressure, the school administration tried to induce me to join the Communist Party. I refused, but to no avail. The principal went so far as to denounce me to the secret police. As I was teaching history as well as Latin, he accused me of having a bad influence on the pupils. Very soon I saw that further resistance was useless, and resigned my position. Then I was evicted from my quarters and summoned to appear in court and account for my conduct. Privately, I learned that the court's decision would go against me, and that I would be placed under arrest. I made good use of the short time remaining, leaving my few things with friends, to be sent on to you. Then I slipped away to West Berlin. Could you send my belongings to me here? I am alone here among strangers, and forced to impose myself on you.

Your old friend,

Fritz Bode.

"Mother, I'll have to take another trip to Berlin and help him out. We used to read how the Romans destroyed their political enemies in the civil war years of Caesar's time. Now we have perpetual civil war in Germany. I'm sure Fritz never thought it would come to this, when he was telling us about Ciceronian statecraft. Perhaps I can ship his packages to East Berlin from here and then carry them into the western sector."

"Just be careful," warned his mother. "You know it'll be dangerous. Aiding fugitives is punishable by five years' imprisonment. You're all I have left, and I don't want to lose you through recklessness."

"You're right, of course," Franz agreed, "but it's not so dangerous as one might think. We'll simply forward the material to Cousin Johann in East Berlin, which is allowed. After that, there's nothing to it but to take a street-car and ride to the western sector of Berlin."

When the shipment arrived at the village station the following week, Franz had the freight papers prepared and arranged for the parcels and suitcases to continue their journey. On Sunday he boarded the train which took him to the eastern sector of Berlin, when he soon found his cousin's dwelling. After exchange of greetings, and some breakfast, Franz learned that the freight had been delivered. He suggested transferring it promptly to the western sector, aided by his cousin Johann. After thanking him, Franz suggested that they separate temporarily, meeting later at an arranged address.

Franz boarded a street-car with the first load, reaching his destination safely. He used a different route for the second trip to avoid being recognized. Late that night, after several hours of nerve-racking work, Franz and his partner completed their self-imposed task.

Here it should be stated that such efforts were commonplace here in the shadow of the Iron Curtain, for a bond of brotherhood united people in the submerged countries of Eastern Europe. It was such close ties of friendship and confidence that repeatedly frustrated the calculations of the Red rulers to accomplish their plans of dividing the people.

Ever since 1950, those in power in East Germany had been working strenuously to introduce a Bolshevik state organization on the Russian model, with the usual demoralizing results. The Soviets had not yet succeeded with their plans because of the presence of West Berlin as an island surrounded by Red territory.

The East Germans were powerfully attracted by Berlin, the "show window" of the west, as the majority of the population still retained a sense of unity with their friends and neighbors.

Mr. Bode had rented a large furnished room in the

suburban district of Grunewald. After the last load had been deposited, Franz stopped to chat with him.

"What a life this is, when people have to sneak around like thieves in their own country just to keep what belongs to them."

"Well," said Mr. Bode, "we are not living under a regime of law. What can we expect from the Red conquerors? They are enforcing their harsh system here with ruthlessness, using their German vassals as examples of cowardly submission to Soviet rule."

"How do you intend to stay in the west, Mr. Bode?"

"First I shall prove to the West Berlin authorities that I am a genuine political refugee. I will furnish evidence that I was in deadly peril, and had no alternative to sudden flight. If I am lucky, it will not be long before I will be permitted to apply for registration as a West German citizen and obtain West German papers."

"I see," said Franz, thoughtfully. "The great hazard is the element of forged documents. It is possible for clever Communist agents to gain entrance to the Federal Republic to carry on their subversive activities. How can the West Berlin authority distinguish the true refugees from the false?"

"Well, they can't, always, but there's no help for it. There are bound to be a few black sheep in the flock of fugitives. Still, the investigating agencies are a state within the state. Here in West Berlin the background of every refugee is carefully checked, and those unable to qualify for admission are denied an entry permit. After that, they can stay in the refugee camps of West Berlin, or else go back to East Germany."

"That's terrible," Franz exclaimed. "Don't you think it awful, Mr. Bode, for innocent people to be driven from place to place in their own country? And this is the twentieth century! What's happening to the farmers and tradesmen whom the Soviets are expelling? Are they also political refugees?"

"No," Mr. Bode answered. "They have a very hard time of it here. Because they have been persecuted by the Soviets for economic reasons only, they are unacceptable as political refugees."

"That's unfair," said Franz indignantly. "Why shouldn't they be accepted? Anyone familiar with Soviet Russian policy knows that their aims can only be achieved by such economic liquidation. All that is left for the Reds to do is to destroy the remnants of peasant society in East Germany. Their most deadly weapon is withdrawal of the material bases of life. When a social group has been denied food, clothing or shelter, it is as good as dead. The local bureaucrats do not understand this. They stick to the false notion that such essentials have nothing to do with politics. On the contrary, these factors are the very basis of Soviet politics.

Wherever the Reds gain a foothold, they begin by cutting off the class enemy from his economic base. Very soon these officials, directing refugee traffic in the western zones, will begin to realize what is happening. As the economic refugees increase in numbers, these officials will be confronted with a grave problem.

"I ask you," Franz inquired, "can a West German citizen expect those former businessmen, farmers and artisans to become slaves in the Communist labor battalions? Everything possible should be done to integrate those unfortunates with the citizens of Western Germany, so that they could make a fresh start in life. The western world must develop a strong sense of solidarity if it is to hold fast against the Red menace. Besides, accepting these displaced persons would be beneficial to the economy. Moreover, such a solution would give the exiles a feeling of working for a cause in which they could believe."

"Yes," Mr. Bode agreed. "But young people are too impatient. You must learn to be more deliberate. What man cannot accomplish at present; time will bring it to pass."

"I hope you're right."

Franz, exhausted, lay down on an old couch and fell into a deep sleep. The next morning, he arose from his makeshift bed, hastily dressed, and bid farewell to Mr. Bode. On his way, he stopped for breakfast in a little West Berlin restaurant.

"Do you take East marks?" he asked.

"Yes, if you will pay five to one."

Franz nodded in agreement. Quietly he consumed his sausage, and washed it down with coffee. A few construction and railroad workers were sitting in a far corner, conversing freely.

He liked this pleasant little place, and gulped in the freedom that was the more precious because soon he would have to give it up again. In imagination, he compared this eating place with the public restaurants at home, where there was no escape from the irritating broadcasts of the Communist radio. Back where he came from, pictures of Stalin adorned the walls. Any one of the attendants might be an informer working for the secret police.

After finishing his meal, Franz paid for it at the exchange

rate of five to one. Pretty steep, he thought without regret. By nightfall he had reached his mother's home in Ostwald. She was glad to learn that his mission had been successful. He had a few days left to attend to some of the more urgent things that needed attention.

Before long, thought Franz, I'll have to get back to the machine station, or they'll be coming after me.

Late the following Sunday night, Franz showed his pass to the watchman who admitted him to the station.

"Fine time to be coming in," he said grouchily.

Franz went straight to his room. Early next morning he was at work again, cleaning and repairing engine parts with his friend Gunther.

"Well, what's new in West Berlin?" Gunther wanted to know.

"Nothing much," Franz answered. "You know as much about it as I do. About the only thing of interest in the Industry Show."

"I'll have to make the trip myself one of these days," he said.

"I don't suppose anything of interest has been happening here at the station?"

"Oh, the youth organization has called a meeting for this afternoon. They have an interesting topic for discussion--<u>Indoctrination and Enlightenment of Youth Concerning Proletarian Higher Education</u>. That's what they call it, anyway," Gunther continued. "Plenty of organizers and educators are coming. The idea is to interest the children of workers and peasants in advanced study. I understand some candidates are to be recruited from this station who are interested in the engineering or agriculture curriculum."

"Well, at least it'll be a change from the daily monotony. I'm curious to hear what they have to say for themselves."

"Well," said Gunther defensively, "nobody can deny that the Soviets do a great deal for young people. They give them every opportunity to engage in intellectual as well as athletic activity. They even provide the expensive equipment needed for sports like motorcycling and horseback riding. Why do you suppose the Soviets are so generous and lavish towards young people?"

"That's easy," Franz replied. "The Communists know that the future belongs to those who have the youth behind them. Then, too, they realize that young people have short memories, concerning events of a few years ago. Furthermore, they don't have the mental maturity for independent political judgments. This gives the Red educators an excellent chance to gain many adherents."

The two boys exerted themselves greatly to finish their repair job in time. Soon the noon bell rang in the station yard. The mechanics filed into the mess hall, recently erected during an extra shift. After lunch, the young men congregated in the assembly hall.

The functionaries were not long in showing up. So were the educators, who were introduced to the staff. Some girls had been seated in the center of the hall. Giggling, they glanced about curiously. They had come in response to the government's campaign to get more women interested in tractors and machinery. In this sector also, the Soviet model was faithfully copied in minutest detail.

Suddenly the audience became silent. One of the leaders was mounting the speaker's stand to open the meeting.

"My young comrades, you are undoubtedly aware that our government is doing everything possible to enable working-class children to attend institutions of learning. It is only by intensive social and technical education that we can develop qualified workers. Let us heed the advice Comrade

Lenin once gave the youth of Russia: 'Learn, learn, and learn some more,' he said. This, of course, holds good for our young people too. Whereas in the capitalist countries only the children of well-to-do parents are able to obtain an advanced education, in our Communist state the children of all workers will attend university schools to the extent of their ability and application. The government recognizes this necessity, and has appropriated tremendous sums for the education of youth. As yet, unfortunately, a high percentage of students in our country are not children of the working class. This is an intolerable situation in a proletarian state. In this field also, the class struggle must be intensified. We know there are many sons and daughters of workers and peasants among you. Some of you have surely given thought to the possibility of further education. There must be some bright boys and girls in this audience who would like to go to college. The government extends financial assistance until the curriculum is completed. Of course, during your term of study you must meet the academic requirements to be entitled to a scholar-ship. It is essential that we got class-conscious workers into the leading posts of our economy and government. By training a better intelligentsia and by making scientific use of all the resources of education we hope to defeat the class enemy in the countryside.

"Do any of you have any questions on this point?" asked the speaker at the close of his remarks.

A girl rose and asked, "What do I have to do if I am interested in studying agricultural engineering, for instance?"

"We will give you the addresses and application blanks of the proper institutions. You can fill out the forms and apply direct to the school for the privilege of taking an entrance examination," he replied.

Other boys and girls were interested in biological studies. One young man asked why only working-class children should be permitted to attend such institutions, suggesting that this was contrary to the principles of democratic freedom for children of any segment to be denied higher education.

At this, the speaker repeated his slogans of political struggle, and harangued his young audience until everybody seemed to be convinced. At the end of the program, the manager of the station thanked the visitors and adjourned the meeting.

The young workers returned to their jobs.

"Well, what did you think of it?" asked Gunther.

"I'll tell you," replied Franz. "The Reds know exactly

how to hitch the youth of a nation to their chariot. They need trained people, and know they cannot carry out a world revolutionary program with illiterates. That is one of the main reasons they spend so much money on education--a very one-sided education. It isn't as though the schools were training young people to be genuine humanists. Quite the contrary. Instead of permitting the student to develop his mind freely, he is oriented in a specific direction. Consequently, nowhere in the Red empire can a young man investigate the fields of science without being influenced by Marxist-Leninist materialism. That is the reverse side of the coin of free education under the Reds. Anyone hungry for knowledge is taught only what is useful to the government. The Communists have no use for the tradition of academic freedom, and they'll make sure that the youth learns nothing about it.

An older worker broke in angrily. "Excuse me, but I can't see why the rest of us should be expected to work through one shift after the other. There is no future for us under this system. We work ourselves to death just so the young fellows can have every luxury at world-youth festivals, so the big propaganda demonstration will go off smoothly. All that stuff is only meant to mislead people in the western world. We of the older generation are supposed to kill ourselves to finance this kind of foolishness. Why Hitler used to trick the young people the same way."

"You should have told him that at the meeting," Gunther suggested.

"I guess you know I've got more sense than that. They would have arrested me for inciting to boycott. No, you can't afford to speak your mind nowadays. That would be plain treason," said the man ruefully.

None of the boys dared to reply. Each kept his thoughts to himself and went silently about his accustomed task.

In the spring of 1953, many people in the Red empire took new hope. This rise in spirits was caused by the death of Stalin, who passed away on March 5. The authorities, despite their strictness, were unable to prevent spontaneous demonstrations of joy. Even some of the Russian soldiers in occupied East Germany marked the event with well-moistened celebrations. Some incautious citizens, however, paid with their freedom for their overenthusiastic reactions.

Stalin's satraps residing in the Eastern European people's democracies were accustomed to receive and execute orders from the Kremlin. Even though the orders, after Stalin's death, emanated from a triumvirate, yet they were carried out more brutally than ever before. Among the masses, feelings rose to the boiling point. Those in power were demanding ever greater sacrifices. The limit of endurance had been reached.

In East Germany, this happened in June, 1953. News that the workers had taken the initiative ran through the country like wildfire. Detachments of Berlin steel and construction workers joined in a great mass demonstration, then marched through the city. The bulk of the population swelled their ranks. Their objective was the seat of the East German government, before which they intended to present the working people's demands. These were the immediate resignation of the government and the holding of free all-German elections. They also wanted abolition of the class struggle and a more reasonable determination of quotas. Where were the bodyguards of the Red rulers now? The popular uprising carried the police along with it, and trampled whatever stood in its path. When the mob in Berlin had reached the East German government buildings in the Leipziger Strasse, the heads of the Russian puppet administration had already made themselves scarce. The few remaining members of the government were seized and publicly manhandled by the mob.

The station where Franz and Gunther worked was in the grip of panic. Some functionaries in the nearby district town had been beaten and lynched by the workers. The farmers would not allow the mechanics from the station in their villages. "Get out of here or we'll kill you like dogs," they threatened the officials, who safely withdrew.

"What do we want with your class struggle? Give us back our farms and our rights!" the people demanded.

In some villages the peasants dealt mercilessly with their tormentors. Wherever the Red leaders showed themselves they were stoned and spit upon. Soon none dared venture out of doors, so terrible became the wrath of the oppressed people. Even in the smaller cities, prisons were broken into and the inmates released. Many poured into West Berlin under cover of the general confusion.

Now it became clear what the true situation was in the people's democracies. As soon as the terror somewhat diminished, the government lost control of the people. The Communists demonstrated to the entire world how far they were from being democrats. Their last resort, of course, could only be the expedient of totalitarian rulers--armed force.

The Russians grasped the situation at once, and decided

to take vigorous measures against the popular uprising. A state of emergency was declared throughout East German territory, and the infuriated workers were soon subdued by the Soviet armored troops. Nonetheless, there were desperate persons who dared oppose this military strength. The next step by the Russian commandant was to proclaim martial law in every town and village of East Germany. Anyone found on the streets after nine o'clock at night without a permit would be shot down. At night the cities and towns seemed deserted. The land was cloaked in silence, and public commerce was paralyzed.

Gunther and Franz had received a leave of absence from the station. They took refuge in the house of Franz's mother and listened to the news broadcasts.

Now that the rebellion had been crushed, everyone wondered what the authorities were going to do. The Soviet overlords had severely reprimanded their East German governors, who now indulged in devastating self-criticism. Within a few days repentant voices were heard on the Communist-controlled radio. The Reds made sure that the former rebels had publicly retracted, and would now carry out Moscow's orders unquestioningly. The rebellion, however, had not been in vain, even if it had not attained its main objective--free elections and abolition of the dictatorship. But unexpected developments compelled the government to make major concessions to the people. Most important of all, the class-struggle theories and the accelerated socialist propaganda had to be dropped. Fugitives living in the west were encouraged to return to their former homes. Tradesmen's shops were given back to them, and farms were returned to their peasant owners. Private enterprise had won back some of the ground it had lost. One thing was certain: the socialist reformers had been plainly told--thus far and no further can you go.

The people now listened with great interest to the radio commentators. Privately, many wondered whether the Russians at last had realized that they could never force the Germans into accepting Bolshevism. Possibly such evidence may have convinced them that free elections were a necessity. Another phenomenon of eastern broadcasts was the confessions made by representatives of the regime.

"We realize now," the penitents would say, "that we failed to respect the true aspirations of the people; that we isolated ourselves from the people instead of working closely with them. From now on, everything will be different."

"Do you believe that, Franz?" asked Gunther. "When the Reds feel strong again, they will squeeze the people harder than they did before."

"We'll have to wait and see."

Harvest time had arrived. The two boys returned to the tractor station and worked hard all day in the fields with the other mechanics. Farm villages stood practically deserted. The fields were ownerless, but the harvest had to be reaped. Some peasants returned after the rebellion, but most of them, lacking confidence in the regime, dared not come back.

Operations at the station had settled down to normal. Slowly the Communists regained full control. In six months, conditions were much as they had been before. Strangely enough, the men were volunteering to work on Sundays and they had agreed to make other sacrifices. The boys realized that the Reds had changed their methods, but the ends sought were the same. They had learned a lesson from the insurrection, and had become more cautious. It was now clear what might happen again if the pant-up fury of the people were suddenly released. The Communists were providing a safety valve; if the popular temper ever boiled over, it would need a vent, a fact evident to the oppressed as well as to the oppressor.

One day Franz was called into the political director's office. Standing alongside the director were two aids.

"These comrades," he told Franz, "Are recruiting young patriots for our people's army, and would like to discuss the matter with you."

This is it, thought Franz. Having already decided to escape to the west, he had no desire to serve as a soldier in the Communist state. He decided to adopt delaying tactics, so he could win enough time to engineer his flight to the west.

"Why, certainly," Franz replied. "I'll be glad to hear what the comrades have to say."

The officers took Franz aside.

"You must have given some thought to the aims and purposes of our organization."

"Yes, I have," said Franz, "but I don't think we need any combat forces. We're under the military protection of the allied powers. Besides, we Germans have had unpleasant experiences with armies in the past."

"What you say is true," one of the officers replied. "But now we are living in a different situation, and a different social order. East Germany has regained its sovereignty. The Soviets are now its friends and allies. Besides, we are creating a new type of army, the first proletarian German army. The officer corps of this force will consist of class-conscious sons of workingmen who will defend the achievements of the socialist revolution."

"I noticed last June how zealously our police were defending the achievements of the state. If the Russians hadn't fought for our socialist achievements, there would be very little to show now."

The officers started in surprise.

"Well, that's beside the point," one of them said. "Those were just growing pains. We've learned our lesson, and we'll make sure that it will not happen again.

"Besides," Franz argued, "by forming a people's army we may be conjuring up the danger of civil war. No one here wants to fight against our brothers in the west. A people's army in the east would encourage the creating of a new army in West Germany, supported by the democratic powers. I really don't believe that we need a people's army."

"You don't understand the meaning of our outfit," said the second officer. "We develop a strong feeling of consciousness in the recruit. The private soldier in our army soon realizes that as a son of the working class, he is fighting for the rights of the working people. His main enemies, he learns, are the forces of reaction and capitalism."

"In other words, it will be an army prepared for civil war."

"No, a people's army."

"In either case, I can't make up my mind at once. Such a step demands careful consideration. I'd better get back to work."

"All right, but we expect you to reach a favorable decision. We'll see you again soon."

"Why not?" Franz answered, and left the office.

The visitors continued with their interviews. One young mechanic after another was worked over by the propagandists for the East German National army. Some mechanics were approached with veiled threats and indirect pressure, others were given glowing promises. Many joined up promptly convinced by their arguments, and with expectations of easy conditions and good pay. Within the next few days, a few of the men volunteered for service.

The recruiting officers had become frequent guests of the station, and slowly gained influence over the workers, aided by the activity of the political directory.

One day an announcement appeared on the bulletin

board, calling a meeting the following evening. Everyone at the station was required to be present.

"What's the meeting for?" Franz asked.

"You'll see at the proper time," was the curt reply.

The next day, at quitting time, the men changed their clothes and went to the assembly hall. The director and some political comrades were already there. Soon the hall was filled with mechanics, and with the following remarks, the director opened the meeting:

"Fellow workers, you know that unity and international solidarity are our only strength. Our French comrades are at this moment fighting a desperate battle against their economic exploiters, and will be grateful for every possible assistance. I believe I am speaking for the comrades present when I propose that we work a special voluntary eight-hour shift on each of the next two Sundays, the proceeds to go to our French comrades in their struggle against reaction. This act will be regarded as a concrete token of international cooperation. Have you any questions in regard to this suggestion? I invite discussion."

"That's all we need," whispered Gunther to Franz. "Why don't you say something? We don't want to give up our Sundays for the aims of international Communism. If you don't speak up," Gunther urged, "the motion will be passed unanimously as usual. Then we can have the fun of digging potatoes or demolishing buildings on our day off."

The director was droning on. "I call upon any comrades who oppose the proposal to state their reasons."

Now's the time, thought Franz, and raised his hand. There was complete silence. He looked around. No one else wanted the floor. His would be the only protest. The chairman was already recognizing him. Franz realized that he would have to defend his position. In a totalitarian state, democratic parliamentary procedure in discussing a problem was held in disfavor by the regime. It looked now that the sacrifices during the June insurrection had been made in vain. The supporters of Bolshevism were again in power, and tormenting the people by subtler methods more fiendish than ever.

The director spoke again.

"What has our young friend to say."

Franz faced the audience:

"Friends, I dare say a large percentage of you would endorse my objection to Sunday work if you knew what was to be done with the money we would be contributing. We should look into this matter more closely before we take action.

Do you know why the French workers went on strike again? I'll tell you. They are on strike because they object to a government bill under which they would receive old-age pensions, not from the present age of fifty-seven, but only after they reach sixty. Our comrades in West Germany also live in a capitalist society. They do not receive old-age pensions until they are sixty-five. Why should we sacrifice our Sundays for something as trivial as this? Our French comrades are better off than we are, having a much higher standard of living than we have. If we are to make such sacrifices, let us do it for our own pensioners, who are in very bad straits and desperately need economic aid."

Franz paused for breath. The spell was broken. The workers began arguing among themselves. "The boy's right," said some. "If that's the case, we object, too. Why should we help foreigners when our own people are so badly in need? We won't agree to Sunday work."

"Why didn't you tell us the real facts?" the director was asked. "You must think we're a bunch of cattle. You're just as arrogant as before the June uprisings."

"That's right," said a young clerk angrily. "That's the way they used to run things. Why don't you draw up a regular

motion, to be adopted if the majority of the workers agree
to it?"

Franz's objection had raised a storm of protest. The chairman called for order.

"Quiet, comrades. Silence!" Slowly the noise subsided.

The political director glared at Franz, then proceeded to
counterattack.

"Comrades, our young friend does not clearly understand
the political background of this situation. We do not propose
such measures for amusement. This is a national project initiated by the government of our country. We are merely trying
to carry it out."

"Don't you know we have a constitution?" Franz retorted. "That the constitution guarantees the workingman a
forty-eight-hour week? We have the right to decide what to
do with our time after the forty-eight hours, especially in a
case like this where volunteer work on Sundays is involved."

"But the government wants--," the speaker began.

"What do you mean," retorted Franz, "'the government
wants'? You are merely trying to carry out orders, isn't that it?
That's the way it used to be under Hitler. Are we still living
in slavery, or in the twentieth century? We're supposed to be

advancing towards socialism. But by your coercive methods, you are strangling liberty and initiative."

"I object to this comrade's remarks," the manager looked at Franz reproachfully. "What you are doing is deliberately inciting the workers to boycott. How dare you suggest that the living standard of workers is higher in capitalist than in socialist countries?"

"I base that statement on official statistics and the conclusions of reputable Soviet scholars," Franz replied. "They have studied the living conditions of workers in every modern state. In comparing the standard of living in eastern European countries with that of the west, they find that the latter is higher--despite the fact that the western countries haven't a socialistic and collective economic structure comparable to the countries of the eastern bloc."

"So, you mean to say that the bourgeois capitalist social and economic structure is superior to ours?"

"I didn't say that," Franz protested.

"We're ready to vote," said many voices from the back rows of the hall. "We don't want to be here all night." Groups of workers began chanting in unison, demanding an immediate vote. The chairman decided to put the question.

"Will all those opposed to this special Sunday shift raise their hands?"

Franz saw an overwhelming majority of hands being raised. He turned pale, wondering how this was going to end.

"All in favor?" the chairman asked. Here and there throughout the audience a few hands were raised.

"The management's proposal has been rejected," declared the director. "The meeting is adjourned."

Chapter XI

Outside the hall, the young machinists crowded around Franz and Gunther.

"That was all right. You gave it to them good and proper. It was about time, too. They're going too far," the boys said.

"Well, you put me up to it," said Franz to his friend. "What do you think is going to come of this?"

"Oh, they can't do anything to you. After all, the whole force backed you up. If they try anything, we'll stand behind you."

"Don't talk nonsense," said Franz. "The authorities will surely demand an accounting, and the management might report me as a provocateur who ruined the Sunday-work project."

"What's done is done. We'll have to see what develops. Good night, Franz."

Still uneasy, Franz went to his quarters. The damp October night was dark and menacing. What did the future have in store for him?

Sunday came, a typical late-autumn day. Gunther and Franz thought about going together to the stadium in town, where an intercity track meet was being held.

"Why don't we go?" Franz had suggested. "I always enjoy these things. We'll have a good time."

"All right, we've nothing much else to do."

The two friends threaded their way through the traffic streaming towards the stadium. Soon they reached the main gate.

"Now we'll have to stand in line for tickets," Franz complained.

"It's better than working extra shifts, anyway," Gunther reminded him.

"Let's not talk about that. You'll spoil my whole day."

At the ticket window, the cashier said, "All we have left are some of the high-priced reserved seats. Everything else is sold out."

"Then we'll take two reserved seats," they agreed.

They fought their way into the stadium and were directed to their seats. Franz looked about him.

"Hey, Gunther, we really came to the right place!"

"What do you mean?"

"Just take a look at our neighbors," Franz whispered.

Gunther glanced discreetly around.

"I feel lost among all this brass," Gunther observed. The reserved section was crowded with Russian officers and decorated functionaries, who were intently watching the preparation for the spectacle. Some announcements were made over the loudspeakers, followed by martial music. Long streamers, in garish colors, were hung along the grandstands, with printed slogans of the regime. The public was used to this sort of thing. Everybody knew that the party in power lost no chance to disseminate its propaganda. At last the actual program began.

"I always like the pole vaulting, and the high hurdles too," Franz remarked. "Think of the training needed to develop that kind of form."

Enthusiasm was aroused by the exciting sixteen-hundred-meter relay. A runner for the Comet Sport Club, by a final sprint, succeeded in coming up from fourth place, to win the event.

Russian officers, sitting near Franz and Gunther, commented on several of the events, being especially critical of the javelin and discus throwers. A youthful first lieutenant remarked to his friend, "Misha, did you see that last man sling his discus? No wonder he can't do any better. But what a splendid physique! They ought to get a decent coach to train these fellows."

The main events were over. To avoid the crowds, Gunther and Franz left a little early. Just as they came out of the gate, Franz noticed his two old classmates, Axel and Rudi. Overjoyed at this chance meeting, he strode happily towards them.

"Well, it's about time! Where have you fellows been keeping yourselves? Meet my friend Gunther." After the introductions, the foursome fell into animated conversation.

"What do you say we walk downtown and find a coffee house?" suggested Rudi.

Franz and Gunther nodded agreement.

"I hear you two work at the state secretariat of the Party," Franz said, after briefly explaining what kind of work he was doing.

"Yes," Axel replied. "We are youth functionaries in the state leadership. It's an important political job, as you can imagine."

"In what way, a political job?" asked Gunther.

"Well, you know, you can't get along any more without politics," Rudi explained. "You see, we go from one training course to another. Being in youth work, we're supposed to bridge the gap between town and country. Through the resolving of traditional contradictions, the entire youth of the state is to be welded into a single community of interests."

"That's marvelous," said Franz sarcastically. "You know your lesson well. I see you haven't been wasting your time in class. But I guess you make a good living at your work. Are you so firmly convinced that you are doing the right thing?"

"In the first few years after the war, I was in doubt, but as time went on, I came to realize that people have to take sides," Rudi replied.

"Are you convinced that you've taken the right side?" asked Franz, cautiously.

"Yes, I am," said Rudi. "You should study the Lenin doctrine. You'll see that these people have really worked out sound proposals that can be applied to our country. The two foremost exponents of Bolshevism have shown how we can lead our people away from catastrophe."

"Do you really believe that?" You should know that the exponents of Communism have carried out an anti-human program in Russia. Moreover, they mean to extend that to the rest of Europe. Unless we fight against it, East Germany will become a carbon copy of the Soviet Union as far as social and economic conditions are concerned."

"Of course," said Axel, "you can't extend every sound Soviet idea to this country, but our Russian friends have a lot of valuable ideas on how to construct a new society."

"But look, Rudi," Franz interposed. "Are you blind, or what? Didn't you find out in June of 1953 what the German people really think? Isn't it obvious that those in power can maintain their control in Central Europe only as long as the Soviet tanks terrorize the population? The East Germans made their position clear to the whole world. Then the puppet government burst like a soap bubble. The jig would have been up with everyone holding your political opinion, if the Red army hadn't saved you. You've got to admit that," said Franz.

"What you say is merely a half-truth," Rudi countered. "The June uprising was a well-planned attack by western capitalists and militarists upon our young working-class state. Agents and provocateurs smuggled in from the west got in their dirty work."

"No, my friend," Franz retorted, "you can't expect any sensible person to believe that. How could these alleged provocateurs have managed to get a majority of the people behind them in so short a time? How could they have incited a rebellion against the present regime so quickly? The people must have been very stupid to follow the "provocateurs" for no good reason, even at the cost of their lives. What you have swallowed is just party propaganda. I say, Rudi, it was a genuine uprising, a cry for help from an oppressed nation, a desperate appeal to world public opinion."

"Do you think it would be better if things went back to the way they were before the political change took place?" Axel asked Franz.

"The main thing I object to, Axel, is the inhuman cruelty of the present methods of government. Such tyranny generates nothing but hatred among the people. For example, everyone who had a thriving little business or property has been expropriated, and then exiled without being awarded the slightest compensation. Even right now many innocent persons are languishing in prisons and labor camps. When governments of civilized nations believe like that today, they do not deserve to be known as democrats or friends of peace and progress, as your group call yourselves. That's plain hypocrisy!" ended Franz indignantly.

"You're just a hopeless reactionary," Axel replied. "If I didn't know you so well, Franz, I'd have to turn you in."

"You're the reactionary, not I," Franz rejoined. "Ultimately, you have to judge people by their actions, not by their propaganda. Look at the way your government conducts itself. These methods are the very opposite of progress or socialism. They represent medieval cruelty, and closely resemble the practices of the Nazis. Your threat to turn me in is typical. As long as such things are possible, there can be no freedom. The only saving feature is that times are good, and that's the important thing for most people."

Gunther interposed. "Don't get so excited. Let's cut out the political arguments. We want to enjoy our day off."

All were in favor of this suggestion. Rudi knew of a cozy little coffee house nearby. The boys entered the long rectangular room and sat down at a large table. The place was about half full. The prices were exorbitant. A band had been brought in for the evening, and was playing some catchy dance music.

Rudi and Axel seemed to have plenty of money. They ordered several rounds of delicacies; and after a while they danced with some girls they seemed to know. Everyone tried to avoid politics. Franz had a fine time talking to Rudi's sister. But the hands of the clock inexorably drew near to midnight.

"Franz," Gunther urged, "show us how the Cossacks dance."

"You have to have the right music," Franz hesitated.

Gunther asked the band to play a <u>zoshakov</u>, and Franz danced until he dropped from exhaustion.

"Where did you learn to dance like that?" asked an officer, one of a group who had watched him delightedly.

"Oh, I learned some Russian dances with a folk-dance group here," Franz lied.

"That's wonderful. You dance like a real Cossack."

"Thank you," said Franz modestly.

"Now you can't get out of it that easily," said a corpulent major. "You must join us at our table. Have a drink and do another dance for us."

Franz thought it wise to comply. The conversation was

carried on partly in German, and in Russian. Everybody joined in. After a few rounds of vodka, Franz performed a second time. Under the tutelage of Serge Andreyevich, the Cossack colonel, he had become an expert at this kind of dancing.

"Ochen khorosho!" exclaimed the major. "You must come to our next party. We're here often on Sunday nights. You can find us just two doors this side of headquarters. Come and see us any time."

"I'll look you up soon," Franz promised.

It was time to leave. The boys said good-bye to the Russians and walked the girl's home.

The next day was Monday. In the morning Gunther and Franz were back at work. That night, Franz found an envelope in his room, bearing the official stamp of the People's Court. Apprehensively, he tore it open. Quickly he read the following words:

> Because of your provocative and inflammatory remarks at a public meeting, the political director of your plant has found it necessary to report you for subversive activity. You are hereby

ordered to appear on Thursday, November 10,

at nine o'clock, in this Courthouse, Room 12,

to answer charges.

(Signed)

Judge, People's Court

Franz's worst fears were realized. Should he answer the summons or try to escape while there was a chance. If he appeared in court he surely would be convicted and deported to a forced-labor camp in Russia with its torture and slavery. Anything would be better than that! He had not forgotten his desperate struggles to escape a few years before. Any risk would be justified to avoid the fate awaiting him.

Calmly he attempted to analyze his great danger. If he tried to leave at once, he would be caught by the police. He also knew that the railway station at home was under surveillance, so were the main approaches to Berlin. He seemed to be trapped.

I still have my papers, he thought, so I should be able to pass through the inspection lines and get into West Berlin. If I show up in court, the least I'll get is a prison sentence. I won't do it. What did Rudi say? People have to take sides.

I've already done it. This letter tells me that I must decide at
once. Where is my place, there or here? How many people
living under Bolshevism have asked themselves that very same
question?

Franz no longer hesitated. As a Christian, he believed in
the eternal values of the divine creative power and of the un-
hampered development of the human spirit. With such faith
he could never assent to the degradation of the individual. He
made his decision irrevocably. Tomorrow I'll board the train
and leave for good.

Despite Franz's decision to escape, the specter of doubt
began to harass him. Had he done right to reject the hand
extended to him? Ostensibly, the Reds were doing everything
possible for the mental and physical development of the youth
and asking nothing in return. But was this actually so? Of
course, nobody had to pay back in money. But the impres-
sionable youngsters were compelled to accept an ideology
alien to their upbringing, thus sacrificing their freedom for
something that was inferior. Franz knew, however, that freedom was priceless. According to Franz, a group of determined
patriots might overthrow the Bolshevik power by exposing
the rottenness of this criminal ideology. But the militarists

in eastern Germany were too powerful and too vigilant. The armed troops stifled every movement towards freedom from its very beginning. Unless help came from without, all resistance was futile.

Franz was young and impatient. He lacked the fierceness and resilience to fight against decades of apparently hopeless resistance. What could he do to at least see on the horizon some results of his efforts? There was one thing he could do. He would escape to the Western world, there to continue the struggle for a just cause among those who believed in the dignity of freedom. What about hundreds of thousands of resistance fighters who had opposed every form of tyranny. A great many had died as martyrs after incredible exploitation and untold suffering at the hands of their enemies. If the Allies had not destroyed the Nazi concentration camps, the inmates would be there now--that is, those who were still alive. The many hundreds of thousands now confined in the labor camps of Bolshevism are confronted with a fate just as terrible. Illegal activity alone would never cause the system to crumble. At the same time, the west could not be expected, without gigantic preparation, to attack the greatest slave state ever conceived by man, because of the spiritual anguish of its victims. So, Franz was confronted with two choices: He might accept the false teaching of Bolshevism and pretend enthusiasm for it, or he could leave the country of his birth to live among people who shared his beliefs, where he could labor in peace and have security of mind.

Since Stalin's death, many changes had taken place in Russia. Malenkov had placed the question of coexistence in the foreground as a rational solution of today's world crisis. The leaders in Moscow had correctly recognized that threats were of no avail against powerful and determined opponents. So, they had decided to try gradual methods, and had discarded the idea of quickly Bolshevizing the world. But their ultimate aim was unchanged. The means of accomplishment seemed to be less aggressive, but below the surface the essential techniques of Soviet propaganda and infiltration remained unchanged.

A loud knocking at the door of his room interrupted Franz's train of thought. Upon opening it, he saw his former classmate, Rudi, now a youth functionary.

"Franz," he said, excitedly, "I've just learned what you've been up to. If you're caught, it will mean at least two years in prison for you. I'm warning you as a friend, get out of here as quickly as you can. It's my duty as a functionary to take you in, but I won't. Because of our friendship, I am rendering you this last service."

"Thank you, Rudi." Tears welled up in the eyes of Franz. Speechlessly they shook hands, forgetting strife and hatred. After a short pause Franz said, "Rudi, why don't you come, too? You're too good to let yourself be exploited by these monsters."

"I can't. By now, I'm too deeply involved in the dictatorship. Besides, I have a family to support. At least, I am assured of a livelihood. I'm sorry, Franz. You may depend on me not to give you away."

"Thank you again for warning me. Do you think I could see my mother again before I leave?"

"You know best. But make sure that you're out of the country before the hearing, or it'll be too late. Good-bye."

These were Rudi's last words as he walked through the door and down the corridor.

Franz spent a restless night. Next morning the station manager ordered him to drive a tractor to a village about thirty miles from the station where a field crew was to take over. Suddenly, his mind clicked with an idea. Here was a perfect opportunity to get away. After driving a while, he reached the highway and headed rapidly for his mother's house.

"Why, Franz, I didn't expect you. What's the matter?"

"I have to go, there's no more time," he answered, and told his mother the whole story. "You ought to come away too," he said. "But I'll have to leave right now."

After a tearful farewell he tore himself away.

"God be with you. I'll soon follow," he heard his mother say as he began walking away.

Franz proceeded to town as fast as was prudent. As he came nearer the depot, he parked the tractor in a nearly alley. He purchased a ticket to a point just beyond Berlin, and the papers he showed were not questioned.

The platform was crowded with travelers. Small groups of Russian soldiers were standing around, some going on leave, and others returning. It could be seen from their baggage that very few went home empty-handed. The express ponderously pulled in. Franz was fortunate to find a seat. Within an hour the train reached the non-familiar inspection post.

The police or the inspectors aren't going to have much luck with me today, thought Franz, who had with him neither money nor baggage. The usual line had formed in front of the guard station. He wondered how many were in the same situation as himself. Two officers were examining papers, while others went through the luggage. At last it was Franz's turn. He showed his pass.

"What is your destination?" asked the officer.

Franz simply showed his ticket.

"What baggage are you carrying?"

"Just a briefcase."

"All right, that's all," said the officer.

With a light heart, Franz passed through the barrier, boarded the waiting train. When he arrived in free West Berlin, he got off. Once there, he looked up some old friends of his father's, and was received kindly by the lady of the house.

"Could I stay here for just a day?" he asked. "I'm trying to get to West Germany."

"Of course, you can. Come in and rest up from your journey."

In the living room, Franz was greeted by Mr. Müller, his father's old friend, who was delighted to see him. Franz gave a short account of his most recent adventures.

"I'll drive you to the airport tomorrow," said Mr. Müller.

"I can order the ticket now by phone." Within a few moments Franz had a one-way plane ticket to Düsseldorf.

"Now let's have some dinner," said his host. The meal was delicious and Franz happily toasted his benefactor's health.

"This is the happiest moment of my life," beamed Franz. "At last I have found the way to self-realization which has been achieved by my faith in people who believe in the dignity of human beings and their inmate right to political freedom. Despite the trials and temptations of the last few years, I know the ideals of liberty and humanism are irreplaceable and beyond price. A comparison of the realities of east and west is the best proof we can ask for."

Next morning Franz bid farewell to his kind friends. Reaching the airport, he boarded a plane which flew across the Iron Curtain from the island that is Berlin. At last, he had emerged from the darkness and tyranny of a political dictatorship into the bright light of freedom.

Today Franz is a <u>free</u> citizen of a <u>free</u> country, contentedly pursuing his chosen vocation.

THE END

ABOUT THE AUTHOR

Franz Haeussler was born in 1930 in northern Germany and raised on country estates. After public school, he attended gymnasium. At age eighteen, he learned how to be an auto mechanic before immigrating to Canada. He practiced his trade for eight years before buying a farm in Grand Valley, Ontario, raising and training three-day event horses.

Printed in the United States
By Bookmasters